NATIVE AMERICAN MYTHOLOGY
A TO Z

Patricia Ann Lynch

Facts On File, Inc.

Native American Mythology A to Z

Facts On File, Inc.
132 West 31st Street
New York NY 10001

Library of Congress Cataloging-in-Publication Data is available on request from Facts On File, Inc.
ISBN 0-8160-4891-6

Facts On File books are available at special discounts when purchased in bulk quantities for businesses, associations, institutions, or sales promotions. Please call our Special Sales Department in New York at (212) 967-8800 or (800) 322-8755.

You can find Facts On File on the World Wide Web at http://www.factsonfile.com

Text design by Joan M. Toro
Cover design by Cathy Rincon

Printed in the United States of America

VB PKG 10 9 8 7 6 5 4 3 2 1

This book is printed on acid-free paper.

CONTENTS

Acknowledgments

I want to thank Brown Publishing Network for providing me the opportunity to share my awareness of Native American traditions and to write this book.

My deepest gratitude goes to North America's First People. May you walk in beauty.

INTRODUCTION

When the first European explorers arrived on the North American continent in the late 15th century, they did not find an empty land. More than 2 million Native Americans representing at least 1,000 different tribes were living in North America. Native Americans inhabited regions ranging from the frozen Arctic to subtropical Florida, from the Pacific Ocean to the Atlantic. They lived on the tundra, in the mountains and woodlands, on the plains and prairies, in the swamps of the Southeast and the deserts of the Southwest. Far from being the single culture labeled "Indian" by Europeans, Native Americans represented a multitude of highly developed cultures and spoke hundreds of different languages.

Wherever they lived, Native Americans of North America developed lifestyles, worldviews, religions, traditions, and mythologies as varied as the environments they inhabited. In the Arctic, where people depended on the creatures of the sea for sustenance, myths identified the powerful beings that controlled the supply of these ANIMALS, who needed to be honored and obeyed. Along the Northwest Coast, people who fished for SALMON developed a mythology in which salmon played a primary role. In the Southwest, where a CORN-based agriculture predominated, legends about corn were prominent. Groups whose lives depended on hunting told stories about the origin, loss, and recovery of game animals. The climate, the weather, the geography, the sources of food, and the people's way of life all influenced the legends people told.

Humans use mythology and ritual to establish a sense of community, identity, and an understanding of their place in the universe. These tools maintain the traditions of a culture and reflect what is most important in people's lives. We read myths not only to learn about the culture in which the myth originated but to discover the hearts and minds of the myth makers. This book explores the surviving mythological traditions of Native North Americans (referred to in this book simply as Native Americans) ranging from the northern border of what is now Mexico into the Arctic Circle and from the earliest known myths to the most recent. The myths of Native Americans give us a glimpse into the ways of life and worldviews of North America's first people.

NATIVE AMERICANS: A BRIEF HISTORY

In the history of a people lie the roots of the people's culture, religion, traditions, rituals, and mythology. Little, however, is known about the early history of Native Americans. Native Americans were not native to the North American continent. Fossil remains of dinosaurs dating back millions of years have been found in North America. However, no fossil evidence has been found of human presence in North America earlier than about 38,000 years ago. Details about the first Americans' arrival are lost in prehistory. Through various scientific methods, however, a picture has begun to develop. Radiocarbon dating of artifacts and sites where animals were killed, DNA studies comparing Native Americans to other population groups, and studies by linguists of similarities and differences among Native American languages have led scientists to conclude that the first humans in North America began arriving from Asia about 40,000 to 35,000 years ago. (These findings conflict with the religious and cultural beliefs of some Native Americans, who dispute this conclusion.)

During the last Ice Age, which lasted until about 10,000 years ago, enough of the planet's water was locked up in glaciers to lower the level of the oceans as much as 300 feet. Land that is now submerged was above sea level. Between Siberia and Alaska a bridge of land called Beringia stretched across what is now the Bering Strait. Based on radiocarbon dating of archaeological sites in the Yukon and along the Pacific coast, it seems likely that bands of Paleolithic hunters migrated across this land bridge. Another theory suggests that some groups crossed the Pacific by boat before the land bridge existed. A site in New Mexico dating back 38,000 years and one in Chile dating back 33,000 years support this theory. People migrating on foot across Beringia could not have reached these sites so quickly. Signs of human habitation on some Pacific islands dating back 20,000 or more years indicate that early humans were capable of crossing long stretches of open sea. According to evidence based on the length of time sites have been occupied, the most recent arrivals—the Inuit and Aleut—migrated across the Bering Sea from Siberia in skin boats and wooden dugout canoes between 2500 and 1000 B.C., after the ocean waters again covered Beringia.

Archaeological, DNA, and linguistic analysis suggests that some waves of people migrating onto the North American continent settled where they first arrived. Others continued on, migrating across the continent and continuing south into Central and South America. They followed the paths that opened up as the ice sheets that covered North America melted and withdrew. As various passageways developed, the first Americans migrated south along the Pacific Coast, east across what is now Canada, and southeast into the heart of the continent. These migrations became part of the mythology of later cultures.

For the first arrivals, called Paleo-Indians, the dominant way of life was nomadic and consisted of foraging and big-game hunting. The game that Paleo-Indians hunted was mammals of the Pleistocene epoch that later became extinct in North America: woolly mammoths, mastodons, saber-toothed tigers, American lions, camels, dire wolves, long-horned bison, horses, and giant sloths. Archaeologists and anthropologists have learned a great deal about the lives and migrations of these early people from artifacts and bones found at campsites and kill sites. Over the centuries, the Paleo-Indians improved the weapons they used to hunt their prey. Spear points chipped from stone, now identified as Clovis and Folsom from the sites in New Mexico where they were found, are among the best known of Paleo-Indian artifacts. Clovis points have been dated as 12,000 to 15,000 years old and have been found throughout North America. Other spear-point cultures were the Sandia (ca. 9100–8000 B.C.), which was also centered in the Southwest, and the Plano or Plainview (ca. 8000–4500 B.C.), which was primarily associated with the Great Plains.

Between 10,000 and 8000 B.C., the Ice Age ended with the final retreat of the northern glaciers. During this time the big-game species that had been the primary prey of Paleo-Indian hunters became extinct. As the climate warmed, new animal and plant species filled in the gaps left by those that died out. The Clovis and other spear-point cultures began to give way to regional variants generally called Archaic cultures, which flourished from about 5000 to 1000 B.C. The Archaic, or Foraging, Period was characterized by migratory hunting, trapping of small game, fishing, and gathering of edible wild plants. As animal prey became scarcer, people became more dependent on plant foods. The cultivation of crops such as squash, beans, and maize (corn) was introduced. In some parts of the continent, people began to settle in permanent villages. During this period, people of the Southeast began making pottery. The practice gradually spread throughout North America.

The change from a nomadic, hunting and gathering culture to a more sedentary, agriculture-based culture was the beginning of what is called the Formative Period. In addition to the establishment of villages and the development of agriculture, the Formative Period was characterized by pottery making, weaving, and trade. Across the continent, cultures became more diverse. Ceremonies and ritual gained increasing importance in people's lives, and carvings in stone expressed people's beliefs. As the people's way of life changed from hunting to agriculture, it is likely that their myths changed as well. The mythology of hunting societies is dominated by tales about the game animals so important to life. Myths of agricultural societies focus more on the fertility of crops and rain making.

In the Southeast, the Ohio River valley, and along the Mississippi River and its tributaries, unique mound-building cultures arose beginning around 1800 B.C. These cultures were characterized by the construction of huge earthworks, some in geometric shapes and others—called effigy mounds—in the form of animals and birds. These structures and the ornaments, pottery, carved figures, and other artifacts found in MOUNDS hint at the wealth of myth and legend of the MOUND BUILDERS, which unfortunately have not survived to the present day.

The earliest mounds were built by the Poverty Point culture (1800–500 B.C.), of which hundreds of sites are located in Louisiana, Arkansas, and Mississippi. The most impressive Poverty Point earthwork is a giant bird with outstretched wings that measures 710 feet by 640 feet. People of a later tradition, the Adena culture (ca. 1000 B.C.–A.D. 200) created mounds along the Ohio River valley from Kentucky to New York State. One of their earthworks, Great Serpent Mound in Ohio—the figure of an enormous snake that extends for 1,348 feet—plays a role in the Hopi migration story. Another group of mound builders, the Hopewell culture (ca. 200 B.C.–A.D. 700) spread throughout much of the East and the Midwest. The Hopewell people established a widespread trading network. Many beautifully crafted artifacts have been found in Hopewell mounds. After the decline of the Hopewell people, the people of the Mississippian culture (A.D. 700–postcontact times) developed one of the most complex societies to arise in North America. Its huge population centers housed thousands of people and were centered on temple mounds larger than the pyramids of Egypt. The trading network of the Mississippian people reached from northern Mexico to Canada. Their burial practices and social system indicate that the Mississippians' religious life and mythology were probably influenced by Meso-American cultures. Although their own ancient myth systems have not survived, the mounds built by these four cultures entered into the mythology of the people who succeeded them.

Separately, in the Southwest, three dominant cultures arose: the Mogollon, Hohokam, and Anasazi. The Mogollon (ca. 300 B.C.–A.D. 1300), whose main area ranged along the Arizona–New Mexico border, were known for the images they left painted on or chiseled in stone (known respectively as pictographs and PETROGLYPHS), their weaving, and their pottery. Although we have no records of the myths and legends of the Mogollon, the images they painted and carved give clues. Representations of deities, ceremonial dancers, supernatural beings, animals, BIRDS, and geometric symbols reflect the richness of Mogollon religious and spiritual life. The Hohokam (ca. 100 B.C.–A.D. 1500) made the Sonoran Desert of Arizona flourish with the extensive canal systems they developed to irrigate their arid homeland. Meso-American influence on the Hohokam was evident in the pottery and the human-shaped ceramic figurines they created, as well as in the Mayan-style ball courts they constructed for sacred games. The Anasazi (ca. A.D. 100–1300) built the great cliff houses and multi-unit dwellings found along canyons and mesa walls throughout what is now called the Four Corners area, where the boundaries of Arizona, New Mexico, Colorado, and Utah meet. The descendants of the Anasazi (some of whom prefer the term *Ancestral Puebloans*) have incorporated legends about the Anasazi and the abandonment of their vast dwellings into their traditions and histories.

For the many different Native American peoples, everything changed following contact with Europeans after Columbus landed in the Americas in 1492. European contact added new dimensions to old mythologies, and new traditions developed. For instance, the introduction of the HORSE by Spanish conquistadores in the 1600s radically changed the culture of the Plains tribes. The oral tradition of the Plains people celebrates the coming of the horse, although it does not attribute its origin to the Spaniards. These animals were too important a gift to have come in such an ordinary way. Many tribes told stories of how a vision seeker acquired horses through supernatural encounters. Of course, the changes that prompted the development of other new Native American myths were far from beneficial. The near-extinction of the BUFFALO caused by European hunters in the 1800s was devastating for the Plains tribes. The loss of the buffalo figures in numerous legends. Displacement and resettlement of tribes had an equally devastating effect. Cultures and traditions were altered or destroyed, native languages died out, and countless Native Americans died from European diseases, warfare, and genocide.

Today there has been a resurgence in the efforts of Native Americans to restore and preserve their traditional cultures, religions, and languages. Ritual and myth, in addition to being links with a people's past, have become alive and vital in the lives of present-day people. Myth is still evolving as modern storytellers add their own dimensions to old tales.

THEMES OF NATIVE AMERICAN MYTHOLOGY

Although details of Native American myths vary from culture to culture, certain themes are universal. Throughout North America there are CREATION ACCOUNTS—legends about the origins of the universe, Earth, heavenly bodies, human beings, animals, and important PLANTS. For almost all tribes—except for those in the arid Southwest—in the beginning the world was covered with PRIMORDIAL WATERS before land was created. Myths abound about diving animals and birds that bring up mud from the bottom of the waters to make the Earth. In tales from the Southwest, four or five worlds of different colors or elements are stacked atop each other, and people ascend from one dying world to the next until they reach the last, present world.

Universally, myths express a reverence for nature and an understanding of the need to honor the animals that gave their lives to sustain human life. Many myths center on instructions about the appropriate ways to approach, take the life of, and thank game animals.

Every culture has its tales of CULTURE HEROES who brought the gift of the essentials of life, such as LIGHT, FIRE, RAIN, game animals, and sacred plants. Culture heroines also exist—women associated with fertility, conception, pregnancy, birth, agriculture, and skills such as pottery, weaving, and basket making. Every culture also has its tales of TRICK-STERS—beings so clever they often outwitted even themselves—who were also often seen as culture heroes. WARRIOR TWINS are a variant of culture heroes found in many different traditions. Regional variations reflect specific cultures. However, the twins' births are typically shrouded in mystery. They are frequently sons of the SUN, attain adulthood rapidly, have supernatural powers, and are capable of feats of magic. Typically, the twins enter on a quest to their father in order to obtain weapons and lore, having many adventures, undergoing ordeals and tests, and slaying MONSTERS in the process. They return to their people triumphant and share the knowledge they have gained—thus assuring the perpetuation of ritual knowledge and traditions.

Along with the origins of life, the origins of death and the nature of the afterworld also play a role in the mythologies of almost every culture. Concepts of life after death vary widely. The Natchez sent their rulers into the afterlife accompanied not only by a wealth of treasures but also by women and servants who had been slain in order to attend them in the next world. For some tribes, the souls of the dead lived on in the spirit world in much the same way they lived on Earth—hunting, tending crops, gathering foods, and fishing.

According to Joseph Campbell (1904–1987), the world's foremost authority on mythology, mythology serves four basic functions: to express the mystery and wonder of the universe, to describe the nature of the universe, to support and pass on cultural traditions and codes of conduct, and to teach people how to live in harmony with their world. The myths presented in this book exemplify these four functions.

SOURCES OF NATIVE AMERICAN MYTHOLOGY

Although at the time of European contact Native Americans were preliterate—without written languages—SHAMANS, storytellers, and elders had been passing down traditions, beliefs, and mythology from generation to generation for hundreds of years. In postcontact times, interested people began to record details of Native American lives, traditions, histories, and legends. The dispersal and extinction of tribes played a role in determining which mythologies were preserved and which were lost. Some tribes had more members than others and thus were able to survive as tribes. Other tribes—such as the Navajo (Dineh) and Hopi—held out longer against the influence of European cultures and have retained their traditions into the present. Present-day storytellers, singers, shamans, and tribal elders of most Native American groups continue the ORAL TRADITION, passing on the stories and rituals that were passed down to them. From such sources come what we know about the "first people"—the name by which most tribes identify themselves.

Among the early recorders were missionaries and traders, who contributed greatly to our knowledge of Native American religion, ritual, and mythology. Franc Johnson Newcomb (1887–1970), for example, spent 25 years at a trading post on the Navajo (Dineh) reservation, where she collected tales from a variety of storytellers. One of the best known recorders of Native American life was the artist and author George Catlin (1796–1872), who in 1832–33 traveled throughout the West painting portraits of Native Americans, collecting artifacts, and recording traditions and ceremonies. Pioneer ethnographers—scientists who study human cultures—spent years in the field recording the history, religion, mythology, songs, ceremonies, arts, daily life, and languages of various tribes.

The accuracy of recorded myths and legends depends largely on these variables: the storyteller, the translator, and the recorder. Native American myths evolved over time, and each storyteller added his or her own variations to a tale. Different storytellers told their own versions of tales, which resulted in the variations of the same tale that exist today. Native American interpreters spoke English and European languages with varying degrees of ability and may have edited tales to reflect what they thought European listeners would prefer to hear. Before tape recorders existed, human recorders developed their own systems for recording Native American languages. This resulted in different spellings for words and names in myths recorded by different people. Recorders, too, added their own biases and points of view. Franc Johnson Newcomb, for example, rewrote the Navajo (Dineh) myths she recorded as stories for children.

CULTURE AREAS

Because ways of life are closely related to environment, Native American groups within a region usually share cultural traits, lifestyles, and often languages. However, the history of Native Americans has been characterized by movement. Through migration and resettlement, many groups unrelated by culture or language became residents of the same geographic area.

Scholars of Native American culture have divided the Americas into what are known as culture areas, which roughly represent common cultures. One system defines the following 10 culture areas for North America including much of what is now Mexico: Arctic, California, Great Basin, Great Plains, Northeast, Northwest Coast, Plateau, Southeast, Southwest, and Subarctic. (See the map page xiv.)

HOW TO USE THIS BOOK

The entries in this book are in alphabetical order and may be looked up as you would look up words in a dictionary. When the English name is used more commonly in myths than the Native American name, the main entry is the English translation; the Native American name is given in parentheses. Alternative names and spellings are also provided in parentheses following the main entry, as are English translations of Native American names. Cross-references are provided to both Native American and English versions of names. Because so many different Native American languages are represented in this guide—and because many languages have died out—no attempt has been made to include pronunciations of Native American names and terms. Cross-references to other entries are printed in SMALL CAPITAL LETTERS. The Index at the back of the book will help you to find characters, topics, and myths.

Time Line of North American Cultures

Note: This time line tracks the evolution of *various* cultures, not a single monolithic and continuous one.

ca. 40,000–10,500 B.C.	Arrival of Paleo-Siberians in North America from Asia and dispersal throughout the Americas
ca. 35,000–8000 B.C.	Paleo-Indian Period
ca. 9200–8000 B.C.	Clovis spear-point culture
ca. 9100–8000 B.C.	Sandia and Folsom spear-point cultures
ca. 9000–1000 B.C.	Desert culture in Great Basin
ca. 8000–4500 B.C.	Plano (Plainview) culture
ca. 5000–1000 B.C.	Archaic (or Foraging) Period
ca. 4000–1500 B.C.	Old Copper culture around Great Lakes
ca. 1800–500 B.C.	Poverty Point culture
ca. 1500 B.C.–A.D. 1500	Formative Period
ca. 1400 B.C.–A.D. 1500	Woodland cultures in East
ca. 1000 B.C.–A.D. 200	Adena culture
ca. 200 B.C.–A.D. 700	Hopewell culture
ca. A.D. 100–1300	Anasazi culture in Southwest
ca. 700–1550	Mississippian (temple mound building) culture along Mississippi River and its tributaries
ca. 1200–1400	Ancestral Apache and Navajo (Dineh) bands migrate into Southwest

1492	Period of European contact begins when Christopher Columbus (Spain; Italian descent) lands in San Salvador in the Caribbean
1512	Colony of New Spain founded, covering present-day Mexico, Central America, the southwestern United States, Florida, the West Indies, and the Philippines; Spanish law gives Spanish land grantees the right to enslave native peoples on granted lands
1540–42	Francisco Vázquez de Coronado (Spain) explores the Southwest and southern Plains; horses are introduced to North America
ca. 1560–70	Formation of Iroquois League of Five Nations by Deganawidah and Hiawatha
1830	U.S. Congress passes Indian Removal Act calling for relocation of eastern Native American tribes to Indian Territory west of the Mississippi River
1832–42	Relocation of Cherokee, Chickasaw, Choctaw, Creek, Seminole, and other eastern tribes to Indian Territory (in what is now Oklahoma)
1838	Potawatomi "Trail of Death," relocation from Indiana to Indian Territory
1838–39	Cherokee "Trail of Tears," enforced march to Indian Territory during which thousands died from disease, starvation, and abuse
1876–77	Sioux War for Black Hills, involving Lakota, Cheyenne, and Arapaho under Sitting Bull and Crazy Horse; Battle of Little Big Horn in 1876; Crazy Horse surrenders in 1877
1889	Ghost Dance movement founded by Northern Paiute prophet Wovoka
1890	U.S. troops massacre some 200 Lakota en route to Ghost Dance celebration at Wounded Knee Creek, South Dakota; last major engagement between Native Americans and U. S. settlers

NATIVE AMERICAN CULTURE AREAS

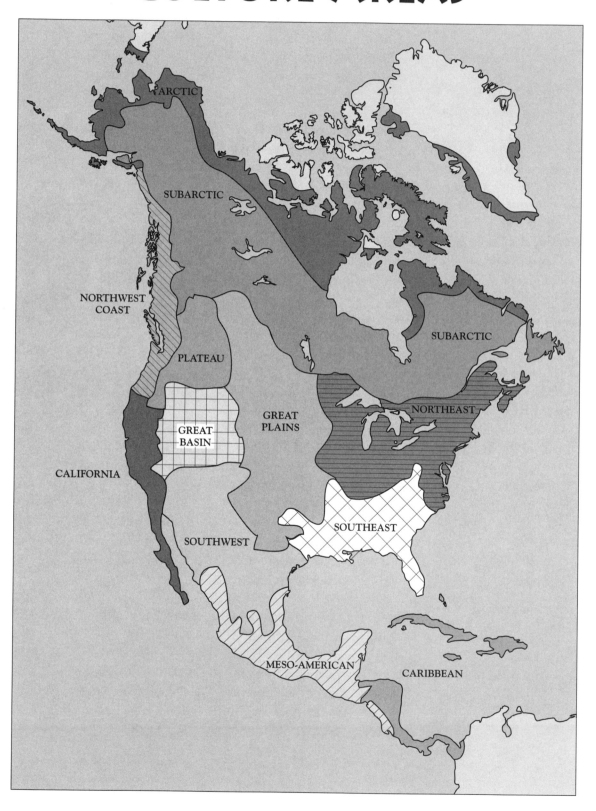

AATAENTSIC (Ataensie, Eagentci)   See SKY WOMAN.

ABOVE-OLD-MAN (Gudatri-Gakwitl) *Wiyot* The CREATOR of the world and everything in it. Above-Old-Man was unhappy with the first people he made, because they had fur and were unable to speak clearly. He decided to destroy the world with a FLOOD. However, CONDOR became aware of Above-Old-Man's plan. He and his sister hid in a basket and were saved. When they emerged after the waters receded, they found the world empty except for birds. In Condor's role as a CULTURE HERO, he and his sister became the ancestors of the human race. (See also HUMANS, ORIGIN OF.)

ACOMA EMERGENCE AND MIGRATION
Acoma Pueblo Acoma Pueblo is one of the seven pueblos inhabited by Keres-speaking people. (The other Keresan pueblos are Cóchiti, Laguna, San Felipe, Santa Ana, Santo Domingo, and Zia.) In the Acoma CREATION ACCOUNT, the people were living in a dark, FOUR-chambered UNDERWORLD. MASEWA AND UYUYEWA, the WARRIOR TWIN sons of IATIKU (the Mother of the Pueblo people), led the people out of the underworld at SHIPAP, the emergence place. The people were soft and weak, and their eyes were closed. Iatiku faced them toward the east, and when the Sun rose the people's eyes opened and they grew in strength.

Iatiku showed the people how to get food in order to live and told them that powerful spirits called KACHINAS would arrive soon. Masewa and Uyuyewa taught the people how to welcome the kachinas with offerings of food and PRAYERSTICKS—ceremonially prepared, decorated sticks to which items such as FEATHERS and shells were attached. When the kachi-nas arrived, they brought gifts of clothing, tools, bows and arrows, and pottery, and they danced all day.

The people did not want to defile the emergence place by continuing to live there, so they left to find a new home. Masewa led them south. The people settled in Kacikatcutia (White House) and called on the kachinas. Again, the kachinas came and danced. After they left, one man imitated them in a comical way. Learning about this mockery, the kachinas became angry and attacked the village the next day. Most of the people were killed. Messengers told the surviving people that the kachinas would never come again unless the people dressed as kachinas and performed the prayers they had been taught. The remaining people quarreled among themselves over whether it was right to impersonate kachinas. They split up into different groups, some of which migrated to other locations. To make it difficult for the people to quarrel again, Iatiku gave them different languages to speak.

Masewa led one group to Acoma, where they established Acoma Pueblo. When the people called the kachinas, the impersonators came and danced in the plaza, and the people's prayers for RAIN were answered.

ADLET *Inuit* Five blood-drinking MONSTERS that were born to a woman who married a DOG. The young woman had turned down many suitors, until finally her father lost patience and told her that if no man was good enough for her, she might as well marry a dog. The next day a new suitor arrived, wearing an amulet of dog claws. She agreed to go with him, and they went to live on a nearby island. She soon began to suspect that her husband was actually a dog that could take human form. Her suspicions about him were realized when she gave birth to a litter of five puppies and five human babies. In one version of the tale, the human babies later became the Adlet. The woman set the puppies adrift in a boat, and they became the ancestors of white people.

In a second version of this tale, the DOG HUS-BAND swam to the home of his wife's father every day to be given food, since in his dog form he was unable to hunt. After a while, the father grew tired of feeding his daughter's family, so he put boulders in the bag with the meat he gave the dog. Weighted down, the dog sank into the sea and drowned. The next time her father came to visit, the woman set her dog children on him, and they killed him. Left with no means of support and 10 children to feed, she decided to send her children off to fend for themselves. She transformed her boots into boats and sent all 10 children out to sea. They became the ancestors of both Native Americans and white people.

ADLIVUN (Qudlivun) *Inuit* The UNDER-WORLD. People who disobeyed SEDNA, a powerful goddess who ruled over sea creatures, were sent to Adlivun when they died. *Adlivun* means "those beneath us." A being named ANGUTA brought the dead to Adlivun.

AHAYUTA AND MATSILEMA (Ahaiyuta and Matsailema) *Zuni* WARRIOR TWINS who were collectively called the Ahayuta. They were the sons of the SUN, created when sunlight struck the foam of a waterfall. The Ahayuta led the first people into the world (see ZUNI EMERGENCE AND MIGRATION). Stories about the Ahayuta contain many elements common to myths about warrior twins, such as making a journey to their father, the Sun, in order to gain power; being able to bring RAIN; and slaying MON-STERS to make the world safe for humans.

One monster the twins slew was CLOUD SWAL-LOWER, a powerful giant. Cloud Swallower's practice was to stand with his legs forming an arch over a pathway. When people came by, the giant would greet them politely and tell them to pass through his legs. Then he would snatch them up and devour them. Grandmother Spider (SPIDER WOMAN) offered her help to the Ahayuta in ridding the world of this monster. While Cloud Swallower pretended to sleep, she wove her web around his head. Blinded by the web, Cloud Swallower was unable to catch the twins, who easily slew him.

Another legend relates how the Ahayuta acquired the ability to make RAIN by stealing rain-making tools—thunder stones, a lightning frame, and arrows—from the Saiyathlia, KACHINA warriors. The Ahayuta sneaked into an initiation ceremony for young warriors, but they were killed during the ceremony. The Saiyathlia cut off the twins' arms and legs and cooked them to feed the youths being initiated. However, the twins' voices remained alive and taunted the Saiyathlia. When the Saiyathlia sneezed, the twins shot out their noses and came back to life. They then slew the Saiyathlia and stole the rainmaking tools.

In another legend, when the CORN MAIDENS fled, taking all the CORN with them, the Ahayuta joined in the search for them. The twins are credited with creating the MILKY WAY through their travels around the world during this search.

AKBAATATDIA (The One Who Has Made Everything) *Crow* The CREATOR, who had responsibility for all natural forces. Akbaatatdia was called by several different names, among them Isaahka (OLD MAN), Isaahkawuattee (OLD MAN COYOTE), Baakukkule (The One Above), and Iichikbaaalee (First Doer).

AKHLUT *Yup'ik* A killer WHALE that took the form of a wolf and went on land to kill people and other animals.

AMALA *Tsimshian* The being that supported the world. According to legend, the world was spinning on a pole held up by Amala as he lay on his back. Amala's strength came from wild duck oil rubbed onto his back. However, the oil was gradually being used up, and when it ran out, Amala would die and the world would end.

AMCHITAPUKA (First Man on Earth) *South-eastern Yavapai* A CULTURE HERO; son of the SUN and grandson of the female CREATOR figure WIDAPOKWI. Shortly after Amchitapuka's birth, a giant EAGLE carried off his mother to feed its eaglets. When Amchitapuka reached adulthood, he learned how his mother had died. In order to avenge her death, he let himself be carried off by the same giant eagle, which dropped him in its nest. Using a powerful blue stone that his father had given him, Amchitapuka slew the adult eagles. He told the eaglets that he was their brother, and eagles never again harmed humans. Amchitapuka became a great chief. Among the deeds with which he was credited was naming the CONSTELLATIONS. The Western Yavapai call him Nyapakaamte (Man Up Above), and the Yavapai-Apache call him Sakarakaamche (Lofty Wanderer).

In the Yavapai-Apache CREATION ACCOUNT, Sakarakaamche grew lonely and wanted a wife, but the only other person in the world was his grandmother. Sakarakaamche idly began rolling a bit of clay around in his hands. He found that he had shaped a female figure. Liking what he had done, he made more human figures. He thought that if the figures were alive, he would no longer be lonely, so he closed his eyes and dreamed of living people. When he opened his eyes, the Yavapai-Apache people filled the canyon. (See also HUMANS, ORIGIN OF.)

AMULET   An amulet, or talisman, is an object that is believed to have special powers to protect or bring good luck. Some amulets had broad powers, providing general protection. Others were used for specific purposes, such as helping hunters achieve success or protecting against headaches. Newborn babies and children were especially supposed to need the protection of amulets.

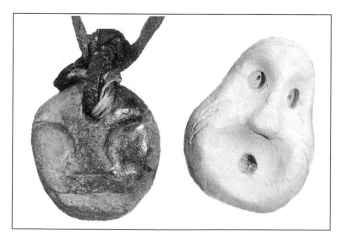

Amulets, such as the Huron (Wyandot) amulets pictured, were worn or carried for protection against harmful spirits and danger. (© Raymond Bial)

Amulets were carried on the person in a pouch or MEDICINE BUNDLE, attached to clothing, hung from a special belt, or kept where their effect was most desired. For example, the Inuit attached amulets to their kayaks to keep them seaworthy.

Belief in the power of amulets was universal across North America. The type of amulet varied from tribe to tribe, from one geographic area to another, and according to the amulet's purpose.

Amulets could be either natural or crafted by hand. Natural amulets were of many kinds: the FEATHERS, beaks, talons, and feet of BIRDS; animal hooves, horns, teeth, and claws; bones; quartz crystals and other stones; CORN ears; plants and grasses; and even human body parts such as dried umbilical cords. The Inuit sometimes used as an amulet the entire stuffed body of a small animal, such as a squirrel or bird. Crafted amulets included engraved stones; figures of people and animals carved from bone, shell, ivory, or wood; and beaded symbols. Amulets worn into battle were frequently shaped like shields.

Amulets made of animal parts were believed to transfer a specific quality or power of an animal—such as a loon's fishing skill or a turtle's longevity—to the person who carried the amulet. Plains warriors wore eagle feathers into battle so that they might acquire the endurance, sharp vision, speed, and ferocity of that bird. Chickasaw hunters carried deer hooves to give them the deer's speed. Animal parts were also carried in order to draw animals closer to the hunter and ensure success.

ANASAZI   (Ancient Ones, Ancient Strangers, Ancient Enemies)   The ancestors of the Pueblo people. (*Anasazi*, a Navajo [Dineh] term, is offensive to many Pueblo people, who prefer the term *Ancestral Puebloans*.) The Anasazi were the builders of the great cliff houses and huge, multi-unit dwellings built along canyons and mesa walls in the Southwest, which were mysteriously abandoned around A.D. 1300. (See BLACK MESA; CANYON DE CHELLY; CHACO CANYON; MESA VERDE.) Various legends explain why the Anasazi left their homes and disappeared. According to one Navajo (Dineh) story, a whirlwind dispersed the Anasazi because they had abandoned the ways of their ancestors. (See also CLOUD SWALLOWER; HORNED WATER SERPENT.)

The Anasazi culture developed around A.D. 100 in what is now called the Four Corners area, where the boundaries of Arizona, New Mexico, Colorado, and Utah meet. Anasazi culture is divided into six periods of development: Basket Maker (A.D. 100–500), Modified Basket Maker (500–700), Developmental Pueblo (700–1050), Classic Pueblo (1050–1300), Regressive Pueblo (1300–1700), and Modern Pueblo (1700–present).

The Basket Maker people were skilled basket weavers who had begun to move from hunting and gathering to agriculture. They cultivated maize (CORN) and pumpkins and lived either in caves or in freestanding structures made of poles and adobe. By the Modified Basket Maker period, agriculture had taken the place of hunting and gathering. The people added bean crops to maize and pumpkins, raised turkeys, and began to make sun-dried pottery. The Modified Basket Makers still lived either in caves or in the open, but they had begun to create homes with both aboveground and underground chambers. The aboveground rooms were used mainly for storage, and the underground rooms probably served as both residences and ceremonial chambers.

During the Developmental Pueblo period, homes increased in size, and stone began to replace the pole-and-adobe method of construction. Aboveground rooms were used as residences, and the underground pit houses became KIVAS, the circular rooms used for ceremonial purposes. It was during the Classic Pueblo period that the great apartmentlike structures, some of which had as many as 1,000 rooms, were constructed. By 1300 these villages had been abandoned. Modern theories about the reasons for this include a drought that lasted from 1276 to 1299 and the movement of Navajo (Dineh) and Apache bands into the area from the north.

When the large Anasazi centers were abandoned, the residents began moving away from the region, establishing new communities in the Rio Grande Valley of New Mexico and the White Mountains of Arizona. This movement characterized the Regressive Pueblo period. Eventually, people returned to the Black Mesa area of Arizona. The period of wandering became part of the Hopi CREATION ACCOUNT (see HOPI EMERGENCE AND MIGRATION). According to tradition, the Hopi people emerged from the previous world through SIPAPU, a cave located variously in the Grand Canyon, along the Little Colorado River, or near where the Colorado and Little Colorado Rivers meet. Following their emergence, the people wandered about in search of a place to live. After exploring the lands and learning about the world, they returned to the center of the universe, Black Mesa. (See also MASAU'U.)

Increasing Spanish influence marked the beginning of the Modern Pueblo period, usually dated from around 1700.

ANGUTA *Inuit* A being who lived with the sea goddess SEDNA in ADLIVUN, the UNDERWORLD. Anguta brought people who died down to Adlivun. After sleeping beside Anguta for a year, some dead souls went on to Adliparmiut (or Qudliparmiut), a deeper and darker place than Adlivun, where they were allowed to hunt. Murderers remained in Adlivun.

ANIMALS Animals were vital to the survival of Native Americans. They were a source not only of food, but also of clothing, tools, utensils, musical instruments, and lodge coverings. In addition to turning furs and hides into clothing, footwear, robes, and shields, Native Americans used sinew for thread; crafted bones into knives, awls, and other tools; used rawhide for bindings and to make drums and drumsticks; and turned hooves into rattles.

Because of their importance, animals are a major presence in the folklore of every Native American cultural group. Numerous tales describe their origin (see BLACK HACTCIN for one example), and tales across the continent explain how animals acquired specific characteristics, such as the RACCOON's face mask or the BEAR's short tail. In myths, animals act as messengers, guardians, advisers, and servants of humanity. They are essentially human—thinking, speaking, and acting as humans do—but also have abilities specific to their animal form. Animals are featured in many CREATION ACCOUNTS, sometimes as the CREATOR of the universe and the human race (see HARE; OLD MAN COYOTE), sometimes as deities helping to regulate conditions (see BEAST GODS).

Native American tradition reflects the view that all the Creator's works—humans, animals, birds, fish,

Effigy pottery vessel, Pueblo Bonito, Chaco Canyon National Monument, New Mexico *(© George H. H. Huey)*

Black-on-white *olla*, ca. 1260–1330, Navajo National Monument, Arizona *(© George H. H. Huey)*

Ceramic jars, Pueblo Bonito, Chaco Canyon National Monument, New Mexico *(© George H. H. Huey)*

Canteen, ca. 1250–1300, Keet Seel, Navajo National Monument, Arizona *(© George H. H. Huey)*

Well-preserved Anasazi artifacts have been found at sites in Arizona and New Mexico.

insects, plants—are equal and share the Earth as part-ners. A show of respect for the spirit of an animal about to be hunted has characterized almost all Native American cultures: Unless they were honored, animals would not consent to their deaths. In a num-ber of myths, animals or powerful beings such as MANITOUS, Holy People, or spirits responsible for game instructed hunters about the rituals necessary for a successful hunt.

Some stories say that before humans came into the world, animal spirits ruled over the Earth and ani-mals could speak. When animals turned the Earth over to people, they lost their ability to speak. Many people, however, could understand animal languages and communicate with animals. Animals were also believed to have supernatural powers and knowledge that they could share with chosen people. Through fasting and other means, a human might have a vision of his or her animal protector, or spirit guide. (See TOTEM ANIMAL; VISION QUEST.)

Marriage between animals and humans is a com-mon theme in Native American folklore. Cultures across the continent have stories about bear spouses, the BUFFALO is a common figure in tales from the Southwest and Plains, and many tales revolve around a DOG HUSBAND (see ADLET; SEDNA). Sometimes the animal spouse transformed itself into human form for a period of time. A dog husband, for example, might be a DOG by day and a human at night. Most tales of animal-human marriages end unhappily, with one of the pair—animal or human—becoming homesick for his or her own world and people before running off. (One such example is BUFFALO WOMAN.)

Many tales involve clever animals that play the role of a helper, a TRICKSTER, or a combination of the two. In various stories, animals—as CULTURE HEROES—brought LIGHT and FIRE to humans, showed them how to survive, and taught them important skills such as weaving. Among the animals that brought light or fire are BEAVER, FOX, MINK, and MUSKRAT. COYOTE is perhaps the most frequently appearing animal character in myths. Across the western part of North America, the coyote is univer-sally respected for its cleverness and ability to survive in a wide variety of environments.

Among the other animals that played roles in various cultures are the BADGER, DEER, ELK, FROG, HORSE, MOUNTAIN LION, OPOSSUM, OTTER, PORCU-PINE, RABBIT, SABLE, SNAKE, TURTLE, WHALE, WOLF, and WOLVERINE.

ANOG ITE   See DOUBLE-FACED WOMAN.

APACHE EMERGENCE AND MIGRATION
Jicarilla Apache   In the beginning, there was noth-ing—no Earth, no sky—only the HACTCIN, supernat-ural beings. The *hactcin* made the Earth first, including both the upper world and the UNDER-WORLD, and then they made the sky. Everyone—spirit people and spirit animals—lived in the dark underworld, where there was no SUN or MOON. The only light came from eagle feather torches that the people carried around. Accounts differ as to how the Sun and Moon were created. In one version, Holy Boy acquired the Sun from WHITE HACTCIN and the Moon from BLACK HACTCIN. In another, the head-men of the tribe created the Sun and Moon, using various materials. In still another version, people and the animals that are active in the daytime held a contest with the night animals. If the day animals won, there would be light; if the night animals won, it would remain dark. After the people and day animals won FOUR times, the Sun rose in the east, and it was light.

Soon, however, the Sun and Moon left the underworld through an opening to the world above—in one version, they left because the people argued and ignored the *hactcin*'s warning to be silent for four days; in another, they left because evil beings tried to destroy them. Nothing the people did made the Sun and Moon return, so they determined to leave the underworld also. In order for the people to reach the upper world, the *hactcin* directed them to make a rep-resentation in sand, or SANDPAINTING, of a land bor-dered by four mountains. The people built four mounds of sand of four different COLORS and placed on each mound leaves, seeds, and fruit of those col-ors—black in the east, blue in the south, yellow in the west, and speckled in the north. The mounds grew into mountains but stopped growing before they reached the upper world, so the people had to build ladders to reach it. In one version of the account, the ladder was constructed from four rays of sunlight brought from the upper world by Fly and SPIDER. In another version, the people first tried to use FEATH-ERS to build a ladder, but these could not bear any

Carvings and paintings on stone, like these Fremont Indian petroglyphs from Nine Mile Canyon, Utah, are found throughout North America. They frequently depict the animals that were essential to human life. *(© Stephen Trimble)*

weight. Four BUFFALO then offered their right horns, and the people were able to climb up the horns to the upper world.

Animals sent to explore the world above reported that it was covered with water. WIND offered to drive back the water if the people would ask for his help. A black storm blew and drove away the waters to the east; a blue storm, the waters to the south; a yellow storm, the waters to the west; and a speckled storm, the waters to the north. This created the four oceans in these directions.

The people and animals then emerged from the underworld. First came six sacred CLOWNS, painted white with black stripes. Next came the *hactcin*, followed by FIRST MAN AND FIRST WOMAN and then 12 MEDICINE PEOPLE, six to represent summer and six to represent winter. All the people and animals fol-

lowed, except for an elderly woman (in one version, two elderly people) who was too frail to climb the ladder. She told the people that when they died, they would rejoin her in the underworld.

After all the people had emerged, they traveled east, south, west, and north until they came to the ocean in each direction. As they went, each tribe stopped and settled where it wanted to live. The Jicarilla, however, continued to circle the emergence place until the *hactcin* became displeased and asked where they wished to live. When the Jicarilla answered that they wanted to live in the middle of the Earth, they were led to a place near Taos, New Mexico, where they made their home.

ARROW BOY *Cheyenne* A boy with supernatural powers who was associated with the disappearance of the BUFFALO and their return. The boy's mother carried him in her womb for FOUR years, and when he was finally born, people knew that he was special. When the young boy killed a chief who tried to take away a buffalo the boy had slain, the people became afraid and decided to kill the boy. He disappeared, and all the buffalo disappeared with him.

The boy traveled into the mountains, where a door in a peak opened for him. Inside the mountain he found a group of MEDICINE men, who told him that they would instruct him in how to become his tribe's prophet and counselor. For four years the boy learned sacred songs, magic, and ceremonies for hunting and warfare. At the end of that time, he was given a MEDICINE BUNDLE and four medicine arrows. Calling himself Motzeyouf (Arrow Boy), the boy returned to the Cheyenne, who were weak and starving. He explained that he had caused the buffalo to disappear, but he had returned to care for his people, and they would never be hungry again. The next morning, the buffalo returned. (In another version of this legend, the Cheyenne prophet SWEET MEDICINE is the protagonist, not Arrow Boy.)

ASDZÁÁ NÁDLEEHÉ See CHANGING WOMAN.

ASH Any of several genuses of TREES in the olive family. Ash trees are valued for their wood and for ornamental uses. Thin strips of split wood from the black ash are used in basket weaving.

In an account of the origin of the Penobscot people, the CULTURE HERO GLUSKAP shot an arrow into a black ash tree. The tree split open, and out of it came the Penobscot, singing and dancing. The black ash (sometimes called brown ash for its dark brown heartwood) is sacred to the Penobscot.

ATIUS TÍRAWA See TIRAWAHAT.

ATOTARHO (Atotarhoh, Thadodaho, Wathatotarho) (fl. 1500s) *Iroquois* The Onondaga chief who became the first head of the Iroquois Confederacy. When the Peacemaker, DEGANAWIDAH, and his disciple HIAWATHA tried to end the bloodshed among the warring Five Nations (the Cayuga, Mohawk, Oneida, Onondaga, and Seneca), Atotarho was the chief opponent of peace. According to legend,

Atotarho was twisted by evil in mind and body. He had snakes growing from his hair and could make birds fall from the sky. His magic was so powerful that Deganawidah and Hiawatha were unable to approach him until they composed and sang a song of peace that hypnotized the evil chief. He then sat quietly, allowing Hiawatha to comb the snakes from his hair and straighten his body.

With his power transformed from evil into good, Atotarho was named the Chief Firekeeper and head of the newly formed league. He became honored for his courage, wisdom, and heroism. Atotarho's name was perpetuated as the official title of the leader of the Iroquois Confederacy. To this day, the chief of chiefs is called the Atotarho.

ATSITSI (Screech Owl) *Blackfeet* A legendary warrior. Before a fight with the Cree, older warriors told the 14-year-old Atsitsi to stay behind; instead, the young boy led them into battle, where they were victorious. He went on to become famous for his deeds in war.

AURORA BOREALIS The northern lights, colorful displays of light in the night sky at high latitudes of the Northern Hemisphere. They can take the form of shifting, luminous curtains, arcs, bands, and patches. They occur when energy particles (electrons and protons) from outside the Earth's atmosphere interact with atoms of the upper atmosphere in the area around the north magnetic pole. (The same effect takes place in the Southern Hemisphere, where it is called the aurora australis, or southern lights.)

To Algonquian-speaking tribes, the flashing lights were the dancing spirits of the dead, which would steal noisy children. People of the Arctic said that the lights were the souls of dead children playing football. According to Lakota legend, a giant named WAZIYA guarded the entrance to the place where the northern lights dance.

AWAKKULE *Crow* Tiny but strong people who acted as helpers but in some tales also played tricks on people. (See also LITTLE PEOPLE; TRICKSTER.)

AWONAWILONA (The Maker) *Zuni* The CREATOR. In the beginning, there was only the void in which Awonawilona existed. He first created mist and then transformed himself into the SUN. The Sun's warmth caused the mist to condense and fall as RAIN, forming the oceans. Taking some of his own flesh, Awonawilona placed it on the water, where it became MOTHER EARTH AND FATHER SKY. These two then created the FOUR-chambered underground womb or four UNDERWORLDS in which the people lived before they emerged into the present world. See ZUNI EMERGENCE AND MIGRATION.

AZEBAN *Western Abenaki* RACCOON, a TRICKSTER.

B

BADGER A burrowing mammal of the Northern Hemisphere, related to the weasel. The small but courageous badger has been known to keep off a pack of dogs until it reaches safety or digs itself into the ground and disappears—a trick it can manage in seconds.

For the Zuni, this sturdy animal was the BEAST GOD symbolizing the south.

In the traditional account of the Hopi migrations (see HOPI EMERGENCE AND MIGRATION), a young girl became ill on the migration to the south. No one could make her well until the oldest clan member went into the forest to find the power to cure her. There he met Badger, who gave him an herb to cure the girl and showed him more herbs, plants, and trees to treat any illness. In gratitude, the clan named itself the Badger Clan. The Badger Clan is one of the four most important Hopi clans and is the custodian of the sacred SPRUCE.

BADLANDS Badlands National Park, South Dakota, is a rugged, eroded area of hills, canyons, and gullies that was once the site of an inland sea. Its numerous fossil beds have yielded the remains of animals that have long been extinct in North America, such as the three-toed horse, camel, saber-toothed tiger, and rhinoceros.

According to Lakota legend, the Badlands were the site of a battle between the UNKTEHI, a race of monsters, and Wakinyan, the THUNDERBIRD. The *unktehi*, who lived in the PRIMORDIAL WATERS from which the Earth emerged, caused devastating FLOODS that endangered the human race. (Another version of the legend attributes the flooding to UNCEGILA, a water serpent.) Angered by the loss of his worshipers, Thunderbird sent down bolts of lightning that dried up the floodwaters and killed the *unktehi*. Their bones were scattered throughout the Badlands, where they can still be found.

BAKOTAHL See KOKOMAHT AND BAKOTAHL.

BEADWAY *Navajo (Dineh)* A ceremonial curing complex, or group of ceremonies (called chants, sings, or ways) conducted to heal illness and restore harmony (*hózhó*) in the universe (see NAVAJO [DINEH] CEREMONIALS). Beadway is included in the HOLYWAY classification of ceremonials, which are used to restore health by attracting good.

The traditional account associated with Beadway involves the adventures of a hero whose mother was Bead Woman, one of CHANGING WOMAN's five daughters. Pueblo people had captured and mistreated the hero. The Pueblo lowered him down a cliff into an EAGLE's nest so that he could steal eaglets for them. They planned to abandon him afterward. Forewarned by the *DIYIN DINEH* (Holy People) about the Pueblo's plans, the hero refused to throw the eaglets from the nest. Although the Pueblo shot fire arrows into the nest, the young man and the eaglets were unharmed. The grateful eagle parents carried the hero up to their home in the sky. Through his adventures there, which involved ignoring the eagles' warnings, doing forbidden things, and defeating the eagles' enemies, the hero gained much knowledge. The eagles taught him both Beadway and EAGLEWAY, offered him one of their daughters as a wife, and eventually returned him to his home. The hero then taught the ceremonials he had learned to his younger brother so that they would be passed on.

BEAR Throughout North America, wherever bears live, they have been honored as powerful figures associated with healing. Because bears hibernate in winter, they are symbols of renewal and seasonal change. The Plains tribes refused to eat bear meat because they considered bears to be their ancestors. Bears were central to the basic rites of many tribes and were celebrated in the initiation of young people—both boys and girls—into adulthood, shamanistic and healing rituals, and hunting practices.

Bear Dances were held by many tribes for a variety of purposes—to heal the sick and those injured in battle, to prepare for war, to welcome and honor bears when they emerged from hibernation in the spring, and to protect people from attacks by bears. A bear KACHINA (which the Zuni call Aincekoko) takes part in the Zuni Mixed Dance held each spring (see also DANCE). For the Zuni, Bear is the BEAST GOD symbolizing the west.

According to Yavapai tradition, Bear was the first great SHAMAN. Tribes of the western subarctic also portrayed the bear as an animal shaman. Among many tribes, shamans with bear power were believed to be the greatest healers of all. Shamans with bear spirit helpers wore bearskin robes and necklaces of bear claws; kept bear claws, teeth, and other body parts in their MEDICINE BUNDLES; and painted bear signs on their faces and bodies.

For the Cherokee, bears were Cherokee of an ancient clan who had been transformed. According to tradition, a young boy of the Ani'-Tsa'guhi clan had a habit of leaving home and remaining in the mountains all day. When brown hair began to grow over his body, his parents asked why he preferred the woods to his home. He spoke convincingly about the good life that could be had living in the woods where food was plentiful and better than the corn and beans available in the settlement. Not only his parents, but the entire clan decided to leave with him and live in the wilderness. When messengers sent by other clans tried to persuade the Ani'-Tsa'guhi to stay, they saw that fur was already beginning to cover the people's bodies. The Ani'-Tsa'guhi told the messengers that from now on they would be called *yanu*, "bears," and that when people were hungry, the bears would come and give them their own flesh. Then they taught the messengers the proper songs with which to call them. The bears' homes were under FOUR peaks of the Great Smoky Mountains, where they held dances every fall before they retired to their dens for the win-

Coastal Alaskan bear totem (*© Joe McDonald/Animals Animals/Earth Sciences*)

ter. Since they had once been human, bears could talk but they chose not to.

Bears appear in hundreds of tales in many different roles. To some Northwest Coast tribes, Bear (Suku) was a CULTURE HERO who traveled the world teaching skills—particularly fishing skills—to humans, naming rivers, creating fish, and killing MONSTERS. In other tales, the bear was itself a monster—usually a giant and often having supernatural powers—that killed people and food animals until it was slain by a hero. In TRICKSTER tales, Bear appears as a slow-thinking, gullible creature that inevitably loses to the trickster animal, such as COYOTE. Humans transformed into bears and bears that changed their form to become humans or other animals are common themes, as are marriages between humans and bears. Bears also figure in myths related to the BIG DIPPER (see DEVIL'S TOWER) and are an important part of the Navajo (Dineh) MOUNTAINWAY ceremonial.

BEAR BUTTE A rock outcropping in the plains east of the BLACK HILLS of South Dakota. Lakota legend says that Bear Butte was formed by the battle between a huge BEAR and UNCEGILA, a female water monster. Uncegila defeated the bear, which collapsed, and the land covered him with soil. He sleeps there in an endless hibernation, the keeper of dreams.

The Cheyenne call Bear Butte Noaha-vose (also spelled Noahvose or Noavosse), the place of MAHEO, the CREATOR. According to tradition, this is where their great prophet, SWEET MEDICINE, received the FOUR sacred arrows that contained the teachings of Maheo and brought blessings to the people.

In Mandan origin stories, Bear Butte was the place where their ancestors were saved from the primordial FLOOD.

BEAST GODS *Zuni* ANIMAL deities associated with the six cardinal DIRECTIONS. North is symbolized by the MOUNTAIN LION; south, the BADGER; east, the WOLF; west, the BEAR; zenith (above), the EAGLE; and nadir (below), the gopher or mole. Curing societies evoke the Beast Gods during retreats. The leader of the Beast Gods is the CULTURE HERO POSHAYANKI, with whom they live in SHIPAPOLINA, a sacred place.

BEAUTYWAY *Navajo (Dineh)* A ceremonial curing complex, or group of ceremonies (called chants, sings, or ways) conducted to heal illness and restore harmony (*hózhó*) in the universe (see NAVAJO [DINEH] CEREMONIALS). Beautyway is included in the HOLYWAY classification of ceremonials, which are used to restore health by attracting good. The traditional account associated with Beautyway follows the story presented in ENEMYWAY, in which two sisters were tricked into marrying elderly men, BEAR and SNAKE. Beautyway relates the adventures of the younger sister, who married Snake.

The young woman fled from her husband but ended up in an underground place that was the home of the Snake People. Over a period of days, the Snake People warned the woman not to do certain things, but she always disobeyed them, causing mischief and getting into difficulties from which the Snake People had to rescue her. For example, she was told not to open some water jars but did so anyway, releasing terrible storms. Through each misadventure, the woman learned the songs, rituals, and sacred objects of Beautyway. When she returned home, she taught Beautyway to her family.

BEAVER Strong swimmers, beavers were viewed as powerful underwater spirits that gave people power over the waters. To some tribes, beavers were a symbol of plenty. In a Nez Perce legend, Beaver stole FIRE from the PINES, jealous guardians of this secret, and gave it to birches, willows, and other TREES. This story explains why fire is created when the wood of trees is rubbed together. In one version of the Blackfeet CREATION ACCOUNT, Beaver was one of the diving animals sent by the Creator, NA'PI, to bring up soil from the bottom of the PRIMORDIAL WATERS in order to create land. Beaver was also one of the diving animals sent for soil by the Cree Creator, WEE-SA-KAY-JAC.

BEGOCHÍDÍ (Begocidi) *Navajo (Dineh)* A son of the SUN who appears in CREATION ACCOUNTS. Begochídí controlled game and domestic animals. He could bring game to hunters he favored and spoil the aim of those he disliked. He was also the first potter. Considered a great mischief-maker among the gods, Begochídí could change into different forms—such as weather, wind, or a rainbow—and move about unseen, playing tricks on people. Besides acting as a TRICKSTER, however, he also took pity on those who suffered from the anger of the gods. When GAMBLING GOD lost all his possessions to the other gods and was exiled to the Moon, Begochídí agreed to help him. He created many kinds of animals for Gambling God and made a new people for him to rule, the Naakaii dineh—the inhabitants of what is now Mexico. He then returned Gambling God to Earth.

BIG DIPPER A star pattern formed by the seven brightest stars in the CONSTELLATION Ursa Major, the Great Bear. The handle of the Dipper corresponds to the Great Bear's tail, and the stars that form its bowl mark the Bear's back and hindquarters. Because of its prominence in the night sky, the Big Dipper has been the subject of many tales related to its origin.

According to Chumash myth, the stars are seven boys who were turned into seven geese. The Seneca tell a story about six hunters who chased a BEAR into the sky, not realizing where they were going. After they caught and killed the bear, they remained in the sky as the stars of the Big Dipper; the bear is the star at the lower outside corner of the Dipper's bowl. A Kiowa legend says that seven sisters and their brother were playing one day when the boy changed into a ferocious bear. To save themselves, the girls climbed into a tree that grew taller and taller until it carried them into the sky, where they became the Dipper's stars. In a variation of this tale, the girls climbed onto a tree stump that grew into a tower of rock, DEVIL'S TOWER. In a similar Blackfeet story, the Dipper's seven stars are seven brothers who were chased into the sky by a bear.

In a Cheyenne tale, a BUFFALO was the villain. In this story, a beautiful girl who was skilled at quillwork adopted seven brothers as her own. On each of FOUR successive days, a buffalo—first a calf, then a heifer, next a large cow, and finally a giant bull—came to them and announced that the buffalo nation wanted the girl. When the boys refused to give up their new sister, the bull prepared to kill them. The girl and her brothers clambered up a tree that grew until it reached the sky, where they safely stepped off. The youngest brother then turned all eight of them into

stars. The girl became the brightest star in the Dipper, where she filled the sky with her beautiful quillwork. The youngest brother became a pale star at the end of the Dipper's handle.

Because of its position close to the north celestial pole, the Big Dipper swings around POLARIS, the stationary North Star, during the night. In this way it serves as a compass, always indicating the north. The Navajo (Dineh) combined the Dipper and Polaris into one constellation called Whirling Male (see also SWASTIKA).

The Dipper also changes position relative to Polaris in different seasons of the year, enabling it to be used as a calendar that signals the changing seasons. The Micmac used the seasonal changes in the Dipper as the basis for a hunting story. Seven birds (represented by the three stars in the Dipper's handle and four stars in the constellation Boötes) began hunting a bear (represented by the four stars of the Dipper's bowl) in the spring. They chased her throughout the summer, but in the fall four of the hunters dropped out. The remaining three birds caught, killed, and ate the bear. During the winter the bear's skeleton floated up, and her life spirit entered another bear. In the spring she would reenter

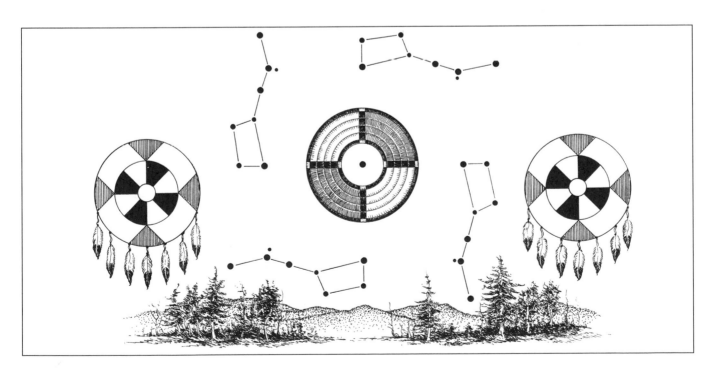

The Big Dipper's motion around the north celestial pole has been used as a calendar. Its changing positions signal the changing seasons. *(Alexander Farquharson)*

the world, and the seasonal hunt would begin again. This myth reflects the concept of bears as symbols of renewal and seasonal change.

Another view of the Big Dipper relates to its position near the MILKY WAY. For the Seminole, who saw the Milky Way as a pathway for dead souls, the Big Dipper was the boat that carried good souls to the City of the West, their final home.

BIG STARWAY *Navajo (Dineh)* A ceremonial curing complex, or group of ceremonies (called chants, sings, or ways) conducted to heal illness and restore harmony (*hózhó*) in the universe (see NAVAJO [DINEH] CEREMONIALS). Big Starway is included in the HOLYWAY classification of ceremonials, which are used to restore health by attracting good.

The traditional account associated with Big Starway involves a family whose daughter married the son of Big Snake and bore him a son. The family followed the SNAKE husband toward his home but could not keep up with him; he continued on without them. While the family camped beside a lake, the baby disappeared, having been swallowed by Big Snake. TALKING GOD brought the woman and her younger brother into the lake, where the WINDS (see NILCH'I) performed a ritual that transformed the infant into an adult. While in the lake, the woman and Younger Brother learned various MEDICINE practices and TABOOS.

Younger Brother, whose adventures form the core of Big Starway, failed to keep the taboos and became ill. He was cured by a performance of NAVAJO WIND-WAY. COYOTE wanted Younger Brother's wife and tried to get rid of Younger Brother by stranding him on a rock that carried him into the sky. When the Star People found Younger Brother, they offered their help. Big Star (S'tsoh, the Navajo [Dineh] name for the planet Venus) taught him the rituals involved in Big Starway and sent him back to Earth. To revenge himself on Coyote, Younger Brother gave him food in which he had enclosed a star. Coyote died after eating the food. In other versions of Big Starway, Younger Brother's wife and sons learned the ceremony from Big Star.

BIRDS Because of their ability to fly, birds were seen as intermediaries between humans and the sky spirits—as messengers that could carry prayers and

pleas up to the gods and return with the gods' blessings and guidance. Powerful flyers such as EAGLES and HAWKS were especially associated with sky spirits. Birds also symbolized the soul. FEATHERS, beaks, bones, talons, and even entire bodies of birds were carried as AMULETS to protect people or to bestow birds' powers on them.

Birds appear frequently as characters in Native American myths. The mischievous BLUE JAY, CROW, and RAVEN are often seen as TRICKSTERS, although both Crow and Raven are also considered CULTURE HEROES who brought LIGHT and FIRE to humanity. Various tales describe the origin of birds (see BLACK HACTCIN for one example) and explain how birds came to have certain characteristics, such as the bald heads of the BUZZARD and TURKEY. In CREATION ACCOUNTS that involve earth-diving animals, water birds such as DUCK, GOOSE, LOON, and SWAN are often included among the divers.

See also CONDOR, HUMMINGBIRD, MAGPIE, OWL, ROADRUNNER, and WOODPECKER.

BISON See BUFFALO.

BLACK GOD (Haashch'ééshzhiní) *Navajo (Dineh)* The god credited with the origin of FIRE. Black God represents fire-making and the control of fire and is also portrayed as the creator of STARS and CONSTELLATIONS. In one version of the Navajo (Dineh) CREATION ACCOUNT, Black God was carefully placing stars in the sky in meaningful arrangements when COYOTE became impatient with the slow process. Coyote snatched up the bag from which Black God was taking the stars (or the blanket on which he had placed them) and tossed the remaining stars into the sky. This explains both the random placement of most stars and the origin of the MILKY WAY.

BLACK HACTCIN *Jicarilla Apache* The leader of the HACTCIN, supernatural beings who were the personifications of the power of objects and natural forces. In the Jicarilla Apache CREATION ACCOUNT, Black Hactcin is credited with making all the ANIMALS, the BIRDS, and the first human beings. He first made an animal out of clay and brought forth all other animals from that animal's body. He assigned each animal the kind of food it would eat and the place where it would live. He next made a bird from clay and swung it around in a clockwise direction, which made the bird dizzy. The bird saw images of birds of many different kinds, which then became real. Black Hactcin assigned each bird the kind of food it would eat and the place where it would live. Taking up some moss, Black Hactcin molded it between his hands and threw it into the river, where it became fish, frogs, and all the other creatures that live in water. Feathers that fell into the water turned into water birds such as the duck.

The animals told Black Hactcin that they wanted a human as a companion because someday the *hactcin* would leave them and someone would be needed to take care of the world. The animals gathered together the objects that Black Hactcin would need to make the first man. Black Hactcin drew on the ground the outline of his own body and dusted it with POLLEN. Inside the outline he placed precious stones and other things that would become the man's flesh and bones: turquoise for veins, red ochre for blood, coral for skin, white rock for bones and white clay for their marrow, opal for fingernails and teeth, jet for the eyes' pupils and abalone for the whites, and a dark cloud for hair. Black Hactcin sent WIND to give the body breath and bring the first man to life. Woman was born when the man dreamed of her.

See also APACHE EMERGENCE AND MIGRATION; HUMANS, ORIGIN OF.

BLACK HILLS

A mountain range that straddles the border of South Dakota and Wyoming. Legends of both the Cheyenne and the Lakota say that long ago the Black Hills did not exist. The flat plains stretched endlessly from horizon to horizon. At that time there was no distinction between people and animals, both of which preyed on each other. To bring an end to this situation, humans challenged all the animals to a race. If the humans won, they would rule over animals and eat them. If the animals won, they would rule over humans and eat them. As humans and animals raced in a huge circle, the pounding of their feet wore a deep rut in the plains and pushed up a huge mound of earth in the center. This mound suddenly erupted, showering debris on the racers and killing many of them. Humans survived and declared themselves the winners. The Black Hills remain as a reminder of the great race that decided the fate of humanity.

BLACK MESA

An Arizona mesa, now part of Navajo National Monument, that is sacred to both the Hopi and the Navajo (Dineh). In Hopi tradition, Black Mesa is the center of the universe, to which the people returned following their wanderings (see HOPI EMERGENCE AND MIGRATION). The mesa is the sacred Female Mountain of Navajo (Dineh) tradition. Black Mesa and the nearby Male Mountain together represent nature's balance. Three intact cliff dwellings of the ANASAZI are preserved in Navajo National Monument.

BLESSINGWAY

(Hózhóó'jí) *Navajo (Dineh)* Rites that are central to Navajo (Dineh) ceremonialism and that govern the system of ceremonials (called chants, sings, or ways) conducted to restore harmony (*hózhó*) in the universe (see NAVAJO [DINEH] CEREMONIALS). These ceremonials are frequently described as the branches of a tree that extend over and protect the Navajo (Dineh) way of life. Blessingway is viewed as the trunk of the tree, deeply rooted and supporting all the ceremonial branches. Blessingway is performed to bless the person who is "sung over" and to ensure general good fortune and good health. Blessingway rites may be performed for weddings, childbirth rites, girls' puberty rites, house blessings, rain ceremonies, and numerous other occasions.

According to tradition, Blessingway was given to the Earth Surface People shortly after they emerged into the present world. The first Blessingway was held by the DIYIN DINEH (Holy People) when they created humans. Blessingway is closely connected with CHANGING WOMAN and is the only ceremony in which she is depicted in SANDPAINTINGS. The Blessingway chant retells the Navajo (Dineh) CREATION ACCOUNT and the origin of the Blessingway ceremony itself. The traditional accounts that form the core of Blessingway are those of Changing Woman, the *diyin dineh*, FIRST MAN AND FIRST WOMAN, MONSTER SLAYER AND BORN FOR WATER, MONSTERWAY, and the NAVAJO (DINEH) EMERGENCE.

BLUE CORN WOMAN   See CORN MOTHERS.

BLUE FEATHER

(Kotcimanyako) *Cóchiti Pueblo* A girl who was responsible for the appearance of the starry sky. After a great FLOOD, the Cóchiti people moved north until the waters receded. At last IATIKU, the Mother of the Pueblo people, told everyone it was safe to return to their home in the south. She gave a closed and tightly tied bag to a young girl named Blue Feather to carry with her, with instructions not to open it. On the way south, Blue Feather was unable to contain her curiosity, so she untied the bag. When she did so, STARS spilled out of the bag and scattered in all directions. Blue Feather quickly reclosed the bag, but only a few stars were left in it. When she reached Cóchiti, the remaining stars were put in their proper places in the sky. This is why only a few stars have names and are known to people. (See also MILKY WAY.)

BLUE JAY Noisy and colorful, the blue jay is a common and widespread bird. Blue Jay is a mischievous deity of the Chinook and other northwestern tribes—a TRICKSTER, braggart, schemer, and clown. Many tales about Blue Jay revolve around his attempts to outdo other creatures.

BORN FOR WATER (Tó bájísh chíní) *Navajo (Dineh)* The second of the WARRIOR TWIN sons born to CHANGING WOMAN (see MONSTER SLAYER AND BORN FOR WATER). His Apache counterpart is CHILD-OF-THE-WATER.

BREATH MAKER (Hisagita misa) *Seminole* A CULTURE HERO who created the pumpkin plant, taught fishing skills, and showed people how to dig wells for water. By blowing his breath toward the sky, Breath Maker created the MILKY WAY to form a pathway for good souls to take as they journeyed to the City of the West after death.

BRYCE CANYON A canyon (now Bryce Canyon National Park) in southwestern Utah that contains brightly colored and unusually shaped spires, pinnacles, and walls created by erosion. According to a Paiute legend, before there were humans, Bryce Canyon was inhabited by LEGEND PEOPLE, whose appearance combined characteristics of humans, birds, animals, and reptiles. Because of the evil nature of the Legend People, COYOTE turned them into the rock structures that can still be seen in the canyon.

BUFFALO The American bison, a large species of wild cattle that once ranged in the millions over much of the United States, northeastern Mexico, and the Canadian extension of the Great Plains. It stands six feet tall at the shoulder and can weigh a ton or more. The name *buffalo* derives from the French word for beef or ox, *boeuf*, which is what French explorers called the huge animal. The Plains tribes depended on the buffalo for almost every necessity of life. Besides meat (and the dung for fuel to cook it) and hides for clothing, blankets, and tipi coverings, the buffalo yielded fat, or tallow, that was burned for light; bones for hoes, awls, other tools, and even sleds; horns for cups, spoons, and other utensils; stomach and bladder for waterproof containers; rawhide for shields, drums, ropes, belts, and bags; and other body parts for a host of uses.

The importance of the buffalo is reflected in the many ceremonies that celebrate it and legends that surround it. The buffalo is the central figure in one of the most important Plains ceremonies, the SUN DANCE. Before a buffalo hunt, a Buffalo DANCE was held in which dancers imitated the movement of the buffalo. The Lakota Buffalo Bull Ceremony (Ta Tanka Lowanpi) was a puberty rite held to purify girls at their first menstruation. According to tradition, BUFFALO WOMAN taught this ceremony to the Lakota.

For the Lakota, all buffalo were descended from Ta Tanka (*ta* meaning "beast" and *tanka* meaning "great" or "large"), a huge buffalo bull that sat in council with the SUN every night. Ta Tanka provided game, rewarded generosity and punished stinginess, was responsible for the fertility of women, and protected unmarried women.

The gift of buffalo to the people plays a significant role in legends about this animal. Stories about the disappearance of the buffalo—with the resultant famine and death—and their subsequent return reflect the crucial importance of this animal for the people who depended on it for their survival. For examples of such stories, see ARROW BOY, BUFFALO WOMAN, FLINTWAY, SWEET MEDICINE, WHITE BUFFALO CALF WOMAN, and WIND CAVE.

BUFFALO-CALF-ROAD-WOMAN *Cheyenne* On June 17, 1876, U.S. Army forces under General George Crook, accompanied by Crow and Shoshone scouts, faced Lakota Sioux forces, led by Chief Crazy Horse of the Oglala, and Cheyenne

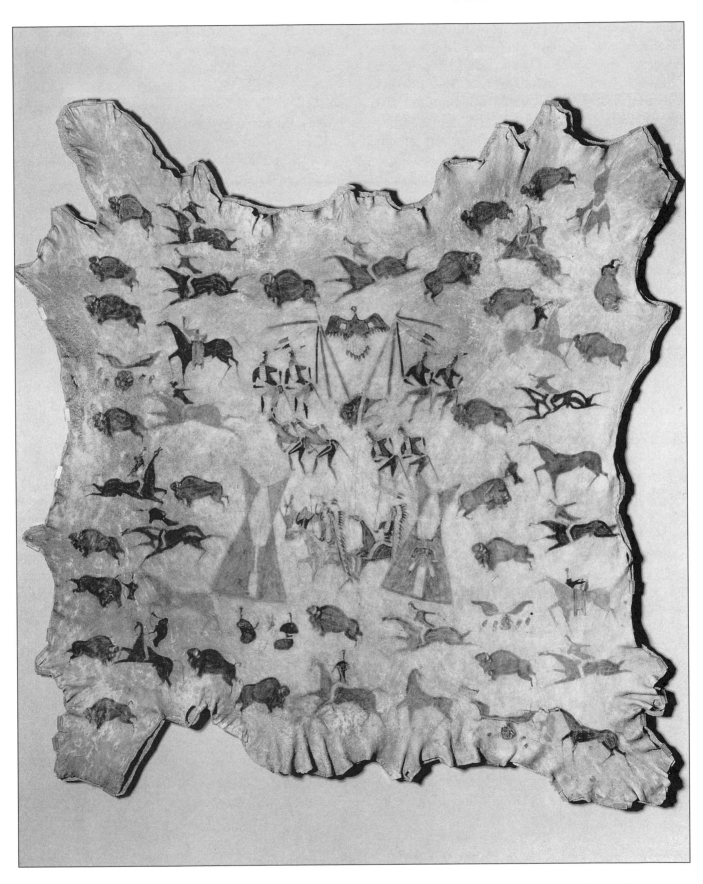

This Shoshone painting on elk skin captures the excitement of a successful buffalo hunt. *(Attrib: Cody, Cadzi [1866–1912], Brooklyn Museum of Art, #64.13, Dick S. Ramsay Fund)*

forces, led by Little Hawk and American Horse. Because the battle that followed was fought on the banks of the Rosebud River in Montana, non-Cheyenne call it the Battle of the Rosebud. Cheyenne call it The Fight Where the Girl Saved Her Brother.

Among the Cheyenne that day was a young woman, Buffalo-Calf-Road-Woman, who had accompanied her husband, Black Coyote, and her brother, Chief Comes-in-Sight, to the battle. When Buffalo-Calf-Road-Woman saw that her brother's horse had been shot from under him and that he was surrounded by the enemy and about to be slain, she uttered a war cry and rode into the heart of the fight. Comes-in-Sight leaped onto the horse behind his sister, and she galloped off with him. Despite soldiers' bullets and Crow arrows, the two escaped unharmed. According to the Cheyenne, General Crook withdrew his forces from the battle because the bravery of Buffalo-Calf-Road-Woman showed him what he was up against facing Lakota and Cheyenne warriors.

BUFFALO WOMAN *Lakota, Pawnee* In Pawnee tales, a legendary figure associated with the scattering of the BUFFALO herds. One of the two wives of a hunter named Without-Wings, Buffalo Woman ran away with her son, who was a calf, and sought refuge with a herd of buffalo. Without-Wings took the form of an eagle and followed her. He changed back into a human and played with his son, but his wife refused to return to him. When Without-Wings persisted in his efforts to regain his wife, the buffalo chief tried to kill him by trapping him inside a hot sweat lodge. Without-Wings escaped by turning himself into a badger and a magpie and then killed the buffalo chief. The buffalo broke up into many herds and scattered, and Without-Wings returned to his people.

The Lakota Buffalo Woman taught the Lakota the Buffalo Bull Ceremony (Ta Tanka Lowanpi), a puberty rite for girls that was held to purify them at their first menstruation. The ceremony originated when Anog Ite (DOUBLE-FACED WOMAN) tried to lure one of Buffalo Woman's daughters to the home of IKTOMI, the TRICKSTER, and a giant named Iya. Buffalo Woman thwarted Anog Ite's plan with the help of the SUN (Wi) and the South WIND (Okaga). When Buffalo Woman saw Anog Ite sneaking around a camp of Lakota, she intervened and taught the people the Buffalo Bull Ceremony so that the Lakota could purify and protect their daughters.

BURNT FACE *Crow* The creator of the first MEDICINE WHEEL. Burnt Face, whose face was scarred by burns he received when he fell into a fire as a child, had lived a lonely life, mocked by other children. When he reached adulthood, he made a journey into the mountains, where he formed large stones into a circle—the medicine wheel—and fasted. A great EAGLE came to Burnt Face, brought him to his lodge, and healed his scarred face. After Burnt Face helped the eagle get rid of an animal that was eating eaglets, he returned to his village and lived a long life. From that time on, people on VISION QUESTS went to the medicine wheel and fasted.

BUZZARD With its bald head, the buzzard, or turkey vulture, is an apt candidate for stories about how it acquired this distinctive feature. In a Choctaw legend about the theft of FIRE, Buzzard hid a burning ember in his head feathers. The feathers were burned off, leaving Buzzard with a bare head—and no fire.

In the Cherokee CREATION ACCOUNT, a buzzard was responsible for the appearance of the Earth. When the Earth was first made, it was soft and wet. Animals living in the crowded upper world were eager to make Earth their home. They sent Great Buzzard to make it ready for them. As he swooped low near the soft Earth, his huge wings struck the ground, gouging out valleys and creating mountains.

In Dakota myth, Buzzard was one of the spirit helpers of TAKUSKANSKAN, the being that personified motion and gave life to things.

CAHOKIA A major center of the MISSISSIPPIAN CULTURE, which flourished from about A.D. 700 until the early 1600s, by which time the centers had been abandoned. The temple mound site at Cahokia, Illinois, near St. Louis, is the largest and most famous of the Mississippian ceremonial and trading centers. Covering some 4,000 acres, the site contains 85 temple and burial mounds. At the height of this culture, around A.D. 1100, the site had an estimated population of 30,000. In the huge plaza in the center of the city is the largest earthwork in the Americas—Monk's Mound—a pyramid more massive than the largest Egyptian pyramid. It measures 700 feet by 1,080 feet at its base and rises in four terraces to a height of 100 feet. Scientists estimate that its construction took more than 300 years. Outside the city was a ring of large cedar posts forming a solar calendar. When lined up with a key post, the posts in the ring marked the spots at which the sun rose at the spring and fall equinoxes and the summer and winter solstices—the dates that mark the change of seasons. Scientists named the circle Woodhenge after Stonehenge, the famous stone circle in England.

See also MOUND BUILDERS; MOUNDS.

Cahokia was the largest city built north of Mexico before the arrival of Europeans. It was representative of one of the most advanced civilizations in ancient America. (*William R. Iseminger, Cahokia Mounds Historic Site*)

CALLING GOD (Hashch'éoghan) *Navajo (Dineh)* The *yei* associated with the west, Calling God is one of the *DIYIN DINEH*, or Holy People, who came up into this world with FIRST MAN AND FIRST WOMAN. Also known as Growling God, Calling God is the equivalent of TALKING GOD in the west.

CANNIBAL Cannibalism is a common theme in Native American mythology. Many stories begin when a man or woman cleans up an accidental injury to himself or herself by licking the wound and then develops an appreciation for the taste of blood. In a tale from California, a combination of the cannibal story and the ROLLING HEAD story, the cannibal ended up devouring his entire body, leaving just his head and shoulders. The cannibal's head then rolled around the countryside eating people.

Some tales seem intended simply to frighten people. An Anishinabe tale describes a cannibal giant who ate anyone who was kind to him. The Iroquois tell of the Stone Giants, who were covered with coats of flint and devoured everyone they met. A Cherokee tale describes an evil cannibal named Nun'yunu'wi (Dressed in Stone), whose body was covered with a skin of solid rock. In another Cherokee tale, water cannibals who lived at the bottom of deep rivers emerged just after dawn and went from house to house looking for someone who was still asleep. They shot the victim with invisible arrows and brought the body underwater to feast on it. To hide the crime, in the victim's place they left a shade of the dead person that talked and acted just as the living person had. After seven days the shade withered and died, and people would bury it, thinking it was their dead loved one.

Tales such as the ones cited may also, however, reflect a greater significance. The story of the fearful cannibal serves to reinforce traditional taboos against the eating of human flesh. Such tales also serve as warnings about the consequences of certain actions, such as incest and murder.

A recurring theme of cannibal stories is that of the cannibalistic woman. In a Pawnee tale, Cannibal Grandmother preferred human flesh to the tougher meat of buffalo and deer. The Kwakiutl and Bella Coola tell about the Wild Woman of the Woods (Tsonoqua or Dzonokwa), a cannibal woman who threatened children but was also known to bestow power and wealth on humans. The archetype of the cannibal-mother is found in folklore all over the world. The symbolism is of the cycle of human existence—life is brought forth and then consumed.

Cannibal tales from some traditions reflect the terrible forces of nature. According to legends of the Cree, Northern Ojibway, and other tribes of the subarctic, the fearsome WINDIGO stalked the woods in winter hunting for human victims. Winter snows come early in the far north, and a hunter caught in a blizzard without shelter could freeze to death. When a hunter failed to return home, the fear was that he had been caught and eaten by a *windigo*—the personification of winter's perils. Starvation was never very far away for people who lived in regions with harsh winters. In some traditions, cannibals—such as the Dakota giant who consumed people in winter—represented the specter of starvation.

Humans were also believed to be in peril from the supernatural. The Kwakiutl Hamatsa, or Cannibal, Ceremony, which is performed in winter, symbolizes the devouring and transformation of humans by the supernatural.

CANNIBAL-AT-THE-NORTH-END-OF-THE-WORLD (Baxbakualanuxsiwae, Bakbakwakanooksiwac) *Kwakiutl* A CANNIBAL spirit featured in the Hamatsa, or Cannibal, Ceremony performed during the winter ceremonial season to mark the devouring of humans by the supernatural. During the ceremony, an initiate of the Hamatsa society makes a spiritual journey to the house of Cannibal-at-the-North-End-of-the-World and is symbolically devoured by him. In the monster's stomach, he is transformed. Captured by members of the Hamatsa society, the initiate is returned to the winter ceremonial house. Possessed by the spirit, he dances wildly, wearing one of the birdlike masks that represent the creatures that live in the Cannibal's house. When the wildness leaves the initiate's body, he returns to a normal life but with a new name and a new identity to signify his transformation.

CANYON DE CHELLY A canyon (now Canyon de Chelly National Monument) in northeastern Arizona that contains the ruins of ANASAZI

Arizona's rock-walled Canyon de Chelly sheltered Anasazi cliff dwellings for a thousand years.
(© CORBIS)

villages and cliff dwellings dating from A.D. 350 to 1300. Its name is derived from the Spanish pronunciation of the Navajo (Dineh) word *tsegi*, "rock canyons." Canyon de Chelly is sacred to both the Hopi and the Navajo (Dineh). According to Hopi tradition, the canyon is where the Hopi emerged from the corrupt Third World into the present Fourth World (see HOPI EMERGENCE AND MIGRATION). For the Navajo (Dineh) the site was where the DIYIN DINEH, or Holy People, taught humans how to live. It is where the people come to restore harmony (*hózhó*) to their minds and spirits through MEDICINE rituals.

CARDINAL DIRECTIONS See DIRECTIONS, CARDINAL.

CEDAR An evergreen TREE with a fragrant aroma and reddish-brown bark. The cedar was believed to have MEDICINE power and was considered sacred by

many tribes. The Lakota burned cedar leaves as incense in ceremonies for Wakinyan, the THUNDER-BIRD. The cedar was believed to be Thunderbird's favorite tree, since he never struck it with lightning. Someone who offered cedar incense when a thunderstorm arose would be protected from harm. Similarly, the Seminole believed that burning cedar leaves cleansed a home of evil intentions.

In the NAVAJO (DINEH) EMERGENCE account, First Man tried to save the people in the Third World from a FLOOD by planting a cedar tree that they could climb to reach the Fourth World. The cedar, however, was not tall enough. (See also FIRST MAN AND FIRST WOMAN.)

In the Arapaho CREATION ACCOUNT, after Mother Corn taught the people the skills they needed to survive, such as how to cultivate CORN, she became a cedar tree.

A tale told by both the Cherokee and their neighbors the Yuchi describes how the cedar got its red color. A wicked magician caused great harm until two brave warriors found and killed him. They cut off his head and carried it home with them, but it remained alive. To kill the head, they were told to tie it to the upper branches of a tree. They tried many different trees, but only when they tied the head to a cedar was it finally killed. The blood that trickled down the tree's trunk gave the cedar wood its distinctive red color.

CHACO CANYON A canyon (now Chaco Canyon National Monument) in northwestern New Mexico that was the center of ANASAZI culture. It contains ruins dating from the peak of that civilization, A.D. 900–1000. The canyon's sites include 13 large villages with hundreds of rooms each. One of the largest is Pueblo Bonito, which contains more than 600 rooms and 40 KIVAS (underground ceremonial chambers). Tree ring dating shows a period of drought around 1150, which probably caused the site to be abandoned. The Hopi identify Chaco Canyon as one of the stops their ancestors made on the migration to their home on Three Mesas to the west (see HOPI EMERGENCE AND MIGRATION). Navajo (Dineh) legends say that it was here that the DIYIN DINEH (Holy People) won back all the people's property from GAMBLING GOD.

CHANGING WOMAN (Asdzáá nádleehé) *Navajo (Dineh)* One of the most important figures in Navajo (Dineh) tradition; the mother of the WARRIOR TWINS known as MONSTER SLAYER AND BORN FOR WATER. Different informants describe the parentage of Changing Woman in different ways. Sometimes her father and mother are given as the SKY and the Earth; at other times, they are given as Long Life Boy (Sa'ah naghai), the personification of thought, and Happiness Girl (Bikeh hózhó), the personification of speech. Combined, the names of the latter two—*sa'ah naghai bikeh hózhó*—mean "an all-encompassing environment of beauty" and express the Navajo (Dineh) goal of life, to live in harmony surrounded by beauty. Long Life Boy and Happiness Girl are identified with the inner forms of all living things.

FIRST MAN AND FIRST WOMAN planned Changing Woman's birth and raised her. First Man held up his MEDICINE BUNDLE toward Gobernador Knob (Ch'óol'íí) in New Mexico at dawn, and that was where Changing Woman was born. When she reached puberty (in FOUR days, according to legend), a puberty ceremony was held for her that formed the basis of the puberty rites held for all young Navajo (Dineh) women.

Changing Woman was the personification of the Earth and the natural order of the universe. She represented the cyclical path of the seasons—birth (spring), maturing (summer), aging (autumn), and death (winter)—and was reborn each spring to repeat the cycle. The various dresses into which she changed corresponded to the changes in the seasons and gave her the other names by which she was known: WHITE SHELL WOMAN, TURQUOISE WOMAN, Abalone Woman, and Jet Woman. Her Apache counterpart is WHITE PAINTED WOMAN.

After reaching womanhood, Changing Woman was impregnated by the SUN and by Water and gave birth to Monster Slayer and Born for Water. Although Born for Water had a different father, he was considered Monster Slayer's twin and with him, a son of the Sun. When her sons were grown, Changing Woman asked for and received the Mountain Soil medicine bundle from First Man. Then she moved to a hogan that had been built for her at the base of El Huerfano Mesa and conducted the first wedding ceremony, the mating of CORN. After this ceremony, she moved to a house her sons had built for her in the west. Growing lonely there, she used the power of the medicine bundle to create the first four clans of the Navajo (Dineh) people from skin she rubbed from various parts of her body. (See NAVAJO [DINEH] EMERGENCE.)

Changing Woman is central to the BLESSINGWAY ceremonial and the girls' puberty rite that is a part of it. Other NAVAJO (DINEH) CEREMONIALS in which Changing Woman plays a part include BEADWAY, EAGLEWAY, MONSTERWAY, and SHOOTINGWAY.

CHIBIABOS *Algonquian* The second brother of the CULTURE HERO MANABOZHO. He lived in the country of souls and was responsible for the dead.

CHIEF MOUNTAIN A 9,080-foot-high peak in northwestern Montana. According to Blackfeet legend, in the beginning Chief Mountain was the only land that was not submerged by a great FLOOD. The Creator, NA'PI, created the present Earth from this spot.

CHILD-OF-THE-WATER *Apache* A CULTURE HERO, son of Water and WHITE SHELL WOMAN. He was conceived at the same time as the culture hero KILLER-OF-ENEMIES, son of the Sun and WHITE PAINTED WOMAN. Child-of-the-Water is usually considered to be the twin brother of Killer-of-Enemies. As often happens in tales of WARRIOR TWINS, the two made a journey to their father, the Sun, and had many adventures hunting and killing MONSTERS in order to make the world safe for humans. In Chiricahua and Mescalero Apache tales, Child-of-the-Water is the dominant culture hero rather than Killer-of-Enemies. His Navajo (Dineh) counterpart is BORN FOR WATER.

CHIRICAHUA WINDWAY *Navajo (Dineh)* A ceremonial curing complex, or group of ceremonies (called chants, sings, or ways) conducted to heal illness and restore harmony (*hózhó*) in the universe (see NAVAJO [DINEH] CEREMONIALS). Like NAVAJO WINDWAY, to which it is related, Chiricahua Windway is included in the HOLYWAY classification of ceremonials, which are used to restore health by attracting good.

The story cycle associated with Chiricahua Windway involves a young hunter who insulted WIND (NILCH'I) without meaning to do so. In revenge, Wind held back the DEER, and the hunter's family began to starve. Eventually, Wind released one deer. The hunter followed it but could not shoot it. After chasing the deer over FOUR different types of cactus, the hunter suffered great pain and lost consciousness. Wind restored him to health. Further adventures of the hunter include marriage to a SNAKE woman, discovery of the cave where the deer were hidden, the shooting of a whirlwind, and a dream warning him not to go to a certain hill. He ignored the warning and went to the forbidden hill, where he met beings that questioned him about the Windway ceremony. Unable to answer their questions, he asked the beings to teach him the ceremony. In this way he learned Chiricahua Windway.

CHOKANIPOK (Man of Flint)   *Algonquian* The third brother of the CULTURE HERO MANABOZHO. Chokanipok had a body as big as a mountain. He fought many battles with his brother Manabozho. Manabozho's arrows tore off pieces of Chokanipok's body, which fell to Earth as pieces of FLINT. When Manabozho finally conquered Chokanipok, pieces of the giant's body were scattered everywhere. This story explains why flint is so common in some parts of the country.

CHULYEN   *Tanaina* CROW, a TRICKSTER who was able to change himself into any type of creature, including a handsome young man. In one tale, Chulyen arrived in a village that was cold and dark because a wealthy man had stolen the SUN and the MOON. Through trickery, Chulyen stole them back and returned them to the village.

CINAUAU   *Ute* CREATOR brothers who determined the conditions under which the Ute would live. The younger brother wanted food for the people to be abundant and the dead to come back to life the morning after they died. The older brother, however, argued that if food were readily available, people would become lazy. He won the argument, so people had to work hard to feed themselves. He also disagreed with his brother about death and decreed that

death would be permanent. To show that this was a mistake, the younger brother killed his brother's son and pointed out that the grief his brother felt resulted from his decision about the permanence of death. The older brother became so angry that the ground shook and a tremendous thunderstorm raged. The younger brother fled for his life to the protection of his father, TAVWOTS.

CIPYAPOS   *Potawatomi* The TWIN brother of the CULTURE HERO WISKE. As the guardian of the afterworld, Cipyapos received the souls of the dead.

CLAN A social unit that marks lineage from a common ancestor. Traditional Native American accounts are often related to the origin of a clan and its relations with other clans. Clan origins frequently involve a lost hunter or a curious youth who found himself in danger and received help and guidance from an ANIMAL. That animal then became the man's spirit guide and the clan's symbol, or TOTEM. There are usually TABOOS against killing an animal that is a clan totem, because of the kinship relationship between the clan members and the animal. Plants and other natural objects may also serve as clan totems. Clans may observe special rituals and have rules concerning marriage and residence within or outside the clan. In general, clan members are not allowed to marry within their own clan.

CLOUD PEOPLE   *Keres, Zuni* Storm spirits (*shiwanna*) associated with RAIN and the fertilization of the Earth. After death, people who had led good lives became Cloud People and—if they were properly remembered and honored—served the living as bringers of rain. If the *shiwanna* were offended, they might decide not to appear, and a drought would occur.

CLOUD SWALLOWER   *Zuni* A mighty giant who devoured people, the souls of the dead, and the thunderheads that brought the summer RAIN. Many heroes tried to kill him, but all failed. Without rain, the rivers dried up, corn withered in the fields, and people began to starve.

AHAYUTA AND MATSILEMA, a pair of WARRIOR TWINS, were determined to kill this MONSTER. As they headed down the trail that Cloud Swallower guarded, they met Grandmother Spider (SPIDER WOMAN). She told them that she would run ahead and sew up the giant's eyes with her web silk. It was Cloud Swallower's habit to pretend to be old and tired so that he could snatch up unwitting people who passed underneath him. When he heard the brothers approaching, he pretended to be asleep and did not stir to brush the spider web from his eyes, so he was unaware that they were warriors who had come to kill him. The heroes quickly slew the giant. But the people, fearing that the rains would never return, had already abandoned their cliff houses and fled to the south and east. This story is one explanation for the disappearance of the ANASAZI.

CLOWNS, SACRED

Clowning societies are a feature of many Native American cultures. Among the Pueblo people, costumed clowns entertain at ceremonies, mocking viewers and themselves, playing games, and performing balancing acts. The entertainment provided by clowns serves a sacred ceremonial function as well. Clowns are guardians of ritual. Although they make people laugh, they also cause them to observe and think about things in new ways. Clowns mock ritual and ceremony, test boundaries by doing forbidden things, make jokes, and generally create disorder. These behaviors show people that the alternatives to traditional social order can be ridiculous and even dangerous. Clowns are often identified as powerful healers. The best-known clowning societies are the following:

Heyoka *Lakota* Sacred clowns whose great spiritual powers came from Wakinyan (THUNDERBIRD). People who dreamed of Thunderbird or whose dreams contained thunder, lightning, or symbols associated with these elements were required to dramatize the vision in a ceremony called the *Heyoka kaga*, "clown making." In their function as contraries, the *heyoka* acted in opposite ways, such as dressing in warm clothes in summer, facing backward when riding a horse, swimming in icy pools in winter while complaining of the heat, and speaking rapidly, slowly, or backward.

Koshare (Kushali) *Keres* A clowning society primarily concerned with crop growth and animal fer-

tility whose members supervise many ceremonies. Koshare—composed mostly of men, but with a few women members—serve for life. Their bodies are painted white with horizontal black stripes around the torso, arms, and legs and black rings around the eyes and mouth. Their hair is smeared with white clay and bound into two horns with cornhusks. The Koshare alternate ceremonial duties annually with another clowning society, the Kwerana. The right side of the Kwerana's body is painted orange and the left side, white. His face is striped orange and black. In the Keresan CREATION ACCOUNT, IATIKU, a female creator figure, created the Koshare by rolling bits of her own skin into a ball.

Koyemshi *Zuni* A group of sacred KACHINA clowns. According to Zuni tradition, while the people were wandering after the emergence from the UNDERWORLD (see ZUNI EMERGENCE AND MIGRATION), a boy had intercourse with his sleeping sister. When she woke up and realized what had happened, she was angry with her brother but could not speak intelligibly. That night she gave birth to 10 children, the Koyemshi, who had bulbous lumps on their heads and were witless. At the new year the Zuni commemorate these events by appointing 10 men to serve for a full year as Koyemshi impersonators during ceremonies. Although they look alike, each of the 10 Koyemshi has an individual identity and name. Popularly called Mudheads, the Koyemshi wear earth-colored, globular cotton masks with knobs on them and packets of corn seeds around their necks. They are contraries who teach by bad example, exaggerating poor behavior and mocking what is held sacred. For example, to make fun of greed and gluttony, they stuff themselves with food during rituals.

Tsuku (Tachuktu) *Hopi* Clowns who commonly entertain during Plaza Dances and provoke the KACHINAS. Their humor frequently involves wordplay, gluttony, and reversal of normal ways of doing things.

Windigokan *Plains Ojibway* Contraries whose name derives from the WINDIGO, a CANNIBAL of the North Woods. Members of the Windigokan Society are usually people who dream of the *windigo* or of thunder. They wear masks with long noses, act in contrary, or backward, ways at ceremonies, and are known for their healing powers.

The distinctive black-and-white striped Koshare are members of one of the best-known Keresan Pueblo clowning societies. *(T. Harmon Parkhurst, Museum of New Mexico)*

COLOR   Colors are both symbolic and sacred to Native Americans and play an important role in mythology and religion. Color often correlates with the cardinal DIRECTIONS. For the Navajo (Dineh), for example, the color of the north is black; of the south, blue; of the east, white; and of the west, yellow. Each direction also had a WIND and a guardian SNAKE associated with it, in the same colors. For the Hopi, the color of the north is white; of the south, blue; of the east, red; and of the west, yellow. The Tewa recognize six directions, each with its own color. The color for the north is blue; for the west, yellow; for the south, red; for the east, white; for the zenith or above, speckled; and for the nadir or below, black.

In the Cheyenne worldview, the colors black, blue, red, white, and yellow have a special status and are referred to as "Cheyenne colors." Other colors have no special significance. For the Cheyenne, black is the color of death and hatred, blue is associated with sky and water, red symbolizes warmth, white is the color of active life and dancing, and yellow represents new life and beauty.

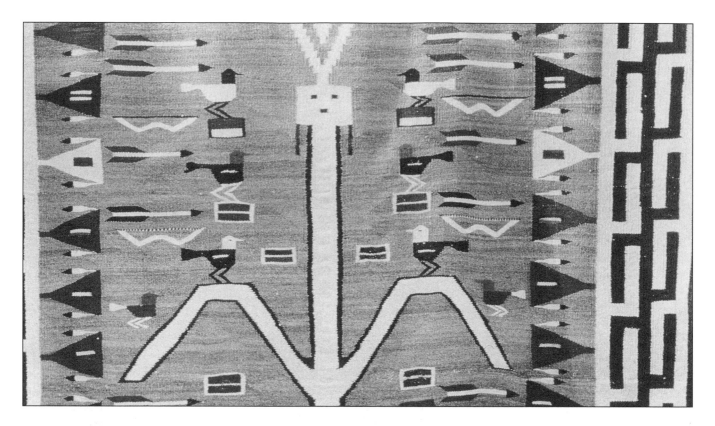

The frequent portrayal of corn plants on objects such as this Navajo (Dineh) rug indicates corn's importance in Native American corn-growing cultures. *(© Stephen Trimble, Courtesy Cameron Trading Post, Arizona)*

CONDOR The largest bird in California, with a wingspan of almost 10 feet. The condor was considered capable of communicating with the supernatural world. In the Wiyot CREATION ACCOUNT, Condor became the ancestor of the human race after surviving a FLOOD sent by ABOVE-OLD-MAN to destroy the first people.

CONSTELLATION A group of stars that appear to form a recognizable shape. Cultures around the world have created stories about constellations. The origin of constellations, such as the BIG DIPPER, is a frequent subject of Native American tales about the night sky. Another common theme is why some stars form patterns and others are randomly placed. COYOTE is often the cause. In the Navajo (Dineh) account, when BLACK GOD (in one version, FIRST MAN) was carefully creating constellations, Coyote became impatient with the slow process and hurled all the stars into the sky at once. In a Pueblo tale, the Great Spirit gave all the animals permission to make star pictures using stones that turned into glittering stars when placed in the sky. Great Spirit asked Coy-ote to carry extra stones for the animals that were too small to carry enough to create their pictures. Irritated by having to carry the heavy bag, Coyote threw whole pawfuls of stones into the sky until they were all gone. Thus, some star pictures were left incomplete and some stars do not form pictures at all. In a Cóchiti Pueblo tale, a young girl named BLUE FEATHER let the stars escape before they could be placed methodically.

The constellations recognized and named by Native Americans are not the same as the 12 constellations of the zodiac and the other constellations recognized and named by ancient European and Near Eastern astronomers. Some, however, correspond to parts of those. In the Navajo (Dineh) tradition, the first constellation that Black God placed in the sky was called Man with Feet Ajar and is a large square in the constellation Corvus the Crow. Other Navajo (Dineh) constellations include Horned Rattler, First Big One (Scorpius), Whirling Male (the Big Dipper plus POLARIS), Whirling Female (the Little Dipper), Slender First One (part of ORION), and Rabbit Tracks (near Canis Major).

CORN In corn-growing cultures across the North American continent, corn has played a major role in both ritual and mythology. People of most cultures performed planting and harvest ceremonies and held DANCES to assure a good harvest, and many still do. Symbols of fertility—corn, cornmeal, and corn POLLEN—have been widely used in ritual, in particular by the Navajo (Dineh) and Pueblo cultures (see SANDPAINTING).

Many tales describe how corn came into being and how people learned to cultivate it. Usually personified as a woman, corn was frequently given to humans by a woman or women, such as the CORN MAIDENS, the CORN MOTHERS, KANENHAGENAT, or MOON WOMAN. In several similar legends, a woman (sometimes called Corn Woman) was killed—frequently beheaded—and her body was dragged around a field. The first corn plants grew from her blood. (See FIRST MOTHER; SELU.)

Not all stories say that the giver of corn was a woman. A dwarf named Fas-ta-chee, whose hair and body were made of corn, gave corn to the Seminole and taught them how to cultivate and grind it. The CULTURE HERO IOSKEHA brought corn to the Huron. TAVWOTS, a rabbit, stole corn and gave it to the Ute. In a White Mountain Apache tale, TURKEY shook the first corn seeds from among his feathers and taught the people how to plant them. The CREATOR gave corn to the Anishinabe, but they did not know how to use it until a man named OKABEWIS was sent to teach them how to live. MAHEO, the Cheyenne creator figure, showed the people how to grow corn.

In the Hopi CREATION ACCOUNT (see HOPI EMERGENCE AND MIGRATION), corn was divinely created in the First World and given to the people. When the First World and then the Second World were destroyed, corn was again given to humanity. Before people left the Third World to emerge into the present world, however, the Creator wanted to discover how much greed and ignorance existed in the various groups of people. He set out ears of corn of various sizes and told the people to choose one to be their food in the Fourth World. The Hopi chose the shortest ear because it reminded them of the original corn given to them in the First World. Hopi corn has small ears growing on stunted stalks; it survives in sandy fields or on rocky hillsides with only occasional rain to nourish it. But it has provided a dependable source of food for countless generations.

In the Yavapai-Apache creation account, the first people emerged from the UNDERWORLD on the first corn plant.

See also PLANTS; THREE SISTERS.

CORN MAIDENS *Hopi, Pueblo, Zuni* Women who were the source of CORN. Corn Maidens personified corn in all its various types and colors. In a Hopi ceremony, sacred CLOWNS ate *piki* (a thin bread made from blue corn flour) that was served to them by Corn Maiden dancers. There are many versions of the Zuni story about the loss of the Corn Maidens. In one tale, they were offended when a priest tried to touch

This Pueblo fresco of a figure holding a cornstalk was painted around 1500 on the wall of a kiva. *(© N. Carter/North Wind Picture Archive)*

the eldest during the Corn Dance. In another version, the people insulted them. Whatever the reason, the Corn Maidens fled, taking all the village's corn with them. Without corn, the people began to starve. In one account, the CULTURE HERO Payatamu, who introduced the cultivation of corn, set off in search of the Corn Maidens. He returned to the village with them after they had been gone for seven years. In another account, the AHAYUTA took part in the search but were unsuccessful. The loss and recovery of the Corn Maidens is dramatized in the Zuni Molawai ceremony, held on the final day of Shalako, a December ceremonial.

CORN MOTHERS *Keres, Tewa* The givers of CORN to the Pueblo people. According to the Acoma CREATION ACCOUNT, when UTSITI, the Creator, made the Earth, he planted the souls of the Corn Mothers in the soil of the newborn world. A spirit called Thought Woman raised them to maturity. When the sisters were grown, Thought Woman gave them baskets filled with seeds and sent them down to the Earth's surface. Corn was the first thing they planted and learned to cultivate, harvest, grind, and cook. They passed these skills on to the Acoma people.

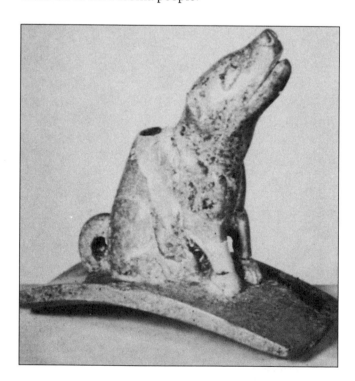

Effigies of Coyote appear on many artifacts, such as this Hopewellian stone pipe from Ohio, carved before A.D. 100. *(Ohio Historical Society)*

In Tewa tradition, Blue Corn Woman and White Corn Maiden brought corn with them when they emerged from the previous world and crawled through the KIVA roof onto the Earth's surface. The Tewa are divided into two groups, Summer People and Winter People. According to tradition, Blue Corn Woman Near to Summer was responsible for the Summer People, who farmed. White Corn Maiden Near to Ice was responsible for the Winter People, who hunted.

Traditionally, newborn Pueblo children were given a Corn Mother—an ear of corn made into a fetish, or AMULET—as a reminder that the Corn Mothers gave life to all living things. People kept the corn fetish for life.

CORN WOMAN See FIRST MOTHER; SELU.

COYOTE A TRICKSTER, CULTURE HERO, and CREATOR figure, perhaps the best known and most widely appearing character in Native American mythology. Mischievous, deceitful, and cunning, Coyote appears in many tales in which he tricks both animals and people. When killed in these stories, Coyote always came back to life. He was also able to change his appearance or exchange skin with men whose wives he desired.

As a culture hero, however, Coyote is credited with bringing FIRE to humans, releasing the BUFFALO into the world, and slaying evil MONSTERS by turning them to stone (see BRYCE CANYON). In a Maidu legend, he introduced work, suffering, and death to the world (see KODOYANPE). In a Zuni tale, Coyote and EAGLE stole LIGHT from the KACHINAS, but Coyote let it escape and thus took away heat from the Earth and caused winter (see also SEASONS, ORIGIN OF). In several tales, Coyote was responsible for the appearance of the night sky (see BLACK GOD; CONSTELLATION). The Chumash refer to POLARIS, the North Star, as SKY COYOTE.

Coyote appears as a companion of the Creator in accounts of the Chinook, Maidu, Paiute, Pawnee, Tohono O'odham, Ute, and other tribes. In the Paiute CREATION ACCOUNT, WOLF created Coyote to be his companion. The two of them piled dirt on the water-covered world and made the land. In the Tohono O'odham creation account, Coyote helped

MONTEZUMA survive a flood that destroyed the world. After the Great Mystery created new humans, Coyote and Montezuma taught them how to live. In the Crow account, OLD MAN COYOTE was the Creator.

In the NAVAJO (DINEH) EMERGENCE account, Coyote (Ma'ii) existed with FIRST MAN AND FIRST WOMAN in the First World. In a different version, he was created in the Fourth World. Coyote was responsible for the existence of death. After the emergence, the people wanted to know their fate. Someone threw a hide scraper into the water, declaring that if it sank, the people would eventually die, but if it floated, they would go on living. It floated. Then, however, Coyote picked up a stone and threw it into the water. He declared that if it floated, people would live forever, but if it sank, everyone would die sooner or later. Naturally, the stone sank, and the people became angry. Coyote explained that if there were no death, there would be too many people and eventually there would be no room to plant corn. The people saw the wisdom of this and accepted the inevitability of death. Coyote plays a key role in the traditional account associated with the Navajo (Dineh) ceremonial BIG STARWAY and also figures in ENEMYWAY.

CRATER LAKE The second-deepest lake in North America, located in Crater Lake National Park in southwestern Oregon and known for its deep blue color. Crater Lake is the remnant of a volcanic mountain that erupted 8,000 years ago. According to Klamath myth, the Chief of the Below World, Llal, and the Chief of the Above World, Skell, had a great battle. They hurled red-hot rocks at each other, causing earth tremors and fiery landslides. Skell drove Llal back into the mountain, which collapsed in on him, leaving a great gaping hole. Rainstorms filled the hole and created Crater Lake.

CREATION ACCOUNTS Accounts of the creation of the world, the first people, and the nature of the world vary according to geography, a people's way of life, climate, and many other factors. A few Native American creation accounts begin with the Earth's creation from a void. The CREATORS in some of these stories are AWONAWILONA (Zuni), EARTHMAKER (Ho Chunk), TAIOWA (Hopi), and TIRAWAHAT (Skidi

Pawnee). In most traditions, however, the Earth already existed in one form or another, almost universally covered with the PRIMORDIAL WATERS. These accounts tell how the world achieved its present form and how humans, ANIMALS, and PLANTS came into being. (See also HUMANS, ORIGIN OF.)

Several themes are repeatedly seen among creation accounts. In accounts of a water-covered world, different beings bring up soil to make the Earth. In the Southwest, people traditionally emerged into the present world from one or more UNDERWORLDS. In Northwest accounts, people descended to the present world through a hole in the sky that is associated with the smoke hole of a tipi. Several common themes are presented here.

Co-creators Frequently, two beings are involved in the creation. Often these are WARRIOR TWINS; less commonly, the two are parents of the world (as in the MOTHER EARTH AND FATHER SKY theme). The Hopi Creator, Taiowa, made SÓTUKNANG to carry out the work of creation for him, and Sótuknang in turn made his own helper, SPIDER WOMAN. In a Paiute account, WOLF created COYOTE as a companion, and the two paddled around the water-covered Earth in a canoe. Tiring of paddling, Wolf and Coyote piled dirt on top of the water until they created the land. In the Mandan creation account, First Creator and LONE MAN created the world together as they walked across the water that covered it. The Penobscot creator figure Kloskurbeh, or GLUSKAP, had the help of Great Nephew. In Northwest Coast tales, XOWALACI created the land and some animals, and his helper First Man created the first woman. In tales of good and evil TWINS, such as IOSKEHA AND TAWISCARA (Iroquois) and KOKOMAHT AND BAKO-TAHL (Yuma), the good twin created all that is good in the world, and the evil twin created evil things.

Earth Diver One of the most common creation accounts, found all over North America, is the earth-diver story, which begins with a water-covered Earth. Various animals and BIRDS attempted to dive to the bottom of the water to retrieve mud or clay from which the world would be created. The first animals failed, but one (usually the fourth) succeeded. Diving animals frequently included the BEAVER, DUCK, LOON, MUSKRAT, OTTER, and TURTLE. For the Cherokee, the successful diver was a water beetle. In the

Arapaho account, Man-Above told Flat Pipe, who floated on the water, to get helpers to make the world. Flat Pipe envisioned the water birds, which then became real. He sent first the ducks, then the geese, and next the swans to dive for soil. All failed. Then Turtle dived and came up with a bit of soil, which he placed on Flat Pipe. The soil spread out and became the world. Among the many earth-diver accounts are those associated with KODOYANPE (Maidu), MANABOZHO (Algonquian, Anishinabe), NA'PI (Blackfeet), OLD MAN COYOTE (Crow), SKY WOMAN (Algonquian), and WEE-SA-KAY-JAC (Cree).

Emergence A common theme in creation accounts of the Southwest is emergence into the present world from a previous world. Both the Hopi and the Navajo (Dineh) describe several worlds stacked on top of each other. Emergence involved climbing up from one dying world into the next, new-born one. For the Hopi, the present world is the fourth; for the Navajo (Dineh), it is the fifth in some versions but the fourth in others. The move to another world was necessary in order to escape from conditions that made the preceding world uninhabitable. The previous worlds were too small for an increasing number of inhabitants, were destroyed by fire or FLOOD, or became corrupt. Southwest emergence accounts include the ACOMA EMERGENCE AND MIGRATION, APACHE EMERGENCE AND MIGRATION, HOPI EMERGENCE AND MIGRATION, NAVAJO (DINEH) EMERGENCE, and ZUNI EMERGENCE AND MIGRATION. Emergence accounts also exist in the Southeast. In the Choctaw and Creek accounts, the people emerged from a hole in the ground at Nunih Waya, the site of a huge platform MOUND in what is now Mississippi.

Re-creation In many creation accounts, the first world was destroyed by its creator—usually by means of a flood—and had to be remade (see ABOVE-OLD-MAN; MONTEZUMA; NESHANU). According to an Inuit story, the first Earth came into being when it fell from the sky, complete with people. The world was dark, there was only dirt to eat, and the people did not know how to die. As a result, the Earth became so crowded that it started to collapse. Then a great flood swept away all but a few people. These survivors realized that life could not go on as before. In exchange for accepting death, they were given

sunlight and seasons (see SEASONS, ORIGIN OF). The Cree Creator, Wee-sa-kay-jac, was forced to re-create the Earth when evil spirits flooded it by releasing all the water within the Earth.

Single Creator Many creation accounts feature a strong Creator who is responsible for creating the world and everything in it, including humans. Among these figures are Above-Old-Man (Wiyot), AKBAATATDIA (Crow), Earthmaker (Akimel O'odham, Ho Chunk, Tohono O'odham), ESAUGETUH EMISSEE (Creek), ES-TE FAS-TA (Seminole), GITCHE MANITOU (Algonquian, Anishinabe), HISAGITA-IMISI (Creek), MAHEO (Cheyenne), Neshanu (Arapaho), TABALDAK (Anishinabe), UTSITI (Keres), and Wee-sa-kay-jac (Cree).

CREATOR A fundamental belief of Native Americans throughout North America was the existence of a higher power above all other spirit beings, all powers of nature, and the natural qualities of humans. This power, or supreme being, was known by various names, including AWONAWILONA, "the Maker" (Zuni); ESAUGETUH EMISSEE, "Master of Breath" (Creek); GITCHE MANITOU, "Great Spirit" (Algonquian, Anishinabe); MAHEO (Cheyenne); Naualak (Kwakiutl); Orenda (Iroquois); TAIOWA (Hopi); Tamanoas (Chinook); TIRAWAHAT, "This Expanse" (Skidi Pawnee); Unsen, "Life Giver" or "In Charge of Life" (Apache); and WAKAN TANKA, "Great Mystery" (Lakota). Generally, the creator did not remain to guide the world or its people but instead left the task to other beings that were created—helpers, spirit beings, and CULTURE HEROES.

A sky-dwelling male creator figure appears in traditional accounts of many cultures. Examples are ABOVE-OLD-MAN (Wiyot); AKBAATATDIA, "The One Who Has Made Everything" (Crow); EARTHMAKER (Ho Chunk, Tohono O'odham); ES-TE FAS-TA, "Gives Everything" (Seminole); KODOYANPE (Maidu); KUMUSH (Modoc); and UTSITI (Keres).

Women, such as the Navajo (Dineh) CHANGING WOMAN, play prominent roles as creators. The Arapaho Whirlwind Woman (Nayaanxatisei) created the world from a ball of mud. In the Pawnee creation account, EVENING STAR helped the Creator make the Earth. Her daughter, Standing Rain, was the mother of the human race. IATIKU is a powerful creator figure of the Keresan Pueblo people. In the HOPI EMERGENCE AND MIGRATION account, SPIDER WOMAN created all living things, including humans. Other female creator figures are SKY WOMAN (Iroquois), WHITE PAINTED WOMAN (Apache), and WIDAPOKWI (Yavapai).

CULTURE HEROES, who are often the first people on Earth, frequently figure as creators who transform the landscape, bring LIGHT and FIRE, create human beings, and introduce agriculture. Two examples of culture heroes are GLUSKAP (Algonquian) and MANABOZHO (Algonquian, Anishinabe).

Pairs of creators or heroes play important creation roles in accounts told widely across the continent. Sometimes these are WARRIOR TWINS, but they may also be brothers (such as the CINAUAU), sisters, father and son, or uncle and nephew (such as Gluskap and Great Nephew). Another common theme is that of TWINS with opposite natures—one a positive, kind figure, and the other evil and destructive. Examples of such pairs include IOSKEHA AND TAWISCARA (Iroquois), KOKOMAHT AND BAKOTAHL (Yuma), and Gluskap and MALSUMSIS (Algonquian). COYOTE appears as a companion of the creator in creation accounts of the Chinook, Maidu, Pawnee, Ute, and other tribes.

In some traditions, there are many creator figures. Navajo (Dineh) creator figures—the *DIYIN DINEH*, or Holy People—include FIRST MAN AND FIRST WOMAN, Changing Woman, BEGOCHÍDÍ, and WIND (NILCH'I). The *HACTCIN* of Jicarilla Apache tradition were supernatural beings who personified the power of natural forces. The *hactcin* leader, BLACK HACTCIN, created the animals, birds, and the first man.

CROW
The large, glossy black crow, with its distinctive caw, is a common character in Native American mythology. Among the stories of some cultures, Crow (known to the Tanaina as CHULYEN) takes RAVEN's place as a TRICKSTER and CULTURE HERO.

A Choctaw tale about the theft of FIRE explains why crows have black plumage and harsh voices. Once, crows had white feathers and sweet singing voices. When Crow tried to steal fire, he took so long deciding how to bring it home that his feathers were charred black and the smoke turned his voice into a harsh caw.

CULTURE HEROES
Virtually every Native American tribe, pueblo, or cultural group has culture heroes or heroines, characters who are responsible for a variety of significant acts: creating humans; bringing CORN, FIRE, or LIGHT; teaching skills; transforming the landscape; and slaying MONSTERS to make the world safe for humans. Common aspects of culture heroes include a birth shrouded in mystery (sometimes with a nonhuman parent, frequently the SUN), rapid growth from birth to adulthood, and supernatural powers. Some culture heroes are AMCHITAPUKA (Yavapai), BREATH MAKER (Seminole), GLUSKAP (Algonquian), ICTINIKE (Iowa, Omaha), MANABOZHO (Algonquian, Anishinabe), OKABEWIS (Anishinabe), and WISKE (Potawatomi).

Culture heroes are frequently WARRIOR TWINS, often sons of the Sun. Twin culture heroes include AHAYUTA AND MATSILEMA (Zuni), IOSKEHA AND TAWISCARA (Iroquois), KILLER-OF-ENEMIES and CHILD-OF-THE-WATER (Apache), MASEWA AND UYUYEWA (Keres), and MONSTER SLAYER AND BORN FOR WATER (Navajo [Dineh]).

Women also figure as culture heroes (or heroines), usually associated with fertility, conception, birth, and the provision of food. WHITE BUFFALO CALF WOMAN gave the Lakota the SACRED PIPE and the BUFFALO and taught them how to worship, marry, and cook. Other female culture heroes are CHANGING WOMAN (Navajo [Dineh]) and WHITE PAINTED WOMAN (Apache).

Not all culture heroes are human. ANIMALS and BIRDS frequently fill this role as well. COYOTE is credited with the origin of some tribes, the release of game, the theft of light, the origin of winter, and the finality of death. Fire was given to the Nez Perce by BEAVER, to the Jicarilla Apache by FOX, to the Anishinabe by MUSKRAT, and to the Ute by WOLF. For some Northwest Coast tribes, BEAR (Suku) was a culture hero who created fish, named rivers, taught skills to humans, and slew monsters. MINK, also a monster slayer, created mountains, lakes, and rivers and stole the Sun. For other tribes in the Northwest and the Arctic, RAVEN brought light to the dark world, taught animals, created and changed parts of the world, and named plants. Great HARE—MICHABO—was a culture hero of Algonquian-speaking tribes.

D

DANCE Dance is a part of almost every Native American ritual, from private curing rites to important ceremonials. Many cultures have organized dance societies. The sacred Dark Dance of the Iroquois, which was given to them by the LITTLE PEOPLE, is performed by members of the Little People Society. Dances are associated with agriculture (see CORN, CORN MAIDENS), ANIMALS and BIRDS such as BEAR and EAGLE, hunting, and healing (see FALSE FACES). The Green Corn Dance is a tradition in many cultures. Members of the Hopi Snake and Antelope societies perform a nine-day Snake Dance in which dancers hold live snakes in their mouths. The snakes are released into the desert at the end of the ceremony to carry messages and prayers to the deities in the UNDERWORLD. During the spring and summer months, Plaza Dances are performed by KACHINAS in Hopi villages. Sacred CLOWNS often perform during these dances. During the winter, Pueblo people hold animal dances (ceremonies named after different game animals) for various purposes: to lure game animals, to propitiate animal spirits, to bring healing, and to bring rain or snow.

See also GHOST DANCE OF 1890; SUN DANCE.

Cherokee dancers at Chehaw National Indian Festival (© Kevin Fleming/CORBIS)

DEER Among Native American groups whose principal source of food was the deer, these game animals play a prominent role in folklore and ceremony. In many tales, deer are female and appear as the wife, mother, or sister of another animal character. In some stories, Deer Woman married a human but left with their son when her husband offended her (usually by criticizing the way she ate). A Nootka tale credits Deer with the theft of FIRE from WOODPECKER, the only being that possessed it. A deer helped OLD MAN COYOTE steal summer and carry it to the Crow people (see SEASONS, ORIGIN OF).

The Zuni WARRIOR TWINS, AHAYUTA AND MATSILEMA, were credited with creating deer by killing Saiyathlia, KACHINA warriors. According to Zuni legend, a group of kachinas called the Kanaakwe were involved in a dispute with other kachinas over hunting rights. The Kanaakwe hid the deer, which led to a challenge by the other group. The Kanaakwe won, making them the givers of deer to the Zuni.

The loss and recovery of this crucial food source is a frequent theme. The Hunter, KANATI, was the keeper of game for the Cherokee. When his twin sons, the THUNDER BOYS, set loose the deer Kanati kept in a cave, there was no food for the people until the Thunder Boys returned and sang songs to recall the deer. In the traditional story cycle associated with the Navajo (Dineh) ceremonial CHIRICAHUA WINDWAY, WIND held back the deer because of an insult from a young hunter, causing the hunter's family to starve.

Another theme is the importance of properly honoring deer. According to Cherokee legend, whenever a hunter killed a deer, Little Deer knew it and arrived there to ask the bloodstains on the ground whether the hunter had asked for pardon for the life he took. If he had, all was well, but if he had not, Little Deer tracked him down and afflicted his body with rheumatism.

DEGANAWIDAH (Deganawida, Dekanawida, Dekanahwideh, Dekanawideh, The Peacemaker) (fl. 1500s) *Huron* The Huron prophet who first conceived the idea of what became the Iroquois Confederacy. According to legend, a Huron woman had a dream in which a messenger came to her and told her that her daughter, though a virgin, would soon give birth to a son. The messenger told her the name by which the boy would be called and said that when he was grown, he would bring news of peace to the people from the chief of the SKY spirits. The prediction came true: Deganawidah was born to the young maiden. He grew quickly. When he was ready, he built a canoe of white stone and left home to fulfill his destiny.

In those days, the Five Nations—the Cayuga, Mohawk, Oneida, Onondaga, and Seneca—were locked in bloody warfare. Horrified by the senseless violence, Deganawidah had a vision in which he saw the Five Nations unified, anchored by the roots of a great Tree of Peace. As he planned a way to bring peace, he placed an eagle FEATHER on the ground to represent his "great idea"—the Five Nations living in harmony under a government of law. Deganawidah traveled among the tribes with his disciple, HIAWATHA, spreading his message. Together, the two forged alliances and taught the Great Law of Justice. An Onondaga chief named ATOTARHO was the last to resist, but he was finally won over. A great council was called, which according to legend took place under a giant PINE on which an EAGLE perched protectively, scanning for trouble with its keen eyes. Fifty chiefs, selected by the women clan elders of each tribe, attended, and the laws of the confederacy were stated and agreed to.

When Deganawidah left the council after the great peace was agreed to, he decreed that no one would succeed him or be called by his name.

DEVIL'S TOWER Devil's Tower National Monument in Wyoming is a great shaft of stone, the core of an ancient volcano, that rises 865 feet from its base. There are several tales about the origin of this distinctive landmark, all of which involve a giant BEAR. (The Plains tribes call the tower Mató Tipila, "Bear's Lodge" or "Bear Rock.")

In a Lakota tale, two young boys who had become lost and were wandering about trying to find their way home realized that Mató, a giant grizzly bear, was stalking them. The boys prayed to WAKAN TANKA, the Great Mystery, to save them. Suddenly the earth under them shook and began to rise. The boys rose with it, higher and higher, until they were out of the bear's reach. Angry that he had lost his prey, the huge bear dug his claws into the rock, leaving the long vertical ridges that mark the tower to this day. Wanblee, the EAGLE, rescued the boys from the tower and brought them home.

Kiowa legends about the tower also account for the origin of the STARS of the PLEIADES and the BIG DIPPER. According to one legend, a spirit in the form of a bear appeared to a young girl and changed her into a ferocious, giant bear that attacked her seven siblings. Seeking to escape, the terrified children climbed onto a rock that began to grow upward, carrying them far beyond their sister's reach. The bear clawed at the rock in fury, gouging its sides, but her siblings rose into the heavens, where they became the stars of the Pleiades. In a different version of the legend, it was a boy who turned into a bear and chased his seven sisters onto a tree stump that turned into a tall tower. Carried to safety in the heavens, the girls became the seven stars of the Big Dipper. (See also CONSTELLATION.)

DIRECTIONS, CARDINAL
The FOUR cardinal (or primary) directions—north, south, east, and west—serve as a means of orientation for almost every Native American cultural group. Some groups recognize six directions: the four cardinal directions plus zenith (above) and nadir (below). Across the continent, the acts of rituals, dances, and ceremonies refer to these directions.

In most CREATION ACCOUNTS, the cardinal directions orient the world and give it concrete reference points. The Navajo (Dineh) set four sacred MOUNTAINS at these four points to mark the borders of their homeland. For many tribes, each direction was also represented by a COLOR. Directions are also linked to the SEASONS, ANIMALS, CLANS, CORN, weather, and other aspects of nature. In Navajo (Dineh) tradition, each direction had a guardian SNAKE that was the color of its direction. For the Zuni, sacred animals guarded each of the six directions (see BEAST GODS). According to Lakota tradition, SKAN, the SKY, instructed the four sons of TATE, the WIND, to establish the four cardinal directions and gave each brother control of the direction he established. Skan also assigned a season to each direction and gave the brothers control over the weather for their seasons.

DIYIN DINEH (*dyin diné, diyin dine'é*) *Navajo (Dineh)* Usually translated as "Holy People," the deities, creators, CULTURE HEROES, and other powerful beings who emerged into the present world with FIRST MAN AND FIRST WOMAN. Among the *diyin dineh* are TALKING GOD, CHANGING WOMAN, MONSTER SLAYER AND BORN FOR WATER, and NILCH'I (WIND). The *diyin dineh* created the Earth Surface People, the ancestors of the Navajo (Dineh), and have the power to help or harm humans. (See also NAVAJO [DINEH] EMERGENCE; YEI.)

DOG Dogs were domesticated by Native Americans about 4,000 years ago. Before the Plains tribes acquired HORSES, they used dogs as pack animals. A packsaddle placed over a dog's shoulders was attached to a device—later called a *travois* by French explorers—consisting of two joined poles that dragged along the ground. A dog could pull a *travois* loaded with as much as 75 pounds of goods. To the Lakota, the dog was the spirit of faithfulness and friendship. Dogs play a role in many myths. The most common theme is marriage between a woman and a dog (see DOG HUSBAND). In Cherokee mythology, the MILKY WAY was created by a dog that stole cornmeal and left a trail of it as he ran off.

DOG HUSBAND Marriage between a woman and a DOG is a common theme in Native American mythology. Marriages between humans and animals are a symbolic effort to merge the human and animal realms. In myths, attitudes of human and animal associates of the couple toward such marriages vary, ranging between grudging acceptance and outright rejection. Frequently in tales of dog husbands, the wife's tribe deserts her. Another theme is the ability of the dog to transform himself into a human by night, so the human woman is unaware that he is a dog.

The nature and fate of the children that result from marriage between a human woman and a dog is different from tale to tale. In an Inuit tale, five of the couple's 10 children were puppies, and five were human babies who became the ADLET—blood-drinking MONSTERS. The mother set the five puppies adrift in a boat, and they became the ancestors of white people. According to a Chippewa legend, the Dogrib people (neighbors of the Chippewa) were descen-

Dogs served as pack animals before horses were brought to North America by the Spanish conquistadores. *(North Wind Picture Archives)*

dants of Copper Woman (the first woman) and a dog. In a Cheyenne tale, the dog father of puppies born to a human woman took them to the sky, where they became the PLEIADES, a familiar star cluster.

DOUBLE-FACED WOMAN (Anog Ite)
Lakota Originally known as Ite, she was the beautiful daughter of FIRST MAN AND FIRST WOMAN and the wife of TATE, the WIND. After giving birth to quadruplets, Ite became pregnant again, but she decided to try to replace Hanwi, the MOON, as the wife of Wi, the SUN. SKAN, the SKY, discovered Ite's intentions and condemned her to live forever with two faces, one beautiful and the other grotesquely ugly. She then came to be called Anog Ite (Double Face). In Oglala legends, Double-Faced Woman originated the skill of quilling—the art of decorating objects with dyed porcupine quills. She developed a method of preparing and dyeing quills and taught the skill to young women.

DREAM CATCHER
Lakota A weblike structure formed of sinew woven within a circular branch and decorated with FEATHERS and often with a precious stone. Hung over a sleeping place or on a baby's cradleboard, the dream catcher was supposed to prevent bad dreams from reaching the sleeper. Bad dreams, troubles, and anxieties, which were thought to have jagged edges, became entangled in the dream catcher's web. Good dreams and thoughts, which were thought to be smooth, could pass through.

DRY PAINTING
See SANDPAINTING.

DUCK
Related to geese and swans, ducks vary greatly in size and abilities. While all are good swimmers, only some varieties are divers. In CREATION ACCOUNTS of various tribes, Duck was one of the diving animals sent to bring soil from the bottom of the PRIMORDIAL WATERS in order to create land. In some versions of the Blackfeet account, Duck was the only animal to succeed in retrieving mud that the Creator, NA'PI, used to create the Earth. In one Arapaho story, although Duck brought up some soil, there was not enough to create land. In another version of the Arapaho account, ducks were the first diving animals sent down for soil, but they could not reach the bottom of the water. In one version of the Crow account, the Creator, OLD MAN COYOTE, asked FOUR ducks to dive for soil. The first three failed, but the fourth and smallest duck succeeded. In another version of the story, rather than being sent by Old Man Coyote, the ducks themselves decided to dive.

E

EAGENTCI (Old Woman, First Mother) *Seneca* The mother of the human race. (See also SKY WOMAN.)

EAGLE A powerful symbol in many Native American cultures, eagles appear in a multitude of tales. Because the eagle was believed to fly higher than any other bird, it was sometimes considered an embodiment of the highest god or as a mediator between the gods and people. Its high flight, which can make it disappear behind the clouds, also caused the eagle to be associated with the sky spirits that controlled rain, wind, thunder, and lightning. Throughout North America the eagle was the representative of the THUNDERBIRD, master of storms.

As one of the BEAST GODS, the eagle symbolized the direction above (zenith) for the Zuni. It was the sacred bird of the Cherokee and figured prominently in ceremonial rituals, especially those relating to war. In one version of the Hopi CREATION ACCOUNT (see HOPI EMERGENCE AND MIGRATION), when the Hopi emerged into the present world, they met a great eagle that gave them permission to live on the land. The eagle told them that whenever they wished to

The form of an eagle in this effigy mound in Georgia can be seen only from above. (*© Georg Gerster/Photo Researchers*)

send a message to the Sun Father, they could use one of his FEATHERS. Eagles play key roles in the Navajo (Dineh) curing ceremonials BEADWAY and EAGLE-WAY. The traditional account of MONSTERWAY relates that when the WARRIOR TWIN Monster Slayer slew Rock Monster Eagle, he changed the eagle's nestlings into the golden eagle and the OWL. (See also MONSTER SLAYER AND BORN FOR WATER.)

Eagle feathers were prized as AMULETS. Plains warriors wore eagle feathers into battle to provide them with the endurance, sharp vision, speed, and ferocity of the mightiest of birds. The famous Lakota eagle feather warbonnet was worn to inspire bravery and to invoke the eagle's power over enemies. It was designed to sway in the breeze to imitate the bird's wing beats. Eagle feathers procured according to ritual by the Navajo (Dineh) were offerings to the DIYIN DINEH (Holy People).

In Eagle Dances, which were held by many tribes, dancers moved and sometimes dressed like eagles. Such dances were held for a variety of purposes: to ensure success in hunting or in war, to make peace and create friendship between tribes, and to cure illness. (See also DANCE.)

According to Iroquois tradition, the Huron prophet DEGANAWIDAH conceived the idea of the Iroquois Confederacy while the Great White Eagle perched protectively above him. An eagle also served as a lookout during the council at which the chiefs of the Five Nations agreed to the laws of the confederacy.

EAGLEWAY *Navajo (Dineh)* A ceremonial curing complex, or group of ceremonies (called chants, sings, or ways) conducted to heal illness and restore harmony (*hózhó*) in the universe (see NAVAJO [DINEH] CEREMONIALS). Eagleway is included in the HOLYWAY classification of ceremonies, which are used to restore health by attracting good. The cycle of stories associated with Eagleway takes place after the birth of CHANGING WOMAN but before her twin sons MONSTER SLAYER AND BORN FOR WATER rid the world of MONSTERS.

After Changing Woman created WHITE SHELL WOMAN and Turquoise Woman from skin rubbed from under her breasts, the two newly created women went to live on a mountain. TALKING GOD gave each of them an ear of CORN and instructed them never to

give the corn away. On a journey to find food, the women met Monster Slayer, who helped them avoid several monsters and took them to his home in the south. After Monster Slayer repeatedly asked what the women were carrying, they finally gave him a grain of corn from each ear. Two CORN MAIDENS then appeared at the house and engaged in a contest with White Shell Woman and Turquoise Woman in which they won Monster Slayer. Together with the Corn Maidens' grandfather, Cornsmut Man, Monster Slayer and the Corn Maidens traveled to the home of the EAGLE People. Cornsmut Man and the chief of the Eagle People submitted Monster Slayer to many tests, which he passed with the help of a guardian WIND. After the hero survived the tests, he was rewarded with the prayers and songs of Eagleway. He also learned the proper ritual method for catching eagles.

BEADWAY is another ceremonial that was taught by the Eagle People.

EARTH-INITIATE See KODOYANPE.

EARTHMAKER *Akimel O'odham, Ho Chunk, Tohono O'odham* The CREATOR. In the Ho Chunk CREATION ACCOUNT, Earthmaker (Ma-o-na) was alone in the void. Whatever he wished for came into existence. In this way, he created LIGHT, the Earth, and everything on the Earth. The only problem was that the Earth was restless. To calm it, Earthmaker created FOUR large serpents that pierced through the Earth's four corners and held it still. Earthmaker then made the first man, but he was displeased with his creation and tossed it aside. It became an evil spirit, Wa-cho-pi-ni-Shi-shik, that copied everything Earthmaker created but in an opposite way. When Earthmaker made DEER, ELK, and BUFFALO, Wa-cho-pi-ni-Shi-shik made evil spirits and MONSTERS that devoured people. Earthmaker sent his four sons, one after another, to destroy the monsters. His youngest son, Little Hare, finally completed the task.

According to the Akimel O'odham creation account, Earthmaker (Cherwit Make) created humans from his own sweat. When the people grew selfish and quarrelsome, Earthmaker became annoyed with their behavior and decided to destroy them with a FLOOD. First, however, he sent the WINDS to warn them to change their ways. All the people except a

SHAMAN named Suha ignored the warnings. South Wind told Suha to make a hollow ball of SPRUCE gum in which he and his wife could survive the coming flood. Suha followed his instructions, and he and his wife floated safely on the waters in their spruce gum ark. They became the ancestors of the Akimel O'od-ham people.

In the Tohono O'odham account, Earthmaker made the world from a small ball of mud on which he danced until it grew to its present size. COYOTE was with Earthmaker from the beginning and helped him create humans.

ECLIPSE The total or partial obscuring of one celestial body by another. A solar eclipse occurs when the MOON passes directly between the Earth and the SUN. Where the cone of the Moon's shadow falls on the Earth, the sun is eclipsed. A lunar eclipse occurs when the Earth is directly between the Sun and the Moon. The Moon is eclipsed as it passes through the Earth's shadow. Because eclipses are unusual and dramatic, people of many cultures tried to explain the phenomenon.

Conflict is a common theme of eclipse legends. For the Miwok of California, an eclipse was seen as a struggle for power between the Sun and the Moon. A Pomo myth relates the story of a BEAR that met the Sun while he walked on the MILKY WAY. The Sun refused to get out of the bear's way, so he fought with it. The Sun was eclipsed during the fight. When the bear continued on and met the Moon—the Sun's sister—another fight occurred, during which the Moon was eclipsed.

Some tribes believed that eclipses occurred when the Sun or Moon was eaten or swallowed by something. For the Nootka, the Door of Heaven swallowed the Sun or Moon; for the Kwakiutl, it was the Mouth of Heaven. In a Cherokee myth, a FROG ate the Sun or Moon. The Tlingit, on the other hand, viewed the Sun and Moon as husband and wife enjoying each other's company during the darkness of an eclipse. Still another view of an eclipse was held by the Tillamook; they believed that spirits talking to the Moon kept it from shining. The Tewa were afraid that an eclipse was a sign that the Sun Father was angry and had left to return to his house in the UNDERWORLD.

Eclipses were often feared or believed to be evil omens. In the western Arctic culture area, diseases were thought to emanate from the Moon. For these people, a lunar eclipse was a sign that an epidemic was about to strike.

EFFIGY MOUNDS See MOUNDS.

ELK The largest member of the deer family, the elk is a powerful animal whose only enemies are humans and mountain lions. The Lakota, Crow, and Assiniboine sought elk power as a love medicine.

ENEMYWAY ('Anaa'jí) *Navajo (Dineh)* A major rite that is used to exorcise the ghosts of aliens, violence, and ugliness (see NAVAJO [DINEH] CEREMONIALS). Enemyway is derived from ancient war ceremonials used to protect warriors from the ghosts of enemies they killed. It is performed to heal people whose illness was caused by contact with an enemy (non-Navajo) ghost.

In the traditional account associated with Enemyway, a young man of the Corn People married a young woman of the Rock Crystal People whose father had magical powers contained in a MEDICINE BUNDLE. The young couple secretly exchanged medicine bundles in order to acquire the man's powers, but the father-in-law switched the bundles back. He then invited the young man and his Corn People relatives to take part in a raid on Taos Pueblo. Without the MEDICINE power, most of the Corn People were killed.

The young man had two nieces whom COYOTE wanted to marry. The man decreed that to win the girls, Coyote had to obtain the scalps of two Taos maidens who had never seen sunlight. Although TALKING GOD tried to prevent the war, the WARRIOR TWIN Monster Slayer led a raid on Taos. Two elderly men who joined the raid, Bear and Snake, succeeded in capturing the maidens. The men then passed other tests in order to marry the girls Coyote had desired but were refused. Then they used TOBACCO smoke to transform themselves into handsome young men and tricked the girls into marrying them. The next morning, Bear and Snake returned to their real forms. The account continues in BEAUTYWAY and MOUNTAINWAY.

ESAUGETUH EMISSEE (Master of Breath) *Creek* The CREATOR and god of the WIND, with power over the breath of life. In the Creek CREATION ACCOUNT, in the beginning the world was covered with the PRIMORDIAL WATERS, and there was no land. Then a blade of grass rose above the surface, followed by solid land. In the center of the land was a great hill, the home of the Creator Esaugetuh Emissee. He used the mud surrounding his home to mold the first people. Because water still covered the Earth, he built a wall on which to dry the people he had made, and the soft mud of their bodies turned into bone and flesh. Esaugetuh Emissee then directed the water into channels so that there would be dry land for humans to live on.

See also HUMANS, ORIGIN OF.

ES-TE FAS-TA (Gives Everything) *Seminole* The CREATOR, who lives in the SKY. Also known as OLD MAN, Es-te fas-ta gave the Seminole people land and rice and prepared them for the coming of Fas-ta-chee, a dwarf who brought them CORN. Es-te fas-ta also gave the Seminole the three MEDICINE BUNDLES that represent the three divisions of the Seminole tribe.

ETIOLOGICAL MYTH A class of traditional stories that explain the origins of things in nature, such as animal attributes, plants, and weather phenomena, or the origins of tribal customs. Etiological myths are commonly called "just-so stories" or "pourquoi tales."

EVENING STAR *Skidi Pawnee* The Skidi Pawnee name for the planet Venus, which appears to be either of two different stars depending on its position relative to that of Earth. As a morning star, Venus rises in the east ahead of the Sun. During its period as an evening star, it is the brightest object in the sky, except for the Moon. As an evening star, Venus becomes visible above the western horizon after the Sun has set.

In Pawnee mythology, Evening Star, who was also called White Star Woman, was beautiful and powerful. Many stars courted her, but she accepted none of them. The great warrior MORNING STAR (the planet Mars), pursued her across the sky from his home in the east, but Evening Star kept placing obstacles in his path. Finally, however, he reached her home in the west. Protected by the FOUR guardian stars of the cardinal DIRECTIONS—Black Star, Yellow Star, White Star, and Red Star—Evening Star still did not submit until Morning Star accomplished tasks she set for him. Then she consented to marry him. They produced a daughter named Standing Rain. When Standing Rain was old enough, Morning Star sent her down to Earth with an ear of CORN to plant. Standing Rain and her husband (who in some accounts was the son of the Sun and Moon) became the parents of the human race. (See also HUMANS, ORIGIN OF.)

In the Pawnee CREATION ACCOUNT, the CREATOR told Evening Star to have her priests sing and shake their rattles. When they did, a storm arose and turned the formless world into a water-covered world. The Creator then sent the Black, Yellow, White, and Red Stars to strike the water with cedar war clubs. When they did, Earth appeared. Evening Star's priests again sang and shook their rattles. A storm arose again, and when its thunder shook the world, the mountains, hills, valleys, and plains were formed.

EVILWAY (Hóchoʼíjí) *Navajo (Dineh)* One of the three classifications into which ritual curing ceremonials are grouped. (The others are HOLYWAY and LIFEWAY.) Evilway ceremonials are performed to drive out evil, cure illnesses caused by ghosts, and combat the effects of witchcraft (see also WITCH). They are also performed to restore imbalances caused by witnessing a death, taking someone's life, or visiting ANASAZI remains. Evilway ceremonials last two, three, or five nights.

See also NAVAJO (DINEH) CEREMONIALS.

F

FALSE FACES *Iroquois* The English term used to refer to Iroquois MEDICINE societies whose members wear MASKS during ceremonies. The term *False Faces* refers specifically to the Society of Faces, one of three medicine societies. (The others are the Husk Face Society and the Medicine Company, or Society of Animals.) The False Faces participate prominently in the Midwinter Ceremony and impersonate spirits in the Green Corn Festival. Their function is to conduct curing rituals for individual patients and to drive disease, witches, and tornadoes away from the entire village.

FATHER SKY See MOTHER EARTH AND FATHER SKY.

FEATHERS Gathered according to set rituals from sacred BIRDS such as the EAGLE, feathers are essential elements of many sacred ceremonies and rituals. They are attached to objects used in ceremonies—such as rattles, MASKS, and PRAYERSTICKS—and are also used as offerings. Because birds can fly and appear to communicate with the SKY spirits, feathers are viewed as a bridge between people and the spirit world. They are believed to help invoke the dead as well as other spirits. For the Pueblo people, feathers represent breath or RAIN. Traditionally, Pueblo prayersticks have feathers attached to them to help bring rain. Feathers are believed to carry breath prayers to the spirits. When the breath prayers join with the breath of the spirits, clouds form. Behind these clouds, the rainmakers do their work.

Feathers were frequently carried or worn as AMULETS. Plains warriors wore eagle feathers into battle to provide them with the bird's endurance, sharp vision, speed, and ferocity. The eagle feather warbonnet of the Lakota was worn to inspire bravery and invest its wearer with the eagle's power. Because of their association with the SUN, the brilliant scarlet feathers from a WOODPECKER's head were considered sacred by West Coast tribes and were used to decorate headdresses, feather belts, and other ceremonial objects. SHAMANS in the Southeast wore TURKEY feather capes and used turkey feather fans.

Chief Joseph of the Nez Perce tribe in ceremonial regalia that includes an eagle feather headdress. *(© Edward S. Curtis/Christie's Images/CORBIS)*

FIRE The importance of fire for human survival, as well as its association with the SUN, contributed to its prominent place in Native American mythology. Many stories tell how people first acquired fire. The Hopi were given fire by MASAU'U, the deity of fire and death. The Creator MAHEO taught the Cheyenne how to make fire. For the Navajo (Dineh), BLACK GOD created fire. In some traditions, fire was the gift of a CULTURE HERO. According to Tohono O'odham legend, MONTEZUMA taught fire-making skills to the people. In a Huron legend, the culture hero IOSKEHA was taught how to make fire by Tortoise and passed the knowledge on to humans. Tales frequently involve the theft of fire from the being that possessed it. Often the bringer of fire was an ANIMAL or a BIRD, such as BEAVER (Nez Perce), COYOTE (many traditions), DEER (Nootka), FOX (Jicarilla Apache), MUSKRAT (Anishinabe), TURKEY (Cherokee), or WOLF (Ute). Grandmother Spider (SPIDER WOMAN) stole fire for the Choctaw. In one Cherokee tale, a water SPIDER was responsible for the gift of fire.

FIRST MAN AND FIRST WOMAN (Altsé hastiin and Altsé asdzáá) *Navajo (Dineh)* Two of the beings from the First World (see NAVAJO [DINEH] EMERGENCE). According to one account, First Man was created in the east from the joining of white and black clouds, and First Woman was created in the west from the joining of yellow and blue clouds. In another account, they were created from two ears of CORN (white for First Man, yellow for First Woman) over which White WIND (NILCH'I ligai) blew to give them life.

First Man and First Woman directed the journey through the worlds up to the present one. Following the emergence into this world, First Man and First Woman built a sweat lodge and sang the Blessing Song. Then First Man built the first hogan (a home), constructed on a model of the world set out by TALKING GOD. The FOUR poles that supported the hogan were made of the four sacred stones: white shell, abalone, turquoise, and black jet. Here the people met to plan what their world would be like. They named the four sacred MOUNTAINS that would become the boundaries of the Navajo (Dineh) homeland.

First Man and First Woman planned the birth of CHANGING WOMAN and, although they were not her parents, raised her. First Man gave Changing Woman the MEDICINE BUNDLE with which she created four of the Navajo (Dineh) clans. After giving Changing Woman the bundle, First Man and First Woman returned to the UNDERWORLD to serve as chiefs of death and witchcraft. (See also BLESSINGWAY; WITCH.)

FIRST MOTHER *Penobscot* A woman associated with the origin of CORN. She sacrificed herself to feed her starving people. First Mother was created when a drop of dew fell on a leaf and was warmed by the SUN. As a young woman she married Great Nephew, the helper of GLUSKAP. She bore him children and thus became First Mother; Great Nephew became First Father.

The people kept growing in number. Because they lived by hunting, the more people there were, the less game there was. Soon the people began to starve. When her hungry children begged First Mother for food, she had none to give them, but she promised that she would make food for them. She told Great Nephew that he must kill her. Horrified by the idea, Great Nephew went to Gluskap for advice, only to be told to do what First Mother asked. First Mother instructed Great Nephew to have two of their sons drag her body back and forth over an empty patch of soil until no flesh was left on it and then bury her bones in the middle of another clearing. She told him to wait for seven moons; then the people would find food to nourish them. Great Nephew and his grieving sons did as she asked. Seven moons later, where her flesh had fallen, the land was covered with corn plants. Where her bones had been buried, TOBACCO grew.

See also SELU.

FLINT A hard gray stone (a type of quartz) that produces a spark when struck. Because of its usefulness in making knives, arrowheads, and other weapons and its importance as a fire-making tool, flint is the subject of various myths related to its origin (see CHOKANIPOK; IOSKEHA AND TAWISCARA). Flint is also personified in several mythological characters, such as the Seneca hero Othegwenhda, who could change himself into many forms; the Pawnee Flint Man, a human who could cause transformation, bring RAIN, and heal illness; and the Stone Giants of Iroquois legend, CANNIBALS whose bodies were covered with coats of flint.

FLINTWAY *Navajo (Dineh)* A ceremonial curing complex, or group of ceremonies (called chants, sings, or ways) conducted to heal illness and restore harmony (*hózhó*) in the universe (see NAVAJO [DINEH] CEREMONIALS). Flintway is included in the LIFEWAY classification of ceremonies, which are used to treat injuries caused by accidents or illnesses related to the natural life process.

The hero of the related traditional account was a young man who was killed by lightning after he had unknowingly spent the night with the wife of White Thunder. The young man's family learned what had happened and discovered that Gila Monster could help them. Gila Monster demonstrated his powers by severing and scattering his own body parts and then restoring them. He restored the hero in the same way; this act forms the basis of Flintway. In a later episode, when the hero was attacked by BUFFALO, he killed Buffalo Who Never Dies. This killing resulted in the death of all the buffalo, which the hero then had to restore. Afterward he was given the MEDICINES, chants, rituals, and sacred items of Flintway.

FLOODS Floods play a frequent role in tales throughout North America. Sometimes the CREATOR destroyed the world with a flood because he was displeased. The Arapaho Creator NESHANU, the Akimel O'odham Creator EARTHMAKER, and the Wiyot Creator ABOVE-OLD-MAN destroyed the world with floods because they were unhappy with the people they had created. In the HOPI EMERGENCE AND MIGRATION account, the Creator destroyed the Third World with a flood because so many people had become corrupt. The Navajo (Dineh) Fourth World was also destroyed by a flood (see NAVAJO [DINEH] EMERGENCE). In an Inuit legend, when the world became so overpopulated that it began to collapse, a flood came and carried away most of the people.

MONSTERS and giants are sometimes responsible for floods. In a Lakota tale, a water monster named UNCEGILA caused a flood when she emerged from the primordial sea. In another Lakota legend, the UNK-TEHI, a race of monsters, tried to destroy the human race by flood (see also BADLANDS). In a Navajo (Dineh) story, Water Monster (Teehooltsoodii, "the one who grabs in deep water") caused a flood when SPIDER WOMAN stole his child.

For other tales involving floods, see BLUE FEATHER, CHIEF MOUNTAIN, MANABOZHO, and TAVWOTS.

FOUR A powerful and sacred number for various Native American cultural groups. In many tales, events take place over four time periods—days, months, years, or ages. For example, CHANGING WOMAN grew from birth to puberty in four days (Navajo [Dineh]); ARROW BOY's mother carried him for four years before giving birth to him (Cheyenne); and the prophet SWEET MEDICINE spent four years learning sacred teachings for his people (Cheyenne). Sweet Medicine received the four sacred arrows of the Cheyenne from MAHEO.

Earth-diver CREATION ACCOUNTS usually involve four animals diving to retrieve soil from under the water in order to create land, with the first three being unsuccessful and the fourth succeeding. Emergence creation accounts often involve four UNDERWORLDS or underground chambers in which the people lived before emerging into the present world. For the Hopi, the present world is the fourth on which they have lived (see HOPI EMERGENCE AND MIGRATION). According to the ACOMA EMERGENCE AND MIGRATION account, the people lived in four underground chambers before their emergence.

For the Navajo (Dineh), the number four has special significance. They set four sacred MOUNTAINS to mark the boundaries of their traditional homeland. In addition, each of the four cardinal DIRECTIONS has a guardian SNAKE, COLOR, WIND, sacred stone, thunder spirit, and so on. According to the NAVAJO (DINEH) EMERGENCE account, four Holy People (Haashch'ééh dineh)—named White Body (TALKING GOD), Blue Body (WATER SPRINKLER), Yellow Body

(CALLING GOD), and Black Body (BLACK GOD)—created FIRST MAN AND FIRST WOMAN.

FOUR BEINGS OF THE NORTH *Pawnee*
Beings that were responsible for the supply of food to humans. Led by READY-TO-GIVE, the North WIND, the Four Beings provided BUFFALO and other game and sent the RAIN to ensure the growth of crops.

FOX The clever fox is a common character in many Native American tales, sometimes as the companion of COYOTE. In Dakota myth, Fox was one of the spirit helpers of TAKUSKANSKAN, the being that personified motion and gave life to things.

Other tales link Fox to the origin of FIRE or sunlight. In a Jicarilla Apache legend, fireflies held the secret of fire. Fox tricked the fireflies, stole the fire from them, and gave it to the human race. In a Netsilik Inuit tale about the origin of LIGHT, Fox had a verbal duel with HARE over whether the world would be light or dark. Fox preferred darkness, and Hare preferred light. Hare—whose words had magical powers—won the duel and was given daylight, but to please both animals, night always followed day.

FROG In Northwest Coast legends, frogs were an important symbol, associated with RAIN, dampness, fertility, and renewal. Haida artists carved frogs on the poles that supported houses to prevent them from falling over. In a Blackfeet CREATION ACCOUNT, Frog was one of the diving animals sent by NA'PI to retrieve soil from under the water to create land. A Cherokee myth explains ECLIPSES by saying that a frog ate the Sun or Moon. In the traditional account

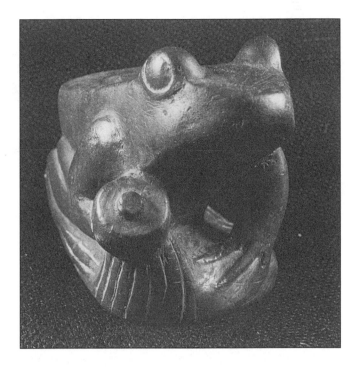

This stone pipe with an effigy of a frog was found at Cahokia, a center of the Mississippian culture in present-day Illinois. *(Cahokia Mound Historic Site)*

associated with the Navajo (Dineh) curing ceremonial HAILWAY, the hero, Rainboy, lost a contest with Frog. Frog won many of Rainboy's body parts. In an Assiniboine story about the SEASONS, IKTOMI declared that winter would last for as many months as there were hairs in his wolfskin robe. Frog objected that no animal could live through that long a winter. He protested that seven (in another version, six) months was long enough. Iktomi flew into a rage and killed him. Dead though he was, Frog held out seven of his toes, and Iktomi gave in.

G

GAMBLING Gambling is a common theme in Native American tales. The Navajo (Dineh) GAMBLING GOD challenged humans and won not only all their possessions but most of the people as well. The main character in the mythology of the Navajo (Dineh) curing ceremonial HAILWAY is Rainboy, who had a weakness for gambling. In a Chumash myth, SKY COYOTE (POLARIS, the North Star) engaged in an annual game with the SUN and other SKY spirits to determine the fate of humans on Earth. In a Zuni tale about the origin of the rain priesthood, people went to the village where the KACHINAS lived to gamble with them. The kachinas won and trapped the losers, who became the UWANNAMI.

GAMBLING GOD (Nááhwíilbiihí, Noqoilpi, The Great Gambler) *Navajo (Dineh)* A god who loved to gamble. When Gambling God came onto the Earth, he found that the humans living here were prosperous, so he became determined to win their property. He challenged the people to games of chance, strength, and skill. Not knowing that Gambling God had the power to turn luck his way, the people accepted his challenge. Soon the god had won not only their property but their women and children as well, and even some of the men. The other gods disapproved of this behavior, so they sent NILCH'I (WIND) to defeat him. Disguised, Nilch'i challenged Gambling God to a contest for the property he had won. Nilch'i won the contest, set the human captives free, and returned their property. Nilch'i then used a bow to shoot Gambling God into the sky, all the way to the Moon. Gambling God went to BEGOCHÍDÍ for help and was granted new animals and a new people to rule. Begochídí then sent Gambling God back down to Earth, where he lived and ruled in what is now Mexico.

GHOST DANCE OF 1890 A religious movement initiated by the Paiute prophet WOVOKA (ca. 1856–1932). In 1889, Wovoka had a vision in which he was given a message of hope and peace for his people. The world would be renewed, the BUFFALO would return, and people would be reunited with their deceased loved ones if they lived without warfare, worked hard, and avoided lying, stealing, and other bad behavior. To bring about this renewal, Wovoka instructed people to meet periodically to conduct five-day rituals of praying, dancing, and chanting. Beginning among the northern Paiute, the movement spread quickly to other tribes.

White settlers and government agents became concerned that the movement would turn violent, so the federal government stepped in to suppress it. The great chief Sitting Bull was one of the first victims of the government's actions. Suppression efforts ended tragically with the massacre by Seventh Cavalry troops of more than 200 Hunkpapa (Teton Lakota) men, women, and children at Wounded Knee, South Dakota, on December 29, 1890.

GITCHE MANITOU (Gichi-manitou, Gitchi Manido) *Algonquian, Anishinabe* The Great Spirit, CREATOR of all.

GLUSKAP (Glooscap, Glooskap, Gluskabe, Kloskurbeh, Klouscap, Kluskap) *Abenaki, Maliseet, Micmac, Passamaquoddy, Penobscot* Among Algonquian-speaking tribes of the Northeast, Gluskap was First Man, a CULTURE HERO, prophet, protector, and TRICKSTER.

Among Gluskap's exploits was the slaying of a host of giants, evil magicians, wicked spirits, CANNIBALS, and witches. He is also credited with teaching a variety of skills to humans: weaving, beadwork, tanning hides, fishing, and hunting. In some tales, a stone canoe carried Gluskap around as he gave names to things, including STARS and CONSTELLATIONS. Gluskap was responsible for the distribution of such essentials of life as food, game animals, fish, and TOBACCO. He also protected EAGLES, which regulated day and night.

Gluskap controlled the seasons. In a myth about the origin of SEASONS, Gluskap traveled to the far north, the home of Winter. By telling stories, Winter put Gluskap to sleep for six months. When Gluskap woke, he journeyed south until he reached the warm lands where Summer was queen. Gluskap captured Summer and carried her north to Winter's home. As Winter again began to weave his story spell, he was overcome by the heat of Summer.

The Penobscot name for Gluskap is Kloskurbeh, "The All-Maker" or "Great Uncle." In the Penobscot CREATION ACCOUNT, Kloskurbeh was put on Earth by the Creator to prepare the land and animals for the coming of humans. At first there were no people on Earth, but one day a young man appeared to Kloskurbeh, calling him Uncle. The youth had been born from the foam of ocean waves, the wind, and the Sun's warmth. He became Kloskurbeh's helper, and together they created many things. One day a young woman appeared who had been born from dew on a leaf and the warmth of the Sun. She and the young man, Great Nephew, married, and she bore him children, becoming FIRST MOTHER. Kloskurbeh taught their children all they needed to know in order to live. Then he went away to the north to stay until he was needed once more. In a slightly different story of the origin of the Penobscot, when the Earth was ready for people, Kloskurbeh shot an arrow into an ASH and split the tree open. The Penobscot people emerged from the tree. To guide the people, First Mother and First Father (Great Nephew) were then created. (See also HUMANS, ORIGIN OF.)

Like some other culture heroes, Gluskap had an evil twin, MALSUMSIS, who killed their mother during childbirth. According to one legend, Gluskap fashioned the Sun and Moon, animals, fish, and humans from their mother's body. Malsumsis created mountains, valleys, serpents, and other things that would inconvenience humans. After Malsumsis made several unsuccessful attempts to slay him, Gluskap sorrowfully killed his brother.

One tradition holds that when Gluskap left humanity, he sang as he paddled off in a canoe. Up to that time, all animals had spoken the same language. After Gluskap left, the different animals could no longer understand one another.

GOOSE A large, long-necked water bird featured in numerous Native American tales. In the Iroquois CREATION ACCOUNT, a flock of geese flew up and caught SKY WOMAN as she fell from the sky world. They carried her safely down to the newly created land. Geese were unsuccessful earth divers in one version of the Arapaho creation account. In a Cherokee myth, geese stole the only TOBACCO plant the people had, causing great suffering.

GREAT BEAR The CONSTELLATION Ursa Major, of which the star pattern known as the BIG DIPPER is a part.

GREAT BUFFALO See BUFFALO.

GREAT GAMBLER See GAMBLING GOD.

GREAT MYSTERY See WAKAN TANKA.

GREAT SPIRIT (Gichi-manitou, Gitchi Manido, Gitche Manitou) *Algonquian, Anishinabe* The CREATOR and highest god.

H

HAASHCH'ÉÉLTI'Í See TALKING GOD.

HACTCIN *Jicarilla Apache* Supernatural beings that personify the power of natural forces and objects. In the APACHE EMERGENCE AND MIGRATION account, nothing existed until the *hactcin* created the Earth—both the above world and the UNDERWORLD—and the SKY. BLACK HACTCIN created ANIMALS, BIRDS, fish, and the first humans. According to Jicarilla Apache tradition, once people all looked alike. The *hactcin* created people's differences in appearance, character, and intelligence. One day the sky appeared to catch fire, and the *hactcin* left the Earth to put out the blaze. They never returned.

See also HUMANS, ORIGIN OF; WHITE HACTCIN.

HADENTHENI AND HANIGONGENDATHA *Seneca* WARRIOR TWINS and CULTURE HEROES who were shunned by their people because they did not know who their parents were. In accordance with the theme of warrior twins, Hadentheni and Hanigongendatha undertook an initiatory journey to find their father and become fully a part of their people.

At the beginning of their quest, the twins climbed a hemlock tree from which a trail led to the SKY. Following the trail, they came to the lodge of Kaahkwa, the SUN, who was their father but did not reveal himself as such. Instead, after a brief stay, he sent them on to the next lodge, the home of an elderly woman who was the MOON. She warned the twins of dangers ahead of them, gave them instructions, and sent them on. Each of the twins' stops prepared them for the next stage in their quest. At the next lodge, they met a man who called himself their uncle. The uncle said that in order to finish their quest and complete their knowledge, they had to

journey to the land of the dead. Before they could do this, though, they had to first be purified and transformed. The uncle then disassembled each twin in turn. He separated their bones from their flesh, purified the bones, and reassembled the twins by blowing on their bones.

After their purification and transformation, the twins traveled on to the longhouse of Hawenniyo, the home of the dead. There they were welcomed, instructed in lore, and watched a performance of the Green Corn DANCE. The twins were then sent back to their village to teach their people all that they had learned. When they arrived home, Hadentheni (the Speaker) sang the songs he had learned and taught the dances to the people. Hanigongendatha (the Interpreter) explained the meaning of the songs and dances. Their people then accepted them fully.

HAILWAY *Navajo (Dineh)* A ceremonial curing complex, or group of ceremonies (called chants, sings, or ways) conducted to heal illness and restore harmony (*hózhó*) in the universe (see NAVAJO [DINEH] CEREMONIALS). Hailway is included in the HOLYWAY classification of ceremonials, which are used to restore health by attracting good.

The related traditional account follows the adventures of Rainboy, who had a weakness for GAMBLING. The shy Rainboy spent the night with the wife of White Thunder, not knowing she was someone's wife. When White Thunder discovered this, he shattered Rainboy with a lightning bolt (or a hailstorm in some versions). The WINDS (see NILCH'I) and other *DIYIN DINEH* (Holy People) restored Rainboy to life. Rainboy had to be restored again when he lost a contest to FROG, who disabled him with hail. Frog won many of Rainboy's body parts, which the Thunders gained back with offerings. In the end,

Rainboy rode lightning, rain, sunbeams, and rainbows to the homes of the *diyin dineh*, who taught him the Hailway rituals. When he returned to his family, he introduced Hailway to the Navajo (Dineh).

HAPPINESS GIRL (Bikeh hózhó) *Navajo (Dineh)* The personification of speech and, in a version of the Navajo (Dineh) CREATION ACCOUNT, the mother of CHANGING WOMAN.

HARE Although related to RABBITS, hares differ from them in several ways. The ears and hind legs of rabbits are much shorter than those of hares. At birth, rabbits are hairless and blind, while hares are furred and their eyes are open.

In a Netsilik Inuit tale about the origin of LIGHT, Hare—whose words had magical powers—won a verbal duel with FOX, who preferred darkness. Hare was given daylight, but in order to please both animals, night always followed. Great Hare (MICHABO) was the principal deity, CREATOR, and CULTURE HERO of Algonquian-speaking tribes. Hare—the grandson of Grandmother Earth—is the hero of a cycle of stories in Ho Chunk mythology in which he performs many marvelous deeds. In a Crow tale, Jackrabbit (which is actually a hare, not a rabbit) was one of OLD MAN COYOTE's helpers in the theft of summer (see also SEASONS, ORIGIN OF).

HARNEY PEAK The highest peak in the BLACK HILLS of South Dakota, 7,242 feet high. Lakota legend says that Harney Peak was the nesting place of THUNDERBIRD. In a vision he had at the age of nine, the famous Lakota MEDICINE man Black Elk (1863–1950) was taken to the peak by spirit guides, and the mountain was revealed to him as the center of the universe for his people.

HAWK These birds of prey vary in size, but all are excellent flyers and have powerful talons for capturing prey. In Cherokee tales, the constant battle between the SKY spirits and the evil forces under the Earth were symbolized by a conflict between Great Hawk (TLANUWA) and Great Serpent (UKTENA). The Tlanuwa often preyed on children, whom they carried to their nests to feed their young. In one tale, a woman rescued her grandchild from a Tlanuwa nest and threw the young hawks into the river, where Uktena began to eat them. When the hawks returned and saw what was happening, they attacked Uktena, dragged it from the water, and slashed it to pieces. Where the pieces landed, they turned into the unusual rock formations that can be seen along the Tennessee River.

HEYOKA *Lakota* Contraries, or backward-acting people, who became *heyoka* after they had dreams of THUNDERBIRD. (See also CLOWNS, SACRED.)

HIAWATHA (Hayenwatha, Heyanwatha, Aiontwatha) (mid-1500s) *Iroquois* A lawgiver, SHAMAN, statesman, and unifier who lived around 1570. The disciple of DEGANAWIDAH, the Peacemaker, Hiawatha is credited with helping to establish the Iroquois Confederacy by uniting the Mohawk, Oneida, Onondaga, Seneca, and Cayuga into the Five Nations. According to some sources, Hiawatha was an Onondaga; others say he was a Mohawk who sought refuge among the Onondaga when his own tribe rejected his teachings. According to legend, he had lived with the Great Spirit and had come down to Earth to help the tribes. In one version of the legend, Ta-ren-ya-wa-gon, (Sky Upholder, Upholder of Heavens) decided to live among people as a human being and took the name of Hiawatha.

When Deganawidah first set out on his mission to bring peace to the warring tribes, he met Hiawatha, a clan leader whose daughters had been killed in the fighting. Deganawidah consoled Hiawatha and told him about his dream of a great Tree of Peace under which the tribes would meet to resolve their differences. Hiawatha joined the Peacemaker in his mission and traveled with him throughout the Iroquois lands, forging alliances. With Deganawidah's vision and Hiawatha's powers of speech, the two succeeded in uniting the tribes and restoring peace.

According to legend, the tribal elders begged Hiawatha to become the head of the confederacy. He responded that he could not, because he had to leave them. He instructed the elders to choose the wisest women in the tribes to be the clan mothers and peacemakers. Then Hiawatha entered his white birchbark canoe, which rose into the sky and disappeared among the clouds.

HIHANKARA See OWL MAKER.

HISAGITA-IMISI *Creek* The CREATOR, known as "Preserver of Breath" and "the One Sitting Above."

HISAGITA MISA See BREATH MAKER.

HOLY PEOPLE *Navajo (Dineh)* The common English translation of *DIYIN DINEH.*

HOLYWAY *Navajo (Dineh)* One of the three classifications into which ritual curing ceremonials are grouped. (The others are EVILWAY and LIFEWAY.) Holyway ceremonials are performed to restore health to the "one sung over" by attracting good. These ceremonials are directed by the *DIYIN DINEH* (Holy People) and are conducted to cure illnesses caused by the anger of the *diyin dineh* and other spirits. Ceremonials in this classification that are still held include BEAUTYWAY, BIG STARWAY, CHIRICAHUA WINDWAY, Hand-Trembling Way, MOUNTAINWAY, NAVAJO WINDWAY, NIGHTWAY, and SHOOTINGWAY. Others, such as BEADWAY, EAGLEWAY, and HAILWAY, are no longer held or are held very rarely.

See also NAVAJO (DINEH) CEREMONIALS.

HOLY WIND See NILCH'I.

HOPI EMERGENCE AND MIGRATION *Hopi* According to Hopi tradition, TAIOWA, the CREATOR, was alone in the endless void. He conceived a plan to bring life to the void and created SÓTUKNANG, whom he called Nephew, to carry out the plan. Following Taiowa's instructions, Sótuknang created the universe, the Earth, land, and water. Then he made his own helper, Kókyangwúti (SPIDER WOMAN). In turn, Spider Woman created the twins PYUYKONHOYA AND PALUNHOYA to help keep the world in order.

Petroglyphs in Mesa Verde, Colorado, include Hopi clan symbols and a drawing representing the migrations of the ancient Hopi clans. *(© George H. H. Huey)*

The Plains warriors represented in this pictograph did not acquire horses until the late 16th century. *(© Christie's Images/CORBIS)*

The First World was Tokpela (Endless Space). Spider Woman created all the living things—TREES, PLANTS, ANIMALS, and BIRDS. From yellow, red, white, and black soil, mixed with her saliva, she created human beings in the image of Sótuknang. At first all the people and animals lived together in peace and happiness. Soon, however, some became fierce and warlike. Sótuknang sent the few people who still lived by the laws of the Creator to safety with the Ant People. The Creator instructed them to observe and follow the ways of the Ant People, who obeyed the plan of Creation. Then he destroyed the First World with fire.

In the Second World, called Tokpa (Dark Midnight), the same thing happened. Again, Sótuknang sent a few chosen people to safety with the Ant People and then destroyed the world by causing it to spin out of control.

The Third World Sótuknang created was Kuskurza (a word that no one can translate). Once more greed, jealousy, and evil broke the harmony of the world. It became so corrupt that Sótuknang had to destroy it yet again, this time with a FLOOD. Spider Woman saved the chosen people by sealing them in hollow reeds that floated on the surface of the water.

For a long time the people floated in boats they made from the hollow reeds. At last land emerged, and the people were on the Fourth World, Túwaqachi (World Complete), the present world. MASAU'U, the deity of FIRE and death, greeted them and gave them permission to live on this world. He explained that first they must find a good place in which to settle. All this was written symbolically on FOUR sacred tablets that Masau'u gave the people.

Each clan was to make four directional migrations,

going to the farthest end of the land in each direction until they came to the place where the land met the ocean, then returning to Túwanasavi (Center of the Universe). All their routes formed a great SWASTIKA. The clans that went north reached the Arctic Circle. The clans that went south reached the tip of South America. Those that went east and west also reached the oceans. During the migrations, some groups forgot their purpose and settled without returning to Túwanasavi. Finally, after centuries of wandering, the people returned and settled on the Three Mesas in what is now Hopi country. PETROGLYPHS and PICTOGRAPHS found throughout the Americas record the migrations of the Hopi clans.

HORNED WATER SERPENT   *Acoma Pueblo*

The spirit of RAIN and fertility who controlled earthquakes and FLOODS. One night Horned Water Serpent abruptly left the people and would not return, regardless of the efforts of the rain priests. Unable to survive the drought that resulted, the people followed his trail until they reached a river, where they established a new home. This account is one explanation for the disappearance of the ANASAZI.

Horned serpents appear widely in Native American folklore. They are often portrayed as battling THUNDERBIRD or other thunder beings (see also UKTENA; UNCEGILA).

HORSE

Although the modern horse evolved in North America about 1 million years ago and spread over land bridges into South America, Asia, Europe, and Africa, by 8,000 years ago it had become extinct in the Americas. Horses were not reintroduced into the Americas until the Spanish conquistadores arrived in the 16th century, when Hernán Cortés landed in Mexico in 1519 with 16 horses. The Spanish explorer Francisco Vásquez de Coronado brought horses onto the Plains in 1541, but more than 100 years passed before Native Americans acquired them in any numbers. Because there was no word for *horse* and the Plains tribes had previously used DOGS as beasts of burden, the horse was referred to variously as Elk Dog, Spirit Dog, Mystery Dog, Medicine Dog, Sacred Dog, and Moose Dog. The horse changed the way of life of the Plains Indians, who became famed for their horsemanship. It enabled hunters to pursue buffalo farther

and faster than ever before, and its strength as a beast of burden allowed nomadic people to travel greater distances and carry more goods with them.

A Blackfeet legend tells how a poor, orphaned boy named Long Arrow brought the horse to the people. Long Arrow was adopted by a chief who told him about powerful spirit people who lived at the bottom of a lake and had mystery animals called Elk Dogs to do their work for them. Every fourth generation a young warrior went to find the spirit people and bring back an Elk Dog for the tribe, but none had ever returned. Long Arrow undertook the quest. A spirit boy befriended Long Arrow and told him the secret of obtaining a gift of Elk Dogs from the spirit chief. Long Arrow successfully returned to his tribe with a herd of horses.

HUMANS, ORIGIN OF

The creation of human beings is the subject of many accounts. In some Native American traditions, the people were already in existence (sometimes in spirit form) and emerged into the world from an underground place. Sometimes people were created in this UNDERWORLD, as in the accounts of the ACOMA EMERGENCE AND MIGRATION, the APACHE EMERGENCE AND MIGRATION, the HOPI EMERGENCE AND MIGRATION, the NAVAJO (DINEH) EMERGENCE, and the ZUNI EMERGENCE AND MIGRATION. The manner of emergence varies. In the Choctaw and Creek accounts, humans emerged from a hole in the ground. Pale and damp, they lay in the sun until their skin darkened. Then they migrated in separate groups—the Cherokee to the north, the Creek and Chickasaw to the east and south. The Choctaw remained in the emergence place. This story explains the origin of the different tribes. (In postcontact times, the Cherokee, Choctaw, Chickasaw, Creek, and Seminole were called the Five Civilized Tribes. They believed themselves to be descended from the MOUND BUILDERS.) In a Northwest Coast CREATION ACCOUNT, the first people emerged from a seashell RAVEN found on the seashore, rather than an underground place. In the Kiowa account, the people came into the world one by one, squirming through a hollow log. Unfortunately, a pregnant woman became stuck in the log, and after that no one else could enter the world. This explains why there were so few Kiowa. According to a Penobscot account, the CULTURE HERO GLUSKAP shot an arrow into an ASH. The tree split open, and from it the Penobscot emerged, singing and dancing.

In other traditions, deities, holy beings, and other powerful beings were the ancestors of humans. In the Skidi Pawnee account, Standing Rain, the daughter of EVENING STAR (the planet Venus) and MORNING STAR (the planet Mars), was the mother of the human race. In an Inuit legend, the children of a woman who had married a DOG became the ancestors of humanity (see ADLET).

Humans were created from a variety of substances. Frequently they were made of mud or clay, as in the accounts of the Yavapai-Apache (see AMCHITAPUKA), Creek (see ESAUGETUH EMISSEE), Yuma (see KOKOMAHT AND BAKOTAHL), and Crow (see OLD MAN COYOTE). In a Northwest Coast tale, First Man brought forth a woman from TOBACCO smoke (see XOWALACI). In the Modoc origin account, KUMUSH created the Klamath, Modoc, Shasta, and other tribes from bones he brought from the home of the spirits. In the Jicarilla Apache story, BLACK HACTCIN made the first man by drawing an outline of his body on the ground, sprinkling it with POLLEN, and using precious stones for the man's body parts. According to Navajo (Dineh) tradition, CHANGING WOMAN created the first FOUR Navajo (Dineh) clans using skin from her own body. EARTHMAKER, the Akimel O'odham Creator, made humans from his own sweat. The Maidu Creator, KODOYANPE, made humans from carved wooden images. In the Comanche creation account, Great Spirit created the Comanche people from swirls of dust gathered from the four directions (see DIRECTIONS, CARDINAL), giving them the strength of powerful storms.

On occasion, the Creator was unhappy with his creation and destroyed the people he had made. A hero named Condor and his sister survived the FLOOD sent by ABOVE-OLD-MAN, the Wiyot Creator, to destroy his first creations; Condor and his sister became the ancestors of humans. NESHANU, the Arapaho Creator, sent a flood to destroy humans who had become wicked, unwise, or disrespectful; he saved those he liked by turning them into grains of CORN and planting them. Earthmaker, the Akimel O'odham Creator, also sent a flood to destroy the people, who had become quarrelsome and selfish. A SHAMAN named Suha and his wife survived the flood by sealing themselves inside a hollow ball of SPRUCE gum. They became the ancestors of the Akimel O'odham people. TABALDAK, the Abenaki Creator, made the first people from stone but decided that he did not like them, so he destroyed the stone people and made new ones from wood.

While individual stories and common themes about the origins of humanity differ, there is a clear and universal concern about how humans came to be and the foundations of the world in which humans live. Origin myths represent humanity's attempt to find our place in the universe—to understand the mystery of life and achieve a sense of identity.

HUMMINGBIRD The smallest of all birds, the hummingbird is known for its amazing flying ability. It is the only bird that can fly backward, hover in place, and fly vertically up and down.

In a Cherokee myth about the loss of the TOBACCO plant, many different animals tried unsuccessfully to recover the plant from the geese that had stolen it. At last, Hummingbird used his small size and swift speed to snatch off the top of the plant with its seeds and, unseen by the geese, return it to the Cherokee. In a Kawaiisu legend, Hummingbird was a curing SHAMAN that COYOTE called to heal his daughter. Coyote paid Hummingbird with tools that became the bird's long beak.

I

IATIKU (Iyatiku, Uretsete, Uretsiti) *Keres* Female CREATOR figure; the Mother of the Pueblo people and of the WARRIOR TWINS named MASEWA AND UYUYEWA. Iatiku was believed to watch over humans to assure their well-being. After UTSITI, the Creator, made the Earth from a clot of his own blood, he planted Iatiku and her sisters in the soil. There they lived in SHIPAP, the dark pre-emergence place. Iatiku sent her sons out of Shipap to find their father, the SUN, and bring LIGHT to the world.

In the ACOMA EMERGENCE AND MIGRATION account of the origin of the Keres-speaking people, Masewa and Uyuyewa led the people out of Shipap, followed by Iatiku and all her people. After the emergence, SPIDER WOMAN gave Iatiku and her sisters a basket of seeds and instructed them in what to do. As Iatiku and her sisters sang a creation song, they threw out seeds that became the things they sang about. From the soil left in the bottom of the basket, Iatiku made the KACHINAS. Later, she made the Koshare (see CLOWNS, SACRED) from bits of her own skin rolled into a ball.

ICTINIKE (Iktinike) *Iowa, Omaha* A CULTURE HERO and son of the SUN. Ictinike offended his father and was ejected from the heavens. He had the power to transform himself into any creature and was also a deceitful TRICKSTER, regarded as the "Father of Lies." Often, in the course of trying to trick other creatures, Ictinike became the victim of his own plots. The Omaha saw him as a war god and credited him with giving them their war customs.

IKTOMI (Iktome, Unktomi) *Assiniboine, Lakota* A CREATOR figure and TRICKSTER; the Lakota SPIDER MAN. Iktomi is described as having the round body of a spider with long, thin legs and strong feet and hands.

In the Assiniboine CREATION ACCOUNT, Iktomi traveled around the water-covered world in a canoe. In one version, he met MUSKRAT, who had a bit of mud in his paws. Muskrat was unwilling to show the mud to Iktomi, but when Iktomi offered to let Muskrat into the canoe, Muskrat revealed what he had. Iktomi took the mud, blew on it, and formed the Earth. In another version, Iktomi sent ANIMALS diving for mud. Only Muskrat was able to reach the bottom. Although Muskrat died in the attempt, when his body surfaced, there was mud on his paws from which Iktomi created the land.

In a story about the origin of SEASONS, Iktomi, together with animal helpers, arranged the theft of summer from a man far to the east who kept this season in a bag. In a tale about the length of the seasons, Iktomi declared that winter would last for as many months as there were hairs in the wolfskin robe he was wearing. FROG protested that no animal could live through a winter that long. He suggested that seven (in some versions, six) months of winter would be long enough. Iktomi flew into a rage and killed him. (In another version, he merely stunned Frog with his club.) Dead though he was, Frog held out seven of his toes, and Iktomi gave in.

The Lakota Spider Man had shape-shifting abilities, often taking the form of an old man or becoming invisible. He could speak with all living things— including THUNDERBIRD—and even with nonliving things such as rocks. In one tale, Iktomi convinced the Lakota to live in separate places rather than close together, which left them defenseless against their enemies. Iktomi just laughed at the trouble he had caused. As a result, the Lakota began to arrange their lodges in a circle with the doors facing inward so that everyone could see if Iktomi entered a lodge.

INUA *Inuit*   Spirit helpers of SHAMANS. *Inua* took the form of animal helpers or animal-like beings. They assisted shamans in many ways: as sources of power, observers of human behavior, informers of broken TABOOS, and aides to communication with ruling spirits. *Inua* were also associated with the power of transformation, enabling humans to take on the appearance of animals and animals to appear as humans or other animals.

IOSKEHA AND TAWISCARA *Iroquois* TWIN grandsons of SKY WOMAN, the mother of humanity. Ioskeha (Iouskeha, Tsentsa), "The White One," was the good twin; he was the CREATOR and CULTURE HERO, father of mankind, and principal deity of the Iroquois. He created the lakes and rivers, freed all the ANIMALS from a hidden cave, and taught the people how to grow CORN and other crops. Tortoise taught him how to make FIRE, and he in turn taught this skill to humans. Tawiscara (Taweskara, Taweskare, Tawiskaron), "The Dark One," was the evil twin, associated with winter. Ioskeha was born in the normal manner, but Tawiscara burst forth from their mother's armpit, killing her. He frequently fought with Ioskeha, trying to undo the good his brother had done. Wounded in a battle with Ioskeha, Tawiscara shed drops of blood that became FLINT, the stone used to make weapons. In a legend of the Mohawk (one of the original five members of the Iroquois Confederacy), Tawiscara tried to build a bridge of stone so that cruel beasts that were associated with winter famine could cross over from their island and eat humans. Bluebird and Sapling played a trick that frightened Tawiscara off, and the bridge disappeared.

KACHINA (cachina, kacina, katchina, katcina, katsina) *Hopi, Keres, Tewa, Zuni* Powerful spirits of the dead that mediate between the human and spiritual worlds and possess the power to bring RAIN and affect fertility and growth. Kachinas can be male or female and come in many forms: ANIMALS, BIRDS, PLANTS, qualities, ogres, demons, and CLOWNS. The term *kachina* is Hopi but has come to be applied generally among the Pueblo people to any masked figure. (The Keres term is *shiwanna*, or CLOUD PEOPLE; the Tewa term, *okhua*; and the Zuni term, *koko*.)

In Hopi tradition, people who have lived properly become kachinas after death. Hopi kachinas were said to live in the San Francisco Mountains near Flagstaff, Arizona, where they remained for part of the year. Around the time of the winter solstice in December, the kachinas began to visit the pueblos to dance and sing for the people in order to summon the "cloud fathers" from the six directions (see DIREC-

Kachina figures made for the tourist trade, such as those shown here, do not represent authentic kachinas because of prohibitions against reproducing anything of a sacred nature. (© *Catherine Karnow/Animals Animals/Earth Sciences*)

TIONS, CARDINAL) and bring rain. In mid-July, after the summer solstice, the kachinas returned to their home. According to the Hopi, long ago, the kachinas came to the pueblos themselves. Now they come no longer, and kachina dancers wearing elaborately painted masks and costumes must impersonate them in ceremonial performances. When the kachina impersonator puts on a mask and costume, that person is believed to become the kachina that is being represented. There are several hundred different Hopi kachinas, each of which is named and has a distinctive mask and costume. Kachinas are of two types: the chief or official kachina (Mon, Mong, or Mongwi) and the ordinary kachina. The chief kachinas play principal roles in the major ceremonies and dance individually, never in groups. Ordinary kachinas dance in groups.

According to Zuni myth, AHAYUTA AND MATSILEMA, the Zuni warrior twins, acquired the power to bring rain by stealing the rain-making tools of the Saiyathlia, kachina warriors. In addition to bringing rain, Zuni kachinas are credited with the ability to increase crops and livestock, ripen CORN, and bring game. Most of the Zuni kachinas were said to live in a village under a lake, KOLHU/WALA-WA, called Kachina Village by non-Zuni. Their chief, PAUTIWA, directed all their activities. When the kachinas were called for, Pautiwa decided which kachinas would go. Kachinas who lived in other villages were not under Pautiwa's control. For example, the Kanaakwe, a group of kachinas believed to live south of Zuni Pueblo, were the enemies of the kachinas who lived in Kachina Village. According to Zuni tradition, both groups hunted in the same areas. The Kanaakwe decided to hide the DEER from the other kachinas, who then challenged the Kanaakwe to a fight. The Kanaakwe won, giving them the right to the deer. As a result, the Kanaakwe supplied deer to the Zuni people, while the other kachinas brought corn, seeds, and other gifts.

The ACOMA EMERGENCE AND MIGRATION ACCOUNT relates how the warrior twins MASEWA AND UYUYEWA prepared the people for the arrival of the kachinas after the emergence into the present world. The story describes how the people insulted the kachinas, how the people and the kachinas did battle, and how the people learned to call the kachinas by impersonating them.

KAMALAPUKWIA See WIDAPOKWI.

KANATI (The Hunter) *Cherokee* Husband of SELU and father of the THUNDER BOYS. Kanati kept the DEER and the other game animals and birds in a cave blocked by a rock. When his sons discovered Kanati's secret, they mischievously let all the game escape. As a result, food, which had been plentiful before, became scarce. The boys were also responsible for their mother's death, which led to the origin of CORN. After Selu's death, Kanati told his sons that he could no longer live with them. Kanati had wolves to hunt for him because of their hunting skills. He sent the Wolf People to kill the two boys. The boys, however, were too clever and managed to kill all but two of the wolves. They then followed Kanati as he traveled and had many adventures.

KANENHAGENAT *Seneca* White CORN, which was given to the Seneca by a beautiful woman. The woman stood on a cliff overlooking a village and sang day and night in order to draw to her a man she wanted as a husband. Because of his age, the man refused to climb the mountain, but the village council convinced him to go. When he found the woman, she told him that their love would cause a plant called *kanenhagenat* to grow and become a major food source for his people. The next morning, the woman had vanished. As she had said, a corn plant grew on the spot where they had met, and the man passed on the knowledge of corn and its cultivation to the village.

KILLER-OF-ENEMIES *Apache* A CREATOR and CULTURE HERO, son of the SUN and WHITE PAINTED WOMAN. He was conceived at the same time as the culture hero CHILD-OF-THE-WATER, son of Water and WHITE SHELL WOMAN. The Jicarilla Apache version of the legend contains themes common to myths of WARRIOR TWINS: making a journey to the Sun and traveling the world killing MONSTERS. His Navajo (Dineh) counterpart is MONSTER SLAYER.

Anasazi ruins at Pueblo Bonito in Chaco Canyon, New Mexico, include a number of kivas, stuctures used for ceremonial purposes. *(© Stephen Trimble)*

KIVA *Pueblo* A ceremonial room, usually circular (although sometimes rectangular), partially underground, and entered by a ladder through the roof. Kivas symbolize the emergence of people from a previous UNDERWORLD and provide a representation on Earth of the original homeland. (The word *kiva* means "world below.") Set into the floor of the kiva is a round, shallow hole symbolic of SIPAPU, the opening through which the people emerged. Climbing the ladder to the hole in the roof symbolizes life emerging from the Earth Mother.

KLOSKURBEH (All-Maker, Great Uncle) *Penobscot* The Penobscot name for GLUSKAP.

KODOYANPE (Earth-Initiate) *Maidu* The CREATOR. In one version of the Maidu CREATION ACCOUNT, TURTLE and Father-of-the-Secret-Society were floating in a boat on the water-covered world. Kodoyanpe climbed down from the sky on a rope of FEATHERS to join them. He sent Turtle diving to bring up soil from the bottom of the water in order to make land. He also called into being Turtle's sister and brother, the SUN and the MOON. Kodoyanpe originally planned an easy, carefree life for people. COYOTE, however, opposed this plan. Before he could be stopped, Coyote introduced work, suffering, and death. Coyote tried to make humans, but he was unable to bring them to life.

In another account, Kodoyanpe and Coyote discovered the water-covered world together and worked to make it livable for humans. They tried to create people from small wooden images, but these did not come to life. Kodoyanpe suspected that Coyote had caused the problem. He found out that he was correct and decided to destroy Coyote. After a long battle, the crafty Coyote managed to defeat Kodoyanpe. However, Kodoyanpe had buried many of the wooden images he and Coyote had created. These now came to life and were the first people.

KOKOMAHT AND BAKOTAHL *Yuma* TWIN brothers born at the bottom of the PRIMORDIAL WATERS. Kokomaht, the good twin, rose to the top of the waters with his eyes closed and proclaimed himself the All-Father, or CREATOR. Bakotahl called to him from under the water and asked whether Kokomaht had kept his eyes open or closed as he rose. Kokomaht, knowing that Bakotahl was evil, lied and said that he had opened his eyes. Bakotahl kept his eyes open as he rose and was blinded by the salt water. Kokomaht then created the cardinal DIRECTIONS and the land. When Kokomaht began to make people out of clay, Bakotahl tried to copy his brother. However, all of Bakotahl's creations had webbed feet, and they became the web-footed birds. Bakotahl became so angry with Kokomaht that he returned to the depths of the water and sent up a whirlwind, the bringer of evil. Kokomaht stomped the whirlwind out, except for a small bit that slipped from under his foot. This contained all the illnesses that afflict people to this day. Kokomaht taught his people how to live, and he also taught them how to die by dying himself. Bakotahl continued to live under the ground. When the ground trembled and volcanoes erupted, people knew that Bakotahl was stirring.

See also HUMANS, ORIGIN OF.

KOKOPELLI (Kókopilau) *Southwest* The humpbacked flute player depicted in PETROGLYPHS, or rock carvings, found throughout the Southwest. Kokopelli symbolized fertility, happiness, and joy. His humpback was actually a bundle in which he carried sacred objects, seeds, and songs. There are many stories about Kokopelli. As a fertility symbol and traveling TRICKSTER, Kokopelli would visit villages, playing his flute, and people would sing and dance all night. When he left in the morning, the crops were plentiful and many women were pregnant. In other legends, Kokopelli was responsible for the end of winter and the coming of spring. When he played his flute, the snow melted, grass grew, and birds began to sing.

Kokopelli is also a part of the HOPI EMERGENCE AND MIGRATION account. Following their emergence into the present world, the Hopi were met by an EAGLE who shot an arrow into two *máhus*, insects that carried the power of heat. The *máhus* began to play melodies on their flutes, and their bodies were healed. The two *máhus* accompanied the Hopi on their migration. The locust *máhu* was called Kókopilau (*kóko* meaning "wood" and *pilau* meaning "hump") because he looked like wood. Carrying a bag of seeds, Kókopilau scattered the seeds over the barren land as he went, playing his flute over the seeds to warm them and make them grow.

KOLHU/WALA-WA (Kohluwala:wa, Kothluwala) *Zuni* A sacred site in northeastern Arizona that is the origin place of the Zuni people and the home of their dead. According to tradition, it is the site of the KACHINA village ruled by the kachina chief PAUTIWA, who received the spirits of the dead.

KOSHARE *Keres* Clowns with black and white stripes. See CLOWNS, SACRED.

These petroglyphs, near Galisteo, New Mexico, include a likeness of Kokopelli, the flute player. (© 1995 N. Carter/ North Wind)

KOTCIMANYAKO See BLUE FEATHER.

KOYEMSHI *Hopi, Zuni* Mudhead clowns. See CLOWNS, SACRED.

KUMUSH (Old Man) *Modoc* The CREATOR of the California tribes. According to the traditional account, Kumush and his daughter went to visit the UNDERWORLD home of the spirits, which was reached by descending a steep road. During the night, the spirits danced and sang on a great plain, but when morning came they returned to their underground home and became dry bones. After six days in the underworld, Kumush decided to return to the upper world and to take some of the spirits with him to create humans, because he was lonesome. He filled a basket with bones that he thought would be good for creating the various tribes of people. On the way up the steep road, Kumush slipped and stumbled twice, spilling the bones. When he refilled the basket for the third time, he told the spirits that they would be happier in his land, where the Sun shone. This time, he was able to reach the upper world. He threw out the bones, naming the different tribes as he did so. Last of all, he threw the bones that became the Modoc. Kumush told the Modoc that they were his chosen people and would be the bravest of all. Then he named all of the ANIMALS, PLANTS, and other foods that people could eat, and these appeared. When he had finished his work and instructed the people in the way to live, Kumush and his daughter traveled along the Sun's road until they reached the middle of the SKY. There they made their home.

L

LEGEND PEOPLE *Paiute* Evil creatures whose appearance combined characteristics of humans, birds, animals, and reptiles. According to a Paiute legend, before there were humans, BRYCE CANYON was inhabited by the Legend People. Because they were so bad, COYOTE turned them into the rock structures that can be seen in the canyon to this day.

LIFEWAY (Iináájí) *Navajo (Dineh)* One of the three classifications into which ritual curing ceremonials are grouped. (The others are EVILWAY and HOLYWAY.) Lifeway ceremonials are held to heal cases of bodily injury or illnesses related to the natural life process. FLINTWAY is included in this classification.
See also NAVAJO (DINEH) EMERGENCE.

LIGHT Associated with FIRE and the SUN, light also figures in Native American myths that tell where it came from and how people acquired it. The creation of light in the form of the Sun and MOON is often credited to a CREATOR figure, such as AWONA-WILONA (Zuni), EARTHMAKER (Ho Chunk), KODO-YANPE (Maidu), MICHABO (Algonquian), or TIRAWAHAT (Skidi Pawnee). CULTURE HEROES—human, ANIMAL, and BIRD—were also credited with bringing light to the dark world. In an Aleut legend, Great Raven created light by throwing pieces of mica into the sky. In many tales, light was acquired by theft; for example, the Tanaina figure CHULYEN (Crow) and the Northwest Coast figure RAVEN stole light for the benefit of their people.

Light was also sometimes won in a contest. In one version of the APACHE EMERGENCE AND MIGRATION account, people and the daytime animals defeated the nighttime animals, who had wanted the world to remain in darkness. In a Netsilik Inuit tale, HARE won a verbal duel with FOX, who preferred darkness. Hare was given daylight, but night always followed so that both animals would be pleased.

LITTLE PEOPLE Tiny people who, in various cultures, were seen as powerful, kindly TRICKSTERS or as dangerous beings. In some traditions, only children or MEDICINE PEOPLE could see them. The Crow viewed Little People (*awakkule*) as helpers who were also known to play jokes on people. The Little People in Seneca tales were responsible for the healthy growth of medicinal plants. Inuit and Yup'ik legends describe tiny people who wore little parkas and trousers made of sealskin or caribou. They lived in underground houses along the seashore. In some Native American tales, the Little People stole human children, and the presence of Little People signaled danger.

All tribes of the Southeast have stories about Little People, who were mischievous and enjoyed pranks but could be deadly when angered. To see a little person was considered a sign of impending death. Numerous stories from the Southeast tell about children who were stolen by the Little People. In some tales, the Little People tested the stolen children and, if they proved worthy, trained them to become medicine people. According to the Seminole, the Little People took care of lost children, feeding them and teaching them how to use herbal remedies. They then returned the children to their parents. Various Cherokee myths describe people who became lost in the wilderness and were found by the Little People, who brought them to their village. After a number of magical experiences, the lost people were led within sight of home by the Little People and warned not to speak about where they had been. People who ignored the warning died soon afterward.

The Lakota Little People, Tree Dwellers (Canotina or Canotili), caused people to become lost in the woods. To see one meant that a close relative was doomed to die.

The Iroquois had a special friendship with the Little People. In Iroquois myth, the Little People were powerful beings who lived deep within the forest and helped control the forces of nature. Long ago, an Iroquois hunter came across two tiny men in the forest. When he gave them a squirrel he had shot, they invited him to dinner in their village. During the feast that followed, the young man watched the Little People perform the sacred Dark Dance and learned its chants and movements, which he later taught to his own people. The Little People told him that in exchange for gifts of TOBACCO, they would join the Iroquois whenever they performed the DANCE. Members of the Little People Society perform the Dark Dance and other rites to maintain the goodwill of the Little People.

LONE MAN *Arikara, Hidatsa, Mandan* A CREATOR figure who traveled with First Creator, making the landforms along the Missouri River. First Creator made the mountains, hills, valleys, and the animals that lived in those places. Lone Man made the lowlands, ponds, streams, and the animals that lived in those places. First Creator and Lone Man argued about whose creations were more useful. According to First Creator, the land Lone Man made was too flat, and he had not provided enough trees. The two came to an agreement that humans should first use the game animals that First Creator had made—the DEER, ELK, and BUFFALO—and when these were not sufficient to feed them, they should use the animals that Lone Man had created, such as BEAVERS and OTTERS.

LONG LIFE BOY (Sa'ah naghai) *Navajo (Dineh)* The personification of thought and, in one version of the Navajo (Dineh) CREATION ACCOUNT, the father of CHANGING WOMAN.

LOON The loon's distinctive black, white, and gray plumage, eerie call, and ability to stay submerged when diving made it a frequent character in Native American tales. Because of its swimming skill, Loon often figured in earth-diver CREATION ACCOUNTS; in both the Anishinabe (see MANABOZHO) and Cree (see WEE-SA-KAY-JAC) accounts, Loon was unsuccessful. The Slavey of northwestern Canada believed that loon and OTTER spirits helped human spirits pass through the Earth to continue their lives in another place.

MAGPIE Related to jays and crows, magpies are highly social and noisy birds. With their long tail and bold pattern of black and white feathers, they are very noticeable.

According to a Cheyenne legend, Magpie helped humans win a contest that determined whether the BUFFALO would eat people or people would eat buffalo. Once, people and animals lived in peace and none of them ate meat. The buffalo came to think that they were the most powerful beings in the world and should be given the right to kill and eat both other animals and people. They challenged the humans to a race. To make the race fairer—since four-legged creatures have an advantage over two-legged humans—it was agreed that the humans could choose birds to race for them. They chose a HUMMINGBIRD, a meadowlark, a HAWK, and a magpie. One by one, the birds dropped out from exhaustion, until only Magpie was left to compete with Running Slim Buffalo Woman, the buffalo's fastest runner. At the last moment, Magpie surged ahead and won the race. Out of gratitude, from that time on, the Cheyenne never hunted or ate magpies.

MAHEO (The Above Spirit) *Cheyenne* The CREATOR of the world and everything in it. In the Cheyenne CREATION ACCOUNT, Maheo sent his FOUR servants to find the Earth. They failed four times, but on their fifth attempt they found a shapeless mass. When they brought the mass back to Maheo, it took the shape of the world with a strange being on it. Maheo told his servants that this being was man, whom he had made to live on the Earth. While Maheo was on Earth with his children—the humans he had created—he taught them how to make stone knives, arrowheads, bone tools and FIRE. Maheo told his children that all the creatures of Earth were put there for them to use, and he showed them how to grow and care for CORN. When he had taught humans how to live, he left and returned to the SKY, where he said he would watch over them.

See also HUMANS, ORIGIN OF.

MAHTIGWESS *Algonquian* RABBIT, a TRICKSTER.

MAIZE See CORN.

MALSUMSIS (Malsum, Wolf) *Algonquian* The evil TWIN brother of GLUSKAP. Before they were born, Gluskap and Malsumsis discussed how they would enter the world. Gluskap said that he would be born as other people were, but Malsumsis announced that he was too great to be born in an ordinary manner—he would burst through their mother's side. That is just what he did, killing his mother in the process.

Both brothers had charmed lives and could be killed only by a secret weapon. They agreed to exchange secrets, but Gluskap did not trust his brother. To test him, Gluskap lied and told him that he could be killed by a blow from an owl's FEATHER. In turn, Malsumsis confided that only a blow from a fern root could kill him. One night, Malsumsis obtained an owl feather and struck Gluskap with it as he slept. Gluskap awoke, admitted that he had lied, and told Malsumsis that it was actually a pine root that could end his life. Soon, Malsumsis again tried to kill his brother, striking him with a pine root as he slept. Unharmed, Gluskap drove Malsumsis off. When Gluskap mused to himself that nothing but a flowering rush could kill him, BEAVER overheard and went to Malsumsis with this news. However, Malsumsis refused to reward Beaver as promised, so Beaver returned to Gluskap and confessed his betrayal.

Saddened and angry, Gluskap searched for Malsumsis and, when he found his brother, killed him by striking him with a fern root.

MANABOZHO (Menabozho, Nanabozho, Waynaboozhoo, Winabojo, Winebozho) *Algonquian, Anishinabe, Ojibway* A powerful and benevolent CULTURE HERO who figures in a multitude of legends, sometimes appearing as a deceitful TRICKSTER. Manabozho had many names and was also identified with the heroes HIAWATHA and GLUSKAP. The origins of Manabozho are as varied as the names by which he was known. In some legends, GITCHE MANITOU, the Great Spirit, created him. In others, he was the son of Mother Earth and Father SUN. A legend of the Menominee (an Algonquian-speaking tribe) gives his father as the North WIND.

In some versions of the Menominee legend, Manabozho was one of triplets. His brothers were Little Wolf and Flint Stone. Flint Stone's birth caused the death of his mother. In a rage, the triplets' grandmother threw Flint Stone away, and his body gave the gift of FIRE to humans (see also FLINT). Little Wolf was later killed, and Manabozho had many adventures trying to avenge his brother's death.

In an Ojibway account, Manabozho had a brother named Wabosso, who disappeared. In yet another legend, Manabozho had three brothers: CHIBIABOS, WABOSE, and CHOKANIPOK (The Man of Flint). Manabozho fought with his brother Chokanipok often and finally defeated him.

In an Anishinabe legend, Manabozho caused a FLOOD that covered the world when he killed the chief of the water MANITOUS, or spirits. To save himself, Manabozho climbed to the top of a PINE where the water could not reach him. To create land to stand on, he asked first LOON, then OTTER, and finally MUSKRAT to dive under the water for soil. All three died in the attempt, but when Muskrat's body floated to the surface, there was sand in his paws. Manabozho used the sand to make a small island that grew larger and larger until the waters were forced to recede from it.

Manabozho traveled around teaching humans such skills as how to make axes, snares, and traps. He taught women how to weave mats and baskets. As many culture heroes do, he slew MONSTERS in order to make the world safe for humans. Manabozho placed FOUR spirits in the cardinal DIRECTIONS. The spirit of the north sent snow and ice to enable winter hunting. The spirit of the south sent warm wind and CORN, melons, and TOBACCO. The spirit of the west sent rain, and the spirit of the east sent the light. (See also SEASONS, ORIGIN OF.)

Some legends say that Manabozho lives on an ice island in the ocean. If he were to leave his home, the world would end, because Manabozho would no longer guide the Sun on its path.

MANITOU (*Manido*) *Algonquian* A supernatural force that pervades the natural world. *Manitous* are spirits that inhabit all living things, as well as natural forces such as WIND and thunder and physical objects such as rocks.

MASAU'U (Masao, Masauwu, Másaw) *Hopi* The deity of FIRE and death. Masau'u ruled the UNDERWORLD and gave fire to humanity. According to the HOPI EMERGENCE AND MIGRATION account, Masau'u was appointed caretaker of the Third World but lost this post because of his lack of humility. The CREATOR, TAIOWA, made him the deity of death and the underworld instead. However, when the Third World was destroyed, Taiowa relented and appointed Masau'u to guard and protect the Fourth World. When the people emerged into the Fourth World, they were met by Masau'u, who gave them permission to live on the land and told them that they must follow their stars to the place where they would settle. He outlined how they would make their migrations, recognize their permanent homes, and make a living when they arrived there. These instructions were symbolically written on FOUR sacred tablets that Masau'u gave to the people. At the end of their migration, the people of the Bear Clan settled at Oraibi (Third Mesa) in northern Arizona, where Masau'u was living. He assigned them the land on which they were to live.

MASEWA AND UYUYEWA (Masewi and Oyoyewi) *Keres* WARRIOR TWINS, sons of the SUN and IATIKU, the Mother of the Pueblo people. In the ACOMA EMERGENCE AND MIGRATION account, Masewa and Uyuyewa led the people from SHIPAP, the pre-emergence place, into the present world. They taught the people how to welcome the KACHINAS. Masewa then led the people on their migration to find a homeland. Stories about Masewa and Uyuyewa contain elements common to tales about CULTURE HEROES and warrior twins, such as making a journey to their father, the Sun, killing MONSTERS to make the world safe for humans, and having power over the RAIN.

In an Acoma Pueblo tale, Masewa and Uyuyewa danced each night at the house of Iatiku to keep the MEDICINE bowl on her altar filled with water, which assured that rain would be plentiful. When Iatiku decided to end the dancing, the brothers departed and remained away for 10 years to prove that only they could bring rain. During their absence, the water in the medicine bowl dried up, the rains failed to come, and people began to die of starvation. When Masewa and Uyuyewa returned, they brought the rains with them and plants grew once again.

MASKS The wearing of masks is a feature of religious ceremonials among many Native American cultures. Masks that represent spiritual beings are often considered to be alive. As ceremonial aids, they are sacred objects that hold great power. Participants in ceremonials wear masks to influence spirits, invoke spirit helpers, honor ancestors, and change their identity. Masks are also used to represent healing spirits and cure illness.

See also CLOWNS, SACRED; FALSE FACES; KACHINAS.

MASTER LOX (Master Leux) *Micmac, Passamaquoddy* WOLVERINE, a TRICKSTER and thief. In tales from the Northeast, Master Lox is often depicted as the companion of WOLF. Master Lox was killed many times but always came back to life.

MATÓ TIPILA See DEVIL'S TOWER.

MATSILEMA (Matsailema) See AHAYUTA AND MATSILEMA.

MEDICINE The power possessed by people, things, and actions. Medicine can be used for good purposes such as healing, controlling game and the

Haida mask with movable parts (© J. Kell B. Sandved/ Photo Researchers)

Iroquois False Face mask (private collection, New York/Werner Forman Archive/Art Resource, NY)

Bella Coola mask with a human face and eagle beak (Provincial Museum, Victoria, British Columbia, Museum No. 2513/Werner Forman Archive/Art Resource, NY)

weather, and seeing into the future. It can also be used for evil purposes such as witchcraft or sorcery. People (usually healers, MEDICINE PEOPLE, and SHAMANS) acquire medicine from spirit beings, ANIMALS, or objects that have power.

MEDICINE BUNDLE A sacred object or collection of objects wrapped in a bundle or contained in a bag. A medicine bundle may be the property of an individual, family, society, clan, or tribe. Associated with each bundle generally are origin stories, rituals, songs, powers, responsibilities, and TABOOS. A caretaker is selected to hold the responsibility for protecting the bundle and performing the sacred rituals attached to it. Because medicine bundles are considered to be alive, they must be treated with respect. Bundles have beneficial powers, such as healing, calling game animals, and bringing success in hunting or war. If not properly cared for, however, they have the power to cause harm.

In the Navajo (Dineh) CREATION ACCOUNT, CHANGING WOMAN used the power of the Mountain

Soil Bundle she received from FIRST MAN to create the first FOUR clans of the Navajo (Dineh).

MEDICINE PEOPLE The English term used to designate Native American healers, SHAMANS, religious leaders, and wise elders.

MEDICINE PIPE See SACRED PIPE.

MEDICINE WHEEL A large spoked circle constructed of stones, examples of which are found in the high country from Canada to Wyoming. The best-known wheel is located on top of 10,000-foot-high Medicine Mountain in the Big Horn Mountains of Wyoming. Its 28 spokes radiate to an outer circle 80 feet in diameter marked by stone cairns. At the summer solstice, the rising point of the Sun is on a direct line with an outer stone marker and one on the inside of the wheel. Prior to the solstice, there are similar alignments with two bright stars in the constellation ORION. Other medicine wheels farther north in Canada were constructed according to

Big Horn Medicine Wheel, located on top of the 10,000-foot-high Medicine Mountain in Wyoming, is a sacred site used by a number of Native American tribes. *(© Georg Gerster/Photo Researchers)*

almost identical designs. This similarity indicates the possible use of medicine wheels as calendars to mark the dates of important ceremonies held at the solstices and equinoxes. Medicine wheels are also places of fasting and meditation for people on VISION QUESTS. Crow legend has it that BURNT FACE originated the medicine wheel.

MESA VERDE A high plateau (now Mesa Verde National Park) in southwestern Colorado that is the site of hundreds of cliff dwellings of the ancient ANASAZI culture. The site was first occupied around A.D. 550. Its population peaked at about 5,000 during the years from A.D. 1100 to 1300. After about 1300, Mesa Verde was abandoned. Most of the cliff dwellings were built between 1190 and the late 1270s. Some are one-room dwellings; the largest is the huge structure called Cliff Palace, containing 217 rooms and 23 KIVAS (ceremonial underground chambers). The second-largest cliff dwelling, Long House, has 150 rooms and 21 kivas.

MICHABO (Great Hare) *Algonquian* The principal deity and CREATOR of Algonquian-speaking tribes. Michabo created the land by taking a grain of sand from the ocean bottom and using it to make an island that he set afloat on the PRIMORDIAL WATERS. The island grew so large that a young wolf that tried to cross it died of old age before reaching the other side. Michabo is credited with the invention of many things, such as picture-writing and the art of knitting fishnets (which he developed after observing a SPIDER weave its web). Originally associated with the dawn, Michabo was a CULTURE HERO credited with ruling the WIND, bringing LIGHT, and causing lightning. See also HARE.

MILGIS (Megis) *Anishinabe* The legendary seashell that led the Anishinabe westward from their original home near the gulf of the St. Lawrence River and the Atlantic Ocean to their eventual home in the Great Lakes region.

MILKY WAY The river of light in the night sky, the great spiral galaxy composed of billions of stars, and the home of our solar system. Our home system of Sun and planets is about two-thirds of the way

Taking advantage of nature, the Anasazi built their cliff dwellings at Mesa Verde under the protection of sandstone overhangs. *(© Harvey Stein/Photo Researchers)*

out from the galaxy's center. Looking toward the constellation Sagittarius, we see vast clusters and clouds of stars, because that direction is toward the center of the galaxy. When we look toward ORION, the Hunter of the winter skies, we see far fewer stars, because that way leads toward the galaxy's rim.

Many Native American tribes viewed the Milky Way as a pathway in the sky. To the Yuma of southern Arizona it was the trail left by an antelope as it raced a deer across the sky. The Pomo of California called it "Bear Foot"—the path on which a mythological BEAR walked.

In many Native American cultures, the Milky Way was a path for the souls of the dead. In Seminole legend, the CULTURE HERO BREATH MAKER (Hisagita misa) created the Milky Way by blowing toward the sky to make a pathway to the City of the West, where good souls went after death. Rain and Rainbow also lived along this path, and the BIG DIPPER was the boat that carried the good souls to their destination. To the Lakota, the Milky Way was the Spirit Road to the land of the dead, guarded by OWL MAKER. To the Skidi Pawnee, the souls of the dead traveled along the Milky Way to the Southern Star, their final home. The Osage also believed that the souls of the dead traveled along this path until they found a star in which to live. In myths of the Iroquois and of Algonquian speakers, this path led to the Village of Souls. The Tewa warrior Long Sash, represented by the stars of Orion's belt and sword, guided ancestors along the Milky Way, the Endless Trail that led south.

The origin of the Milky Way is told in tales from various cultures, such as in the Seminole legend of Breath Maker already cited. In a Navajo (Dineh) tale, BLACK GOD was arranging the stars neatly when COYOTE grew impatient and threw them all into the sky, creating the Milky Way. In an Akimel O'od-ham story, Earth Shaman (Tcu-unnyikita) dipped his walking stick in ashes, drew it across the sky, and created the Milky Way. According to a Zuni legend, it was created when the WARRIOR TWINS called the AHAYUTA traveled around the world in search of the missing CORN MAIDENS. A Cóchiti Pueblo story tells of a girl, BLUE FEATHER, who opened a bag entrusted to her, releasing all the stars. In a Cherokee tale, some people chased away a DOG that had been stealing their cornmeal. The white trail of cornmeal that dropped from the dog's mouth as it ran became the Milky Way, which the Cherokee call "Where the dog ran."

MINK

A member of the weasel family, minks are aggressive and skillful hunters. Among Northwest Coast tribes, Mink appears in tales as a TRICKSTER. In his role of CULTURE HERO, he is also credited with creating mountains, rivers, and lakes; stealing the SUN; and killing MONSTERS.

MISSAPOS

(Big Rabbit, Great Hare) *Ojibway* A TRICKSTER who could change his form in order to trick both humans and other animals. See also HARE; RABBIT.

MISSISSIPPIAN CULTURE

One of the most complex societies to arise in North America. Also called the temple MOUND BUILDERS, the Mississippian people developed an agriculture- and trade-based culture that flourished along the Mississippi River valley from about A.D. 700 to postcontact times. It spread throughout most of the Southeast from Florida to Oklahoma and as far north as Wisconsin. The culture was characterized by sprawling centers housing thousands of people and centered on huge temple MOUNDS that rivaled the pyramids of Egypt. Some mounds in these centers held the homes of the rulers as well as temples; others were used for burials. Archaeological excavations of the mounds have yielded a wealth of treasures—copper sheets embossed with images of bird people, engraved shell ornaments, marble images, carved wooden figures, and many other relics of a highly developed culture. One major center of the mound builders was CAHOKIA in present-day Illinois.

The Natchez people were the last remnant of Mississippian culture. Their ruler was called the Great SUN and lived on one of the mounds that surrounded the central temple mound. His brothers were called Suns and his sisters, Woman Suns. When a noble died, many of his closest relatives and associates gave up their own lives and were buried with him.

The mounds erected by the Mississippian people became part of the mythology of tribes that came later. According to the Choctaw CREATION ACCOUNT, the first humans emerged from a hole in the ground at the great platform mound at Nunih Waya in Mississippi. The Choctaw considered this mound the Great Mother. According to tradition, as the Choctaw people wandered in search of a homeland, they took with them the bones of their elders who had died. When they reached Nunih Waya, they placed their ancestors' bones on the ground, covered them with cypress bark to create the great mound, and planted the surface of the mound with trees. To symbolize the renewal of their world, the Choctaw held their Green Corn Dances at the mound (see also DANCE).

MONSTERS

In Native American mythology, monsters come in all sizes and shapes and frequently can shift shapes at will. Stories of CANNIBALS and giants (and cannibalistic giants) appear in the mythology of most cultures. ROLLING HEADS are bodiless heads that roll across the land chasing people who wronged them. Also common are water monsters, which are frequently serpents, such as HORNED WATER SERPENT, UKTENA, UNCEGILA, and the UNKTEHI. Inuit legends tell of the ADLET, blood-drinking monsters that were born to a woman who had married a DOG.

In many cultures, the world was full of monsters before humans came. WARRIOR TWINS were born for the purpose of slaying these monsters in order to make the world fit for humans to live in. In Zuni legend, AHAYUTA AND MATSILEMA were responsible for slaying CLOUD SWALLOWER, a giant that devoured the rain clouds and caused a great drought. The traditional account associated with the Navajo (Dineh) ceremonial MONSTERWAY relates the adventures of MONSTER SLAYER AND BORN FOR WATER as they traveled the world slaying monsters. Other examples of warrior twins include KILLER-OF-ENEMIES and CHILD-OF-THE-WATER (Apache), MASEWA AND UYUYEWA (Keres), and PYUYKONHOYA AND PALUNHOYA (Hopi).

MONSTER SLAYER AND BORN FOR WATER
(Naayéé neizghání and Tó bájísh chíní) *Navajo (Dineh)* The WARRIOR TWIN sons of CHANGING WOMAN. One day, as Changing Woman slept, the sunshine made her pregnant with Monster Slayer. The next day, when she went to bathe, the water made her pregnant with Born for Water. Although the two boys had different fathers, they were called twins and both were considered sons of the SUN. The purpose of their birth was to rid the world of the MONSTERS that made it unfit for humans.

The boys made a long, hazardous journey to their father, the Sun. (Such a journey is characteristic of many Native American traditions of warrior twins.) They were helped in this adventure by various beings, including the Arrow People, Wind's Child (Nilch'i biyázhi), WATER SPRINKLER, and SPIDER MAN. In the Sun's home, the twins underwent many trials to prove to the Sun that they were his children. At last the Sun accepted them and offered them jewels, livestock, plants, flowers, and many other things. The twins said that they wanted only weapons and FLINT garments, leggings, headgear, and wrist guards. The Sun gave them what they asked for. He also placed agate in them to protect them from injury and gave them PRAYERSTICKS—ceremonially prepared sticks to which FEATHERS and other items were attached. Sun told them that Born for Water, the younger, would watch the prayersticks while Monster Slayer, the elder, went out to kill monsters. If the prayersticks began to burn, Born for Water would know that his brother was in danger and needed help.

After the twins left the Sun's house, they had many adventures slaying monsters. The traditional background of the Navajo (Dineh) ceremonial MONSTERWAY relates the twins' exploits. Monster Slayer also figures in the traditional accounts of EAGLEWAY and ENEMYWAY.

MONSTERWAY *Navajo (Dineh)* One of the traditional story cycles that are part of BLESSINGWAY (see NAVAJO [DINEH] CEREMONIALS). In his daily travels across the sky, the SUN had relationships with many different women, who subsequently gave birth to MONSTERS. The existence of these monsters made the world unfit for humans to live in. MONSTER SLAYER AND BORN FOR WATER, the WARRIOR TWIN sons of the Sun and CHANGING WOMAN, made a journey to find their father. From him, they obtained weapons and armor so that they could fight the monsters. After passing the Sun's tests and receiving many gifts, the twins set out to rid the world of monsters.

The first monster the twins slew was Big God (Yé'iitsoh). Following this success, they killed Horned Monster (Déélgééd) and Rock Monster Eagle (Tsé nináhálééh), whose practice was to swoop down and carry people off to feed his nestlings on top of SHIP ROCK. Monster Slayer turned the children of Rock Monster Eagle into the golden EAGLE and the OWL.

When Monster Slayer had slain all the monsters, NILCH'I, the WIND, told him that four still remained: Old Age Woman (Sá), who caused people to become old and feeble; Cold Woman (Hak'az asdzáá), who represented winter; Poverty (Té'é'i dineh), who used up and wore out possessions; and Hunger Man (Dichin hastiin), who caused hunger. Monster Slayer set out to destroy these last monsters, but each in turn convinced him that they were necessary for life on Earth, so he spared them.

MONTEZUMA (Moctezuma, First Man)   *Tohono O'odham*   A CULTURE HERO (not to be confused with the Aztec emperor of the same name). In the beginning, the Great Mystery created the Earth and everything that lived on it. He formed an image from clay and dropped it into a hole that he had dug. Out of the hole emerged Montezuma, followed by all the tribes. Montezuma taught the people everything they needed to know in order to live—how to make FIRE, cultivate CORN, weave baskets, and create pottery. In those days winter did not yet exist. Humans could speak with animals and lived in peace with them. Then one day COYOTE warned Montezuma that a great FLOOD was coming. Coyote told Montezuma to build a dugout canoe in order to save himself. While all other living things died in the flood, Coyote and Montezuma survived.

After the flood subsided, the Great Mystery again created humans and other living things to fill the Earth. He put Montezuma in charge of them. Once more, Montezuma (with Coyote's help) taught humans how to live, divided them into tribes, and gave them laws. Montezuma's power, however, made him corrupt. He began to rebel against the Great Mystery, declaring himself Chief of the Universe and ordering people to build him a house that reached to the heavens. The ways of the world changed: Humans began to hunt and kill animals and to fight among themselves. As a warning to stop this behavior, the Great Mystery moved the Sun farther away from the Earth. For the first time, winter, snow, and ice came to Earth (see also SEASONS, ORIGIN OF). The Great Mystery then made the Earth tremble, and Montezuma's house collapsed. Still, Montezuma continued to rebel. At last, the Great Mystery summoned people from across the ocean to come in ships and destroy Montezuma.

MOON   Because of the mysterious phases through which it passes monthly, the Moon figures prominently in Native American mythology. The creation of the Moon is usually linked with the creation of the SUN by a CREATOR figure, such as KODOYANPE

The face of this Inuit mask represents the spirit of the Moon. The border around the face symbolizes air, the hoops signify the levels of the cosmos, and the feathers represent stars. *(Sheldon Jackson Museum, Sitka, Alaska, Werner Forman Archive/Art Resource, NY)*

(Maidu), First Man (see NAVAJO [DINEH] EMERGENCE), or TIRAWAHAT (Skidi Pawnee). The APACHE EMERGENCE AND MIGRATION account offers several versions of the origin of the Moon and Sun. Various tales involve the theft of the Sun and Moon, such as stories about CHULYEN (Tanaina) and RAVEN (Northwest Coast).

The Moon was seen by some tribes as female and by others as male. In Lakota myth, Hanwi, the Moon, was the wife of Wi, the Sun. In Inuit tales, the Moon is frequently the brother of the Sun, who is female.

The Moon was often associated with RAIN. The Haida, Kwakiutl, and Tlingit saw the Moon as a woman carrying a bucket. Whenever she knocked over her bucket, it rained.

The Moon was sometimes associated with death and disease. According to a Caribou Inuit legend, Moon helped PANA, the woman who kept the souls of the dead, to return the dead to new lives on Earth. In the Western Arctic culture area, diseases were believed to come from the Moon, and a lunar ECLIPSE predicted an epidemic.

Among the western Inuit, TATQEQ was the Moon Spirit who influenced the ocean tides and currents, controlled the supply of game, and brought good luck to hunters. For the Yup'ik, a TUNGAK was a powerful spirit that lived on the Moon and controlled the supply of game animals. SHAMANS made spirit journeys to the Moon to ensure a sufficient supply of game.

Many people who look at the Moon's surface see a face—"the man in the Moon." Native Americans of the Southwest saw a HARE or RABBIT in the Moon's light and dark patches. Other tribes saw a FROG.

MOON WOMAN *Pawnee* The bringer of CORN and the BUFFALO. Once, before the people had corn and buffalo for food, a famine occurred. A young man fasted on the hill near Moon Woman's cave. She came to him and directed him to drink from a pool of water. In the water, he saw reflected the images of women of different ages, representing the different phases of the MOON. Moon Woman gave the young man several gifts, one of which was a bowl of corn to feed his people. She also taught him many things, including the ceremonies to summon the buffalo. When the people performed the ceremonies, buffalo emerged from Moon Woman's cave. Afterward, the cave disappeared, and the people were afraid that there would be no more buffalo. They scattered and became the different bands of the Pawnee.

MORNING STAR *Skidi Pawnee* The Skidi Pawnee name for the planet Mars. Morning Star was the first and most powerful being placed in the sky by TIRAWAHAT, the CREATOR. Dressed as a warrior, Morning Star was covered with red dust and stood on a bed of red-hot FLINT. Desiring the beautiful EVENING STAR for a wife, Morning Star pursued and eventually won her. Through their daughter Standing Rain, Morning Star and Evening Star became the ancestors of the human race (see also HUMANS, ORIGIN OF).

MOTHER EARTH AND FATHER SKY In some traditional accounts, Mother Earth and Father Sky are the CREATORS. In the Navajo (Dineh) SHOOTINGWAY ceremonial, a SANDPAINTING depicts Father Sky in black, decorated with symbols for the SUN, MOON, several CONSTELLATIONS, and the MILKY WAY. Mother Earth is depicted in blue, with the four sacred plants—CORN, squash, beans, and TOBACCO— growing from a spring. A line of sacred POLLEN, symbolizing positive energy, connects their mouths.

MOTZEYOUF See ARROW BOY.

MOUND BUILDERS The name given to the cultures that made the groups of earthen MOUNDS found in the Ohio and Mississippi River valleys. The four mound-building cultures that have been recognized are the Poverty Point (1800–500 B.C.), Adena (1000 B.C.–A.D. 200), Hopewell (200 B.C.–A.D. 700), and Mississippian (A.D. 700–1600). The mound builders were the ancestors of the Cherokee, Chickasaw, Choctaw, Creek, and Seminole.

See also CAHOKIA; MISSISSIPPIAN CULTURE.

This Navajo (Dineh) sandpainting shows Father Sky and Mother Earth surrounded by the Rainbow God, a symbol of protection. Father Sky is adorned with symbols for the Sun, Moon, Milky Way, and several constellations. Mother Earth bears symbols for corn and other plants growing from a spring. (*National Anthropological Archives*)

Great Serpent Mound in Ohio, like other effigy mounds, contained rich caches of Hopewellian artifacts. *(© Georg Gerster/Photo Researchers)*

MOUNDS   Large earthworks found throughout the eastern part of North America. Some are geometric in shape; others, called effigy mounds, are in the form of ANIMALS and BIRDS. The reason for their construction is unknown. Adding to the mystery is the fact that the shape of the largest mounds can be recognized only when seen from above.

The earliest mounds were constructed in northeastern Louisiana between 1800 and 500 B.C. by the Poverty Point culture. The most impressive Poverty Point earthwork is in the shape of a giant bird with outstretched wings. This mound is more than 70 feet high and measures 710 feet by 640 feet. Other Poverty Point sites have been found elsewhere in Louisiana and in Arkansas and Mississippi.

Another mound-building culture, the Adena, lasted from about 1000 B.C. to A.D. 200. Adena mounds are located along the Ohio River valley from Kentucky to New York State. In addition to burial mounds in the shape of domes or cones, the Adena people constructed animal-shaped effigy mounds. Great Serpent Mound near Chillicothe, Ohio, is the figure of an enormous snake with a coiled tail wriggling toward the north with its mouth open, trying to swallow a huge egg. The effigy extends for an amazing 1,348 feet. Some Hopi believe that this mound was created by their ancestors during their migration (see HOPI EMERGENCE AND MIGRATION).

The Adena culture was followed by the Hopewell culture, named after a large mound in Ohio excavated in the 1800s. The Hopewell culture lasted from about 200 B.C. to A.D. 700 and spread throughout much of the East and the Midwest. In addition to burial mounds 30–40 feet high, the Hopewell people built large effigy mounds and enclosed areas of land with earthen walls 50 feet high and 200 feet across at the base. These enclosures were laid out in a variety of shapes—circles, squares, and octagons.

At a site along the Iowa-Wisconsin border, the Hopewell people built about 200 massive mounds. The most impressive of these are representations of huge birds and a group of mounds called the Marching BEARS. The Marching Bears group consists of 13 effigy mounds constructed along an arc around an east-west line. Astronomers believe that the Marching Bears represent the movement of the BIG DIPPER around POLARIS, the North Star. On early spring evenings, the Dipper is directly over the top of the arc, and in late summer the Dipper is over the bottom position of the mounds.

The mounds have entered into the traditions and mythology of the people who came after the MOUND BUILDERS. When Muskogee and Seminole singers and dancers perform during the Green Corn Ceremony, they do so on earthen mounds. The Creek describe an ancient battle during which their warriors emerged from a mound and defeated a Cherokee war party. In turn, the Cherokee say that in ancient times, when they needed help in warfare, they would go to the Nikwasi Mound (near Franklin, North Carolina) and ask the Nunnehi (Immortals) for assistance. Bearing magic weapons, the Nunnehi would emerge from the mound and join the Cherokee warriors.

According to the Choctaw, the great platform mound at Nunih Waya in Mississippi was the place where Great Spirit created the first people, who crawled out of the mound. Choctaw legend also says that when the Choctaw people were wandering in search of a homeland, they carried along the bones of their ancestors. When they reached Nunih Waya, they placed the bones on the ground and covered them with cypress bark, creating the huge mound. To symbolize the renewal and purification of their world, the Choctaw held their Green Corn ceremonies in this place.

MOUNTAIN LION Known variously as cougar, panther, and puma, the mountain lion is the largest of the wild cats, measuring six to eight feet long and weighing 100 to 175 pounds. In the Keres

CREATION ACCOUNT, Mountain Lion guarded SHIPAP, the pre-emergence place. In the Tewa tradition, supernatural beings living in SIPOFENE, the pre-emergence place, sent a man to explore the upper world. He returned to SIPOFENE as Mountain Lion. For the Zuni, Mountain Lion was the BEAST GOD associated with the north.

MOUNTAINS, SACRED Throughout North America, various mountains are held sacred by different groups. Some mountains are featured in CREATION ACCOUNTS. Others are places where sacred teachings were given to the people, such as BEAR BUTTE and MOUNT SHASTA. BLACK MESA in Arizona is sacred to both the Hopi and the Navajo (Dineh). For the Hopi, Black Mesa is Túwanasari (Center of the Universe), to which the Hopi clans returned after their migrations. (See HOPI EMERGENCE AND MIGRATION.) For the Navajo, Black Mesa is the Female Mountain, which with the nearby Male Mountain represents the balance of nature.

The traditional Navajo (Dineh) homeland is bounded by FOUR sacred mountains that symbolically stand at the cardinal DIRECTIONS (although they are not located geographically in these exact directions). These mountains are Mount Blanca (Tsisnaajiní, "Dawn Mountain" or "White Shell Mountain"), the sacred mountain of the east; Mount Taylor (Tsoodzil, "Blue Bead Mountain" or "Turquoise Mountain"), the sacred mountain of the south; the San Francisco Peaks (Dook'o'oslííd, "Abalone Shell Mountain"), the sacred mountain of the west; and Mount Hesperus (Dibé nitsaa, "Big Mountain Sheep" or "Obsidian Mountain"), the sacred mountain of the north. Within the borders formed by the four sacred mountains, there are three other sacred mountains: El Huerfano Mesa (Dzil ná'oodilii), where CHANGING WOMAN gave birth to MONSTER SLAYER AND BORN FOR WATER and lived in the first hogan; Gobernador Knob (Ch'óol'íí), where Changing Woman was found; and Mount Graham (Dzil naatsis'áán, "Big Seated Mountain").

In the APACHE EMERGENCE AND MIGRATION account, in order for the people to leave the UNDERWORLD, the HACTCIN (supernatural beings) instructed them to make a SANDPAINTING of a land bordered by four mountains. These mountains grew, and eventually the people were able to use them, together with ladders, to reach the upper world.

MOUNTAINWAY *Navajo (Dineh)* A ceremonial curing complex, or group of ceremonies (called chants, sings, or ways) conducted to heal illness and restore harmony (*hózhó*) in the universe (see NAVAJO [DINEH] CEREMONIALS). Mountainway is included in the HOLYWAY classification of ceremonials, which are used to restore health by attracting good. At the end of the traditional account associated with the ENEMYWAY curing complex, two sisters had been tricked into marrying two elderly men, BEAR and SNAKE. The traditional account of Mountainway follows the story of the older sister, who married Bear, and her descendants. (BEAUTYWAY carries on the story of the younger sister.)

After fleeing Bear, Older Sister was cared for by First Earth People. She also gave birth to a female bear cub and saw the Mountainway ceremonial. The *DIYIN DINEH* (Holy People) took her on a series of journeys, during which she learned powerful things. She encountered her husband, Bear, and had to flee again, leaving her daughter with the Bear People. After marrying a man of her own people, she bore a son who was stolen and raised by a bear. The son learned secret knowledge from the bears but eventually fled from them and rejoined his own family. He had two sons of his own, Owl Boy and Reared-within-the-Mountain.

Owl Boy became a great and powerful hunter. Reared-within-the-Mountain was captured by Utes but was rescued by TALKING GOD and other *diyin dineh*. He made many journeys to the *diyin dineh* and

acquired a great deal of knowledge. Afterward, he taught all that he had learned to his family, then returned to live with the *diyin dineh*.

MOUNT SHASTA A dormant volcano in the Cascade Range of northern California, 14,162 feet high. Mount Shasta is sacred to many groups, including the Hupa, Karuk, Modoc, Pit River, Shasta, and Wintu. The mountain figures in many CREATION ACCOUNTS and is believed by several tribes to be the home of the CREATOR.

MUSKRAT With its rudderlike tail and partially webbed hind feet, the muskrat is a powerful swimmer. In the CREATION ACCOUNTS of the Anishinabe (see MANABOZHO), Blackfeet (see NA'PI), Cree (see WEE-SA-KAY-JAC), Crow, and other tribes, Muskrat was the only diving animal that succeeded in bringing up from the bottom of the PRIMORDIAL WATERS a bit of mud that was used to create land. In an Anishinabe tale about the origin of LIGHT, FIRE, and water, Muskrat gave fire to the world by stealing a burning coal from the old chief who kept these three elements for himself.

MUYINWA *Hopi* The deity that controlled the growth of PLANTS. One of the "cloud fathers"—the chiefs of the six directions (north, south, east, west, above, and below)—Muyinwa was the bringer of RAIN. He was associated with the direction below and sent beans, squash, and melons to the Hopi people. Muyinwa's sister, TIH-KUYI-WUHTI, was the mother (or keeper) of game animals and controlled their supply.

N

NANABUSH (Nanaboozhou, Nanabozho, Nana-push) *Algonquian, Anishinabe, Ojibway* See MANABOZHO.

NA'PI (Old Man) *Blackfeet* The CREATOR of the world and everything in it. Na'pi, with the help of FOUR animal assistants, created Earth from soil brought up from the bottom of the PRIMORDIAL WATERS. In one version of the traditional account, the four ANIMALS were BEAVER, OTTER, DUCK and MUSKRAT; in another, Fish, FROG, Lizard, and TURTLE. One by one the animals dived below the surface to try to bring up soil from beneath the waters. The first three attempts ended in failure, but the fourth diving animal (in different versions, Duck, Muskrat, or Turtle) was successful. Na'pi took the soil that was brought up and placed it on the water, where it spread out to form the land. Na'pi came from the south and traveled north, making animals and BIRDS and placing rivers, lakes, and mountains. When he rested at night, he left his outline in the rocks on which he lay. One day Na'pi made a woman and a child from clay and taught them which PLANTS and animals they could eat.

See also CREATION ACCOUNTS; HUMANS, ORIGIN OF.

NATURAL BRIDGE A famous natural bridge of rock that spans Clear Creek in Virginia. According to legend, enemies pursued a band of Mohegan to the chasm through which Clear Creek runs. Backed up against the chasm, the Mohegan prayed to the Great Spirit for help, and a bridge formed across the chasm. While the women and children went across the bridge to safety, the warriors stayed to fight. They defeated the enemy.

NAVAJO (DINEH) CEREMONIALS The Navajo (Dineh) have a complicated system of ceremonials (called chants, sings, or ways) that serve a variety of purposes: to protect people from evil or accidents, promote harvests, ensure general well-being, and restore harmony (*hózhó*). Each of these ceremonial complexes is composed of individual parts that can be kept or deleted according to the individual patient's circumstances. Some parts are required and appear in every performance of a given chant. Ceremonies range from one to nine nights. Most are conducted by singers (*hataalii*) or chanters who are experts in the performance of specific ceremonies. Ceremonies combine many elements: song, dance, oral storytelling, prayer, purification, ritualistic items such as the MEDICINE BUNDLE, PRAYERSTICKS, body painting, and SAND-PAINTING. Ceremonies generally include a recounting of the traditional adventures of a CULTURE HERO ensuring that the person who is "sung over" will return to a healthy, happy life as the hero did. In ceremonies that involve sandpainting, the person who is the subject of the ceremony may walk over or sit on the sandpainting or apply parts of it to his or her body.

An early researcher and recorder of Navajo (Dineh) ceremonials distinguished between rites, in which a rattle is not used, and chants, in which a rattle accompanies the singing. However, the distinction is more one of focus. The two major rites—BLESSINGWAY (*hózhóó'jí*) and ENEMYWAY (*'anaa'jí*)—have a different focus from the chants. Blessingway is preventive in nature and invokes positive blessings. It protects against misfortune by ensuring good luck, order, health, and prosperity for people and everything that concerns them. Enemyway is used to exorcise the ghosts of aliens (non-Navajo), violence, and ugliness. The chants, on the other hand, focus specifically on curing.

Ceremonies are classified according to their pattern, traditional associations, and the cause of the illness toward which the cure is directed. HOLYWAY ceremonies are used when the illness is caused by offenses against spirits and the *DIYIN DINEH* (Holy People). They restore health by attracting good. EVIL-WAY ceremonies are used to exorcise evil when ghosts have caused the illness. LIFEWAY ceremonies are used to treat injuries resulting from accidents.

For the traditional accounts associated with some ceremonies, see BEADWAY, BEAUTYWAY, BIG STARWAY, CHIRICAHUA WINDWAY, EAGLEWAY, FLINTWAY, HAIL-WAY, MONSTERWAY, MOUNTAINWAY, NAVAJO WIND-WAY, NIGHTWAY, and SHOOTINGWAY.

NAVAJO (DINEH) EMERGENCE *Navajo (Dineh)*

There are several different versions of the Navajo (Dineh) CREATION ACCOUNT, all of which involve a series of UNDERWORLDS through which beings ascended until they reached the present world. In some versions, the present world is the fifth; in others it is the fourth.

The First World was black with FOUR corners. Over each corner hung a column of cloud—black, white, blue, or yellow. First Man was formed at the northeast corner, where the black and white clouds met. First Woman was formed at the southwest corner, where the yellow and blue clouds met. (See also FIRST MAN AND FIRST WOMAN.) The creatures that lived in this world were the *NILCH'I DINEH*—Air-Spirit People or Mist People who had no definite form. The *nilch'i dineh* began to quarrel among themselves. As a result, the entire population moved upward into the Second, or Blue, World. The beings that lived there were also at war, and the world was filled with suffering and unhappiness. First Man made a magic wand of jet, turquoise, abalone, and white shell to carry the people up to the Third, or Yellow, World. After they had been living there for a time, the people became corrupt and lived in unnatural ways. A great FLOOD destroyed this world. To save the people, First Man made a tall mountain, but it did not reach the next world. On top, he first tried planting a CEDAR, then a PINE, and next a male reed. None

grew tall enough. Finally, First Man planted a female reed, and the people climbed up through its hollow stem and into the Fourth, or Glittering, World.

The people's first act in the new world was to build a sweat lodge and sing the Blessing Song. First Man then constructed the first hogan, or dwelling. With soil brought up from the Yellow World, the sacred MOUNTAINS were created. After the mountains were in place, the *DIYIN DINEH*, or Holy People, put the SUN and MOON in the SKY, created night and day, and made all the necessities of life. BLACK GOD created the STARS and CONSTELLATIONS.

The BLESSINGWAY ceremonial is a complex of the sacred narratives surrounding the creation of the Navajo (Dineh). Other stories related to the Navajo (Dineh) emergence include those of CHANGING WOMAN, FIRST MAN AND FIRST WOMAN, and Changing Woman's WARRIOR TWIN sons, MONSTER SLAYER AND BORN FOR WATER.

NAVAJO WINDWAY *Navajo (Dineh)*

A ceremonial curing complex, or group of ceremonies (called chants, sings, or ways) conducted to heal illness and restore harmony (*hózhó*) in the universe (see NAVAJO [DINEH] CEREMONIALS). Like CHIRICAHUA WINDWAY, to which it is related, Navajo Windway is included in the HOLYWAY classification of ceremonials, which are used to restore health by attracting good.

The traditional account associated with Navajo Windway involves the adventures of a young man whom the WINDS (see NILCH'I) chose to race with TALKING GOD. SNAKE People kidnapped the hero, but the *DIYIN DINEH* (Holy People) rescued him. Most of the young man's adventures occurred when he violated TABOOS by hunting in forbidden territory or attending ceremonies that were forbidden to him. He was often severely injured, and various beings had to restore him to life and health. Through these experiences, he learned the curing rituals that make up Navajo Windway. He returned from his adventures to teach his family what he had learned. He then left and became part of the wind.

NESHANU *Arapaho*

The CREATOR. Shortly after creating the Earth and the creatures that lived on it, Neshanu became aware that some people were wicked, unwise, and disrespectful. He decided to destroy the bad people with a FLOOD, but he wanted to save those who were good and pleasing to him. He turned the good people into grains of CORN, which he planted both on Earth and in the SKY. After the flood, Neshanu harvested an ear of sky corn and changed it into Mother Corn. He sent her to Earth to recover the good people, whom he had changed into corn seeds. After Mother Corn released the people, she taught them the skills they needed to survive, such as how to cultivate corn and perform important ceremonies. Then she became a CEDAR tree.

NIAGARA FALLS Great falls of the Niagara River on the border between the United States (western New York State) and Canada (southeastern Ontario). The Seneca and Huron name for the falls, *Nee-ah-gah-ra*, means "Thundering Waters."

In Iroquoian legend, the falls were created after a conflict between THUNDERBIRD and Great Snake Monster, who were the powers of SKY and Earth. According to legend, a young Seneca woman was fleeing an undesirable marriage when the river's swift current dashed her canoe against the rocks. Thunderbird spread his wings and rescued her just as the canoe broke apart. Before returning the woman to her village, he told her that the source of illness among her people was a giant SNAKE coiled under the village. The people moved their village to a new location, but Great Snake Monster soon found them again. To protect the people, Thunderbird hurled a lightning bolt to kill the serpent. When the bolt struck him, the monster thrashed around with such force that he scooped out a huge basin, creating the horseshoe-shaped falls. According to some stories, the sound of the falls was the roar of a water spirit who needed to be appeased every year with the sacrifice of a maiden in a canoe.

NIGHTWAY *Navajo (Dineh)* A ceremonial curing complex, or group of ceremonies (called chants, sings, or ways) conducted to heal illness and restore harmony (*hózhó*) in the universe (see NAVAJO [DINEH] CEREMONIALS). Nightway is included in the HOLYWAY classification of ceremonials, which are used to restore health by attracting good. It is an extremely complex and elaborate ceremonial, performed only in winter. Two traditional accounts form the background for Nightway: the "visionary" version and the "stricken twins" version.

The hero of the visionary version is a young man named Bitahatini, whose brothers scoffed at the visions he had. While his older brothers were away hunting, Bitahatini had a vision of them killing a CROW and a MAGPIE that were the keepers of game animals. As a result, there would be no more game to hunt. When Bitahatini revealed his vision to his brothers, they discounted it as usual, but the vision proved to be true. The *DIYIN DINEH* (Holy People), in the form of mountain sheep, led Bitahatini off to their home, where they taught him the rituals of Nightway. Bitahatini returned home, taught Nightway to his younger brother, and left to live with the *diyin dineh*.

In the stricken twins version, a young woman spent FOUR days with TALKING GOD before he left her. The woman later gave birth to TWIN boys. When the twins grew up, developed a habit of wandering. After one adventure, they returned disabled: One was blind and the other was lame. Unwilling to support the boys, the family sent them away. Talking God watched over the boys and brought them to the home of the *diyin dineh* for a cure. However, because the boys did not know the proper offerings to make, the *diyin dineh* refused to help them until tests revealed that Talking God was their father. The first healing ritual failed when the boys cried out after being told to remain silent. The boys' tears at this failure turned into song, and the *diyin dineh* called them back. They cured the twins and taught them the Nightway rituals. The boys went home to teach the rituals to their family and then returned to live with the *diyin dineh*.

NILCH'I (Wind) *Navajo (Dineh)* One of the original Holy People (*DIYIN DINEH*) who emerged into this world with FIRST MAN AND FIRST WOMAN (see NAVAJO [DINEH] EMERGENCE). Although *Nilch'i* is customarily translated as "WIND," the concept is far more powerful than that. *Nilch'i* refers to the air and the atmosphere, both still and in motion. It is associated with breath, speech, thought, and the power of motion. In addition, it is the means of communication among all elements of the living world. In Navajo (Dineh) emergence and CREATION ACCOUNTS, Nilch'i appears as the source of life. White Wind (Nilch'i ligai) gave life to First Man and First Woman by blowing over two ears of CORN. Nilch'i entered CHANGING WOMAN to give her life.

According to tradition, Nilch'i enters a person at the moment of conception, enabling the baby to move, grow, breathe, and live. Nilch'i enters and leaves the body through the spiral whorl patterns on the fingertips and toes and the whorl pattern of the hair on top of the head. The final act in the BLESS-INGWAY ceremonial is to breathe in the air at dawn to fill the individual with the Holy Wind Spirit.

Nilch'i lives in the FOUR cardinal DIRECTIONS marked by the four sacred MOUNTAINS of the Navajo (Dineh). A wind is associated with each mountain and each direction: White Wind (east), Blue Wind (south), Yellow Wind (west), and Black Wind (north).

Nilch'i is said to have released humans from captivity under GAMBLING GOD.

NILCH'I DINEH (*nilch'i diné, nilch'i dine'é*) *Navajo (Dineh)* The Air-Spirit People who lived in the First World (see NAVAJO [DINEH] EMERGENCE). There were 12 groups of *nilch'i dineh*—dark and red ants, dragonflies, various types of beetles, bats, and locusts.

NIMAKWSOWES *Abenaki* SABLE, the traveling companion of the CULTURE HERO GLUSKAP.

NOAHA-VOSE (Noahvose, Noavosse) See BEAR BUTTE.

NOQOILPI See GAMBLING GOD.

NORTHERN LIGHTS See AURORA BOREALIS.

NORTH STAR See POLARIS.

NYAPAKAAMTE See AMCHITAPUKA.

OKABEWIS (Messenger) *Anishinabe* The man sent by the CREATOR to teach the first people how to live. Before Okabewis came, the first people had no knowledge. Okabewis taught them how to make FIRE, cook meat, and cultivate and use CORN and TOBACCO. He also taught them religious practices such as fasting and how to heal the sick by means of dreams and visions.

OLD LADY SALT See SALT WOMAN.

OLD MAN *Blackfeet, Crow, Seminole* In Blackfeet tales, Old Man was a deceitful, lazy TRICKSTER. One tale describes how Old Man talked FOX into letting him pluck out all of Fox's fur except for his tail fur. Old Man claimed this trick was a new method of catching BUFFALO. When the buffalo saw Fox, they laughed so hard that they died of exhaustion. Old Man skinned and butchered the buffalo, but Fox made no move to help him. Old Man angrily gave Fox a push. When Fox fell over, Old Man realized that, without fur for protection, Fox had frozen solid in the cold.

Old Man (Isaahka) was also one of the names of the Crow CREATOR, AKBAATATDIA, and of the Seminole Creator, ES-TE FAS-TA.

OLD MAN COYOTE (Isaahkawuatte) *Crow* One name given to the Crow CREATOR, AKBAATAT-DIA. In the beginning, the world was covered with the PRIMORDIAL WATERS. Old Man Coyote wanted to create land, so he asked the DUCKS to dive for mud. The first three ducks were not successful, but the fourth was. After creating the land, Old Man Coyote used more mud to create First Man and First Woman. He called First Man Cirape (or Shirape) and referred to him as his younger brother. The children of First Man and First Woman were the first people. (See also HUMANS, ORIGIN OF.)

Old Man Coyote was also responsible for the origin of SEASONS. In a Crow legend, winter and summer were kept in separate bags by a woman who lived in the south. She would release only winter to Crow country, while to the south it was always summer. Old Man Coyote—with the aid of Jackrabbit, DEER, and WOLF—stole the bag containing summer and brought it back to Crow country. The two eventually agreed that each land would have both summer and winter.

OPOSSUM The only native North American marsupial (a mammal whose young are carried in a pouch on their mother's body). The most distinctive feature of the opossum is its long, naked tail. The origin of this feature has been the subject of Native American tales. In a Choctaw legend about the theft of FIRE, Opossum was the first animal to try to steal fire from the people who possessed it. He hid a piece of burning wood in the thick fur of his bushy tail. However, his fur caught fire, and the people who owned fire saw him. They took the fire away from him and drove him off. Poor Opossum discovered that all the fur of his tail had been burned off, leaving it naked, as it is to this day.

ORAL TRADITION A method of passing down knowledge—such as laws, history, traditions, and TABOOS—in spoken form. Native Americans had no written language, although picture writing was used. In preliterate societies such as those of the Native Americans, storytellers—keepers of the oral tradition—passed down the tales of their people from generation to generation. In postcontact times,

Europeans began recording these tales. Differences in the spellings of Native American names and different versions of myths were frequently the result of records made by different researchers.

ORIGIN OF HUMANS See HUMANS, ORIGIN OF.

ORIGIN OF SEASONS See SEASONS, ORIGIN OF.

ORION The Hunter, a familiar CONSTELLATION in the winter sky, characterized by three closely spaced stars that mark his belt and three fainter stars suspended at an angle from the belt to form his sword. These six stars found their place in the starlore of various tribes.

The Wasco saw the three stars of Orion's belt as three men in a canoe. Other tribes saw these stars as three animals. To both the Kumeyaay of California and the Yuma of Arizona, the stars were an antelope, a deer, and a mountain sheep. The Chemehuevi of California viewed the belt stars as three mountain sheep and the sword as an arrow shot at them by a

Owl and other figures are etched on a Passamaquoddy birchbark basket. *(Smithsonian Institution, Department of Anthropology, Neg. No. 76-17262)*

pair of hunters. A Chinook tale describes a race between a large canoe (the belt) and a small canoe (the sword) to catch a salmon in the Big River (the MILKY WAY). In Tewa mythology, the belt and sword formed the belt and sash of Long Sash, a warrior who guided people along the Endless Trail, or Milky Way.

OTTER The playful otter is well known for its swimming ability. It has been known to swim underwater for a quarter of a mile without coming up for air. In one version of the Blackfeet CREATION ACCOUNT, Otter was one of the diving animals that tried to bring up soil from the bottom of the water to create land. Otter was also one of the earth divers sent by MANABOZHO (in the Algonquian and Anishinabe traditions) and by WEE-SA-KAY-JAC (a Cree figure). The Slavey of northwestern Canada believed that otter and LOON spirits helped human spirits pass through the Earth to continue their lives in another place.

OWL Owls are nocturnal hunters characterized by silent flight, deeply hooked bills, sharp talons, and enormous eyes in fixed sockets. Almost universally, across cultures and times, owls have symbolized wisdom. The owl plays diverse roles in Native American mythology. In many tales, the owl appears as a wise and friendly spirit, often a helper of the MOON. The Pawnee viewed the owl as a protector during the night; an owl's hooting was a warning against danger. To the Delaware, the hooting of a screech owl was a sign of good luck in hunting. In a Blackfeet tale, Screech Owl (ATSITSI) was a legendary warrior famed for his fighting skills. The Menominee told about receiving the gift of MEDICINE from an owl. To honor the owl, the Menominee and several Plains tribes performed an Owl DANCE, in which the dancers mimicked an owl's behavior.

In other cultures, the owl was associated with death. In a Northwest Coast legend, Owl called out the names of people who were soon to die. To the Cherokee and Creek, the cry of a screech owl signaled impending death. The Cherokee viewed owls as the embodiments of ghosts or witches. In Lakota tradition, OWL MAKER (Hihankara) was an elderly woman who guarded the entrance to the MILKY WAY, over which the souls of the dead passed. In Apache stories, Owl was an evil, destructive MONSTER.

A Navajo (Dineh) legend accounts for the origin of the owl. According to the story, when the hero Monster Slayer slew Rock Monster Eagle, he changed the EAGLE nestlings into the golden eagle and the owl (see also MONSTER SLAYER AND BORN FOR WATER).

In an Arapaho tale, THUNDERBIRD, who symbolized summer, challenged WHITE OWL WOMAN, the winter bird, to a contest to determine which was the more powerful. White Owl Woman's thick, swift, snow-producing white clouds overcame Thunderbird's towering black clouds, so her powers were proven to be greater than his.

OWL MAKER (Hihankara) *Lakota*   An elderly woman who guarded the entrance to the MILKY WAY, which was the Spirit Road to the land of the dead. As the souls of the dead passed along the Milky Way, Owl Maker looked for identifying tattoos on each soul. If she did not find the correct marks, she cast the spirit from the path. When it fell back to Earth, it became a wandering ghost.

P

PALUNHOYA (Palongawhoya) See PYUYKON-HOYA AND PALUNHOYA.

PANA (The Woman Up There) *Caribou Inuit* A woman who lived in the SKY and kept the souls of the dead, who were reborn in her house. With the help of MOON, the dead came back to Earth, where they lived new lives as humans, animals, or fish.

PASSACONAWAY (Papisseconewa) (ca. 1580–1666) *Pennacook* A powerful chief and prophet credited with magical powers. Passaconaway was chief of the Pennacook tribe and the leader of a federation of more than a dozen tribes in what is now New Hampshire. According to legend, Passaconaway could bring a tree to life from its ashes and make dead wood blossom. In summer he could turn water to ice and in winter cause ice to burst into flame. It was said that he could make the trees dance and the rocks move, bring dead serpents to life, and turn himself into a burning fire. Tradition has it that late in Passaconaway's life, a sledge drawn by wolves appeared at his lodge. He mounted the sledge and was carried to the top of the highest peak. In a blaze of fire, he then ascended to the heavens.

PAUTIWA *Zuni* The chief of KOLHU/WALA-WA or KACHINA Village, which was at the bottom of a lake to the west of Zuni Pueblo. Most of the Zuni kachinas lived in this village. Pautiwa controlled the ceremonial calendar and directed all kachina activities. No kachina of the village could sing or dance for the Zuni without his permission. When the Zuni wanted the kachinas to come, they sent PRAYER-STICKS—decorated sticks prepared ceremonially as offerings to accompany prayers and pleas—to the village. Pautiwa then decided which kachinas would visit, sing, dance, and bring gifts. Pautiwa was thought of as kind and benevolent, and humans appealed to him for help when they were in trouble. He also received the spirits of the dead.

PAYATAMU *Pueblo* A CULTURE HERO who introduced the cultivation of CORN to the Pueblo people. In one legend, Payatamu was responsible for the return of the CORN MAIDENS after they had fled, taking all the corn with them and leaving the people to starve.

PEACE PIPE See SACRED PIPE.

PETROGLYPHS Etchings or carvings in rock. Petroglyphs found throughout North America include symbols of stars, the Sun, the Moon, animals, people, mountains, rain, corn, THUNDERBIRD, lightning, spirits, and other representations. Some sites contain many images. The Jeffers Petroglyph Site in Jeffers, Minnesota, contains some 2,000 carvings in 203 clusters, some of which date from 3000 B.C. Petroglyphs found throughout the Southwest frequently feature KOKOPELLI, the humpbacked flute player, as well as horned serpents, spirals, and footprints. Petroglyphs left by the various Hopi clans during their migrations (see HOPI EMERGENCE AND MIGRATION) have been found from the Arctic Circle down to South America and across the North American continent.

Petroglyphs also record more recent tribal history. On the walls of Largo Canyon in New Mexico, Navajo (Dineh) carvers recorded scenes of Kit Carson's 1803–04 campaign against their people, in which government troops burned crops and slaughtered sheep and other livestock. A petroglyph in British Columbia, clearly made after contact with Europeans, depicts a three-masted ship.

PICTOGRAPHS Paintings on stone, similar to PETROGLYPHS.

PINE Any of the members of the large genus of trees that occur throughout North America. Pines are resinous, cone-producing evergreens with pointed needles of varying lengths.

According to Iroquois tradition, the council of chiefs of the Five Nations held the historic meeting at which they agreed to the laws of the newly formed Iroquois Confederacy under a giant pine tree.

In a Nez Perce legend, the pine trees jealously guarded the secret of FIRE. BEAVER managed to steal the fire and, as he ran away with the pines in pursuit, passed it on to the birches, willows, and other trees. This story explains why fire is created when wood is rubbed together.

In the NAVAJO (DINEH) EMERGENCE account, First Man tried to save the people in the Third World from a FLOOD by planting first a CEDAR and next a pine tree that they could climb to reach the Fourth World. Neither tree, however, was tall enough. (See also FIRST MAN AND FIRST WOMAN.)

PLANTS As an essential of life, plants are often viewed as gifts from the CREATOR or the spirit world. For many cultures, the THREE SISTERS—CORN, squash, and beans—as well as TOBACCO are considered sacred. Many tales describe the origin of these and other plants (see FIRST MOTHER; SELU).

A Cherokee legend explains the power of plants to cure disease. According to the Cherokee, every

Petroglyphs (ca. 1300–1650) at Petroglyph National Monument, New Mexico (*© George H. H. Huey*)

plant on Earth is responsible for curing a specific human ailment.

See also TREES.

PLEIADES   A cluster of stars in the CONSTELLA-TION Taurus the Bull. Familiarly called the Seven Sisters, the cluster actually consists of between 300 and 500 stars, although only six are visible to the unaided eye. (Various theories have been presented about why, if only six stars are visible, ancient legends around the world always refer to seven. The missing seventh may be a variable star that has dimmed to invisibility.) Because they are so conspicuous, the Pleiades' place in starlore is universal.

The myths of some groups refer to only six stars. For the Yurok of California, the Pleiades were six women who lived upriver at the end of the world. The Tachi Yokuts, another California tribe, saw the stars as five girls and their husband. Other tales attempt to account for the missing star. For example, the Iroquois described the Pleiades as seven brothers but explained that one brother had fallen back to Earth as a shooting star. In a Nez Perce legend, there were seven sisters, but one, teased by the others, covered herself with a veil so that no one could see her. The Huron saw the cluster as seven sisters in a basket, one of whom chose to sit in the back of the basket with her husband, where she was difficult to see. These sisters, the Singing Maidens, came to Earth to sing and dance on early evenings in autumn (when the cluster is close to the horizon).

In a Kiowa tale, seven children being chased by a BEAR were carried up to the heavens on a rock that grew taller and taller, becoming DEVIL'S TOWER. The children remained in the sky as the Pleiades. In a Cheyenne story, a young woman who had been visited at night by a young man discovered that he was actually a DOG that transformed itself into a human (see DOG HUSBAND). The young woman gave birth to seven puppies, which at first she rejected but soon began to care for. When the puppies were old enough to run, however, their father took them away to the sky, where they became the Pleiades.

POLARIS   (North Star, Pole Star)   The star that currently marks the Earth's north celestial pole. Because of its location at the north celestial pole,

Polaris appears to remain stationary in the sky while the CONSTELLATIONS, stars, and other celestial objects wheel around it. Its stationary position marked it as the stable center of the universe in many cultures. Many Native American groups, such as the Omaha, envisioned a pole or pillar from the Earth to the North Star that held up the sky and maintained world order.

Because Polaris marks the location of the sky's north pole and the direction north, it serves as a guide for travelers during the night. For the Pomo, it was the eye of the Creator, Marumda, who watched people from his home in the sky. When people traveled at night, they kept track of Marumda's eye. The Chumash identified Polaris with SKY COYOTE, a powerful being who gambled with the SUN each year for the fate of people on Earth.

POLE STAR   See POLARIS.

POLLEN   Plant pollen is a sacred substance used ceremonially in Native American rituals. It symbolizes life, fertility, and renewal. As part of a rite, pollen is sprinkled on objects, SANDPAINTINGS, dancing grounds, and trails to make them holy. Pollen might also be sprinkled on the top of a person's head and touched to the mouth. The type of pollen used varies from group to group. Pollen from cattails, corn, oak, PINE, piñon, sunflowers, and tule (a cattail rush of the Southwest) is used.

For the Navajo (Dineh), corn pollen is the food of the DIYIN DINEH (Holy People) and is offered to them as a gift in all rituals, but especially during BLESSINGWAY ceremonials. The pollen of the tule is the most powerful MEDICINE of the Apache and is a part of various rites. Tule pollen was sprinkled on crops to aid their growth, used to heal illness and cure wounds, and painted on moccasins to help travelers find their way. In the Jicarilla Apache CREATION ACCOUNT, when BLACK HACTCIN created the first man, he began by dusting the outline of a human body with pollen.

PORCUPINE   Covered with a protective coat of slender, sharp, hollow quills, the porcupine escapes its enemies by raising its bristles threateningly. Native Americans valued porcupine quills for quillworking, a process in which dyed quills were used to decorate a wide variety of items—moccasins, knife sheaths, tobacco bags, buffalo robes, and ceremonial clothing. Legends often describe quillworking as the sacred gift of a culture hero or heroine such as Anog Ite, the DOUBLE-FACED WOMAN.

Porcupine appears in various tales as the companion of COYOTE or BEAVER. In Plains Indian tales, Coyote frequently went buffalo hunting with Porcupine and tricked him out of his share of the meat. In Micmac mythology, Porcupine controlled cold weather.

POSHAYANKI *Zuni*

A CULTURE HERO and leader of the BEAST GODS. Poshayanki is considered the founder of the Zuni curing, or MEDICINE, societies, which are responsible for healing the sick and which participate in curing ceremonies. He lived in a sacred place called SHIPAPOLINA with the Beast Gods and some KACHINAS.

PRAYERSTICKS

Decorated sticks prepared ceremonially as offerings to accompany prayers to bring RAIN or restore health. Prayersticks vary in length, shape, painting, carving, and the objects that are attached to them, such as shells and FEATHERS. They are often blessed with TOBACCO smoke or sacred cornmeal or by other rites. Prayersticks are placed in

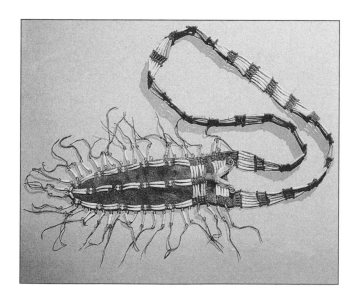

Cedar bark pouch embroidered with glass beads (acquired from Russian traders) and porcupine quills (Inuit, Athapascan) *(Werner Forman/Art Resource, NY)*

springs, in fields, under trees and shrubs, in caves, on altars, or in any other place where spirits might see them and answer the prayers breathed into them.

Prayersticks are used frequently by the Pueblo people. The ACOMA EMERGENCE AND MIGRATION account relates how after the people emerged from the UNDERWORLD, the WARRIOR TWINS MASEWA AND UYUYEWA taught them how to welcome the KACHINAS with offerings of prayersticks and food. During ceremonies that are still held, kachina impersonators plant prayersticks dedicated to the spirits they are impersonating.

The Apache and Navajo (Dineh) also use prayersticks. When the warrior twins MONSTER SLAYER AND BORN FOR WATER went to their father, the SUN, for assistance, he gave them prayersticks that would warn them of danger.

The Tohono O'odham hold annual prayerstick ceremonies at the places where they first settled. These ceremonies are held to bring rain and to keep the world in order. During the ceremony, clowns with healing powers circulate among the people (see also CLOWNS, SACRED). At the end of the ceremony, prayersticks are given to everyone.

PRIMORDIAL WATERS

In many CREATION ACCOUNTS, the Earth was originally covered with water. Frequently the primordial waters were the home of monsters, such as the female water serpent UNCEGILA and the huge, cattlelike *UNKTEHI*. Such accounts focus on the creation of solid land.

In most creation accounts involving primordial waters, diving ANIMALS or BIRDS bring up soil from underwater. KODOYANPE, the Maidu CREATOR, sent TURTLE diving for soil. NA'PI, the Blackfeet Creator, sent FOUR different animals. The first three were unsuccessful, but the fourth animal (in various versions of the tale DUCK, MUSKRAT, or Turtle) succeeded. OLD MAN COYOTE, the Crow Creator, used ducks. In the story of SKY WOMAN, the Iroquois mother of humanity, Turtle instructed the other animals to dive for soil. Only Muskrat was successful. WEE-SA-KAY-JAC, the Cree Creator, sent BEAVER, OTTER, and Muskrat diving for soil. All three drowned in the attempt, but Muskrat's body rose to the surface with mud lodged between his claws. In a similar Anishinabe account, MANABOZHO sent LOON,

Otter, and Muskrat diving. Although all three drowned, Muskrat's body floated to the surface with sand in his paws.

Not all creator figures used diving animals to retrieve soil. The Algonquian Creator, MICHABO, used a grain of sand to create an island that he placed on the waters. The island grew until it formed all the land. In a Paiute account, WOLF and COYOTE became tired of paddling around the world in a canoe. They piled dirt on top of the water until they created land. In the Mandan account, First Creator and LONE MAN created the world as they walked across the water that covered it. The Yuma creator figure Kokomaht and his TWIN brother were created at the bottom of the primordial waters. After they rose to the surface, Kokomaht created the land and many other things (see also KOKOMAHT AND BAKOTAHL). In the APACHE EMERGENCE AND MIGRATION account, before the people emerged from the UNDERWORLD, they sent animals to explore the world. The animals reported that it was covered with water.

WIND offered his help and sent four winds that drove back the water and uncovered the land.

PYUYKONHOYA AND PALUNHOYA
(Poqánghoya and Palongawhoya) *Hopi* WARRIOR TWINS, considered war deities. In keeping with the role of warrior twins, they made a journey to their father, the SUN, and slew a giant bird. SPIDER WOMAN created the twins in the First World to keep the world in order when life was put upon it. Pyuykonhoya's task was to put his hands on the new Earth and make it solid. Palunhoya's task was to send out sound so that the whole world would be an instrument of sound that could carry messages. The twins' places were at the north and south poles, where they kept the world balanced. When SÓTUKNANG, the assistant of TAIOWA, the CREATOR, wanted to destroy the Second World, he commanded the twins to leave their posts. The world spun off balance and out of control. (See also HOPI EMERGENCE AND MIGRATION.)

QANEKELAK *Bella Bella*   A killer WHALE, or Orca, that changed into a human. In the beginning, Qanekelak's upper body was human and his lower body was that of a whale, but he became totally human when he ran his hands over himself. Qanekelak was credited with creating the DOG and with naming the animals and people.

A Tlingit totem pole bears an image of a killer whale. *(© 2000 Ray Bial)*

RABBIT Rabbit commonly figures as a TRICK-STER in Native American tales, such as the Ojibway MIS-SAPOS, who changed his form in order to trick people and animals, and TAVWOTS, who in Paiute and Ute tales had many adventures on a journey to fight the SUN. For the Cherokee, Rabbit (Tsistu) was a trickster and deceiver who was often beaten at his own game by his intended victims. In a Cherokee tale reminiscent of a familiar Aesop fable, Rabbit and Terrapin, or TURTLE, had a race in which the clever Terrapin outwitted Rabbit and won. Terrapin had his family members and friends—all of whom looked exactly like Terrapin—hide along the path of the race and run out just before Rabbit reached them. As the exhausted Rabbit topped the last ridge, he saw Terrapin cross the finish line. Rabbit never guessed how he had been tricked.

Among the Algonquian-speaking people of the Northeast, Mahtigwess the Rabbit was considered a powerful trickster with magical powers. Another Algonquian tradition held that WABOSE, the third brother of the CULTURE HERO MANABOZHO, was changed into a rabbit.

RACCOON In many tales the clever Raccoon appears as a TRICKSTER. Abenaki stories about Raccoon (AZEBAN) portray him as trying to outwit other beings in order to obtain food. In a tale that explains a raccoon's distinctive mask, Raccoon ate all his grandmother's stored acorns, so she struck him with a fire poker, burning the markings onto his face.

RAIN Vital to survival, especially for people living in the desert Southwest, rain plays an important role in both religion and mythology. Beings with the power of bringing rain are frequent characters in Native American folklore. One such group of beings,

the CLOUD PEOPLE (*shiwanna*) were thought to be the bringers of rain to the Keres-speaking Pueblo people and the Zuni. After death, members of the Zuni rain priesthoods were thought to become UWANNAMI, cloud spirits represented by clouds, fog, dew, and rainstorms. In the Navajo (Dineh) tradition, THUNDER SPIRITS were responsible for the life-giving rain. In the Pawnee tradition, the FOUR BEINGS OF THE NORTH sent rain to assure the growth of crops. For the Inuit, a powerful spirit named SILA controlled the weather and brought rain and storms.

A common theme in tales of WARRIOR TWINS, such as AHAYUTA AND MATSILEMA (Zuni) and MASEWA AND UYUYEWA (Keres), is the twins' ability to make rain. The withdrawal of rain and the subsequent drought and suffering are also common themes. One of the monsters slain by Ahayuta and Matsilema was CLOUD SWALLOWER, a giant that devoured the thunderheads that brought rain and thus caused a great drought. In an Acoma Pueblo tale, HORNED WATER SERPENT—the spirit of rain and fertility—abruptly left the people and would not return.

RAINBOW Because a rainbow appears to connect the Earth and the SKY, it has frequently been viewed as a bridge between the two. For the Navajo (Dineh), the rainbow was a bridge between the human world and the world of the DIYIN DINEH (Holy People).

According to the Wyandot, a rainbow carried the world's first animals from the Earth to the sky when they became afraid that Winter would take over the world. Unfortunately, the animals burned the bridge to prevent Winter from following them, so they were unable to return when Summer defeated Winter once again. The rainbow's ashes became the MILKY WAY.

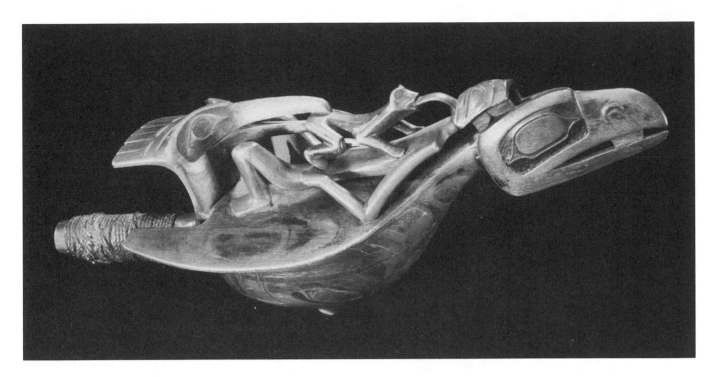

This Tlingit wooden rattle is carved in the shape of a raven. (© Christie's Images/CORBIS)

In the Keres CREATION ACCOUNT, a rainbow formed the gateway through which the people emerged from SHIPAP into this world.

RAIN PRIESTS　See UWANNAMI.

RAVEN　Similar in appearance and habits to the common CROW, the raven is far larger than its relative, measuring 21–27 inches. Ravens are known for their aerial acrobatics. They soar high, tumble and roll in the skies, and even chase EAGLES and HAWKS. Raven is an important figure in the mythology of many Native American cultures. He assumes a variety of roles: a TRICKSTER who cannot be trusted, a CULTURE HERO who brings LIGHT or FIRE to humans, and a CREATOR.

In a Northwest Coast story in which Raven is both a trickster and a culture hero, the world was all in darkness except for one village that had LIGHT. In order to win the chief's daughter as his wife, Raven was determined to steal the light for his people. When he managed to reach the village of light, he used great trickery to steal the caskets that contained the MOON, STARS, and SUN. When Raven returned to his people and opened the casket containing the

Moon and stars, the people were amazed and delighted, and the chief gave Raven his favorite daughter as a wife. Raven asked the chief what he had to offer for an even better light. The chief responded that he would give his second daughter. Raven then opened the casket of the Sun. From that day on, the Sun, Moon, and stars shone in the sky, and Raven lived happily with his two wives. A legend told by an Arctic people, the Aleut, credits Great Raven with creating light by throwing pieces of mica into the sky.

In Dakota myth, Raven was one of the spirit helpers of TAKUSKANSKAN, the being that personified motion and gave life to things. A Northwest Coast tribe, the Haida, call Raven Nankilslas (He Whose Voice Is Obeyed). The Haida relate stories about Raven's travels as he went about the world changing it into its present form, teaching animals, and naming plants. Others saw Raven as the primary Creator. The Inupiaq, an Arctic tribe, told how Raven created their homeland by harpooning a great WHALE, which floated to the ocean's surface and became land.

In a Northwest Coast CREATION ACCOUNT, Raven was walking along the beach feeling lonely because the world was so empty. Suddenly a large clam emerged from the sandy beach. The clam slowly opened, giving off a bubbling noise. Tiny people emerged from the shell and greeted Raven. Delighted with these new creatures, Raven sang a song of greeting to the first people. (See also HUMANS, ORIGIN OF.)

READY-TO-GIVE *Pawnee* The North WIND, leader of the FOUR BEINGS OF THE NORTH. Ready-to-Give sent game to hunters.

ROADRUNNER Commonly associated with the desert landscape, the roadrunner is an unusual bird. Large in size—measuring 20–24 inches—the roadrunner has a long neck and tail, a long, pointed bill, and a bushy crest on its head. It escapes from predators and chases its own prey of lizards, snakes, and birds by running swiftly on its long legs.

An Apache myth relates how Roadrunner became the leader of the birds. When the birds got together to discuss the need for a leader to speak for them, they considered several possibilities. They first selected Oriole because of his beautiful feathers, but they soon rejected him because he did not speak much. They rejected Mockingbird because he was too talkative and tended to mock things. Next, they considered BLUE JAY but decided he not only talked too much, he was a braggart as well. Finally, they chose Roadrunner, who not only spoke well but could use his speed to get to meetings quickly.

ROLLING HEAD A special category of CANNIBAL or MONSTER tales, involving bodiless heads that roll around the land pursuing people. In some tales, the rolling head was originally a person who developed a taste for blood and human flesh by licking a wound. The person ended up consuming his or her entire body until only the head was left. In other tales, the rolling head was the victim of cannibalism, often by family members; the victim's head then pursued those who had wronged him or her.

S

SABLE The sable, or marten, is a tree-climbing member of the weasel family, a swift and fierce hunter of the northern forests. Sable (Nimakwsowes) was the traveling companion of the Algonquian CULTURE HERO GLUSKAP, who taught Sable to hunt and gave him special powers.

SACRED CLOWNS See CLOWNS, SACRED.

SACRED MOUNTAINS See MOUNTAINS, SACRED.

SACRED PIPE A religious object with an ancient history in the beliefs, ceremonies, and rituals of tribes throughout North America. The most sacred of such pipes are those that were given to an entire tribe or nation, such as the Sacred Pipe of the Lakota, which was the gift of WHITE BUFFALO CALF WOMAN. The origins of sacred pipes include visions and gifts from holy beings, various animals, or feathered creatures. Generally, sacred pipes are kept by people who care for them according to traditional rituals. The pipes are rarely brought out into the open. They may be owned by individuals, families, clans, bands, or entire tribal groups. Pipes identified as being used only for specific ceremonial purposes include the SUN DANCE pipe and the peace pipe.

SAKARAKAAMCHE See AMCHITAPUKA.

SALMON *Northwest Coast* An important food fish that hatches in freshwater rivers, spends its adult life in the ocean, and returns to fresh water to spawn and die. Tribes of the Northwest Coast depended heavily on the various species of Pacific salmon.

A Haida legend reflects the important concept of respect for and gratitude toward the animals that offer themselves to humans as food. Once, when food was scarce, a woman had only a small, rotten bit of salmon left to feed her son. He ate just a small bit and threw away the rest, which angered the Salmon King. To teach the boy a lesson, the Salmon People captured him, named him Salmon Boy, and kept him in their ocean home for a year. There, the boy learned that to ensure the renewal of the salmon, all of the bones and uneaten flesh must be returned to the

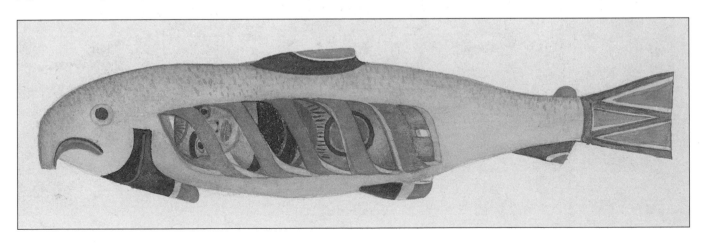

Tutchone carved wooden salmon with the figure of a human inside it, from Sitka, Alaska *(National Anthropological Archive)*

river. When Salmon Boy rejoined his people, he became a SHAMAN and spent his life healing people and teaching them to honor the salmon so that the fish would live again and return each spring.

SALT WOMAN   (Salt Mother, Old Lady Salt)

Keres, Navajo (Dineh), Zuni The goddess of salt. According to the Navajo (Dineh), Salt Woman was one of the DIYIN DINEH, or Holy People. She traveled around the world leaving deposits of salt wherever she rested.

In a Zuni legend, Salt Woman once lived on the seashore, but she became upset when people gathered salt without offering anything in return. She left the ocean and went to live in the mountains. Whenever she stopped by a pool to rest, she made it salty, which is why so many basins of water in the Southwest are bitter. At last she settled near a large lake near Zuni (ZUNI SALT LAKE), where she met and married Turquoise Man. They lived there happily until the people who had followed Salt Woman from the ocean found them and troubled her again. She told the people that she would leave them forever, and she and Turquoise Man entered a mesa by breaking through a wall of sandstone. The arched portal through which they passed can still be seen today. In one version of this tale, Salt Woman gave salt to the priests who had followed her and instructed them in the proper way to gather salt.

SANDPAINTING   A ceremonial rite practiced by a variety of cultures, including the Apache, Arapaho, Cheyenne, Navajo (Dineh), and Pueblo peoples. Sandpainting, more correctly called dry painting, involves the creation of an image by sprinkling dry materials—crushed minerals, corn POLLEN, ground flower petals and leaves—onto the ground or the floor of a hogan or KIVA. Perhaps the best-known

A Navajo (Dineh) sandpainting serves as a temporary altar created for a ceremonial. *(© Charles Herbert/Photo Researchers)*

sandpaintings are those created for Navajo (Dineh) healing ceremonials. Various traditional designs are associated with the mythology of each ceremonial. (See MOTHER EARTH AND FATHER SKY for a description of a sandpainting done for the SHOOTINGWAY ceremonial.) Among the Pueblo peoples, sandpaintings are created for private kiva rituals. The Arapaho and Cheyenne create these paintings during SUN DANCE ceremonies.

In the APACHE EMERGENCE AND MIGRATION account, the HACTCIN directed the people to create a sandpainting representing a world bordered by FOUR mountains, which then grew, enabling the people to climb from the pre-emergence place into the world above.

SEASONS, ORIGIN OF The origin of the seasons is the subject of myths of various groups. Some accounts credit a CREATOR figure with establishing the seasons deliberately. Assiniboine accounts describe how IKTOMI, the SPIDER, created the seasons by stealing summer from a man who kept it in a bag and determined the length of the seasons. In the Ute tradition, the CULTURE HERO WOLF created the seasons. In a Tohono O'odham legend, the CREATOR made the seasons when, as a warning to the rebellious MONTEZUMA, he moved the Sun farther away from the Earth. According to a Lakota legend, SKAN, the SKY, ordered the FOUR sons of TATE, the WIND, to establish the cardinal DIRECTIONS. He then assigned a season to each direction and gave each brother control over the season that corresponded to his direction.

A Tsimshian legend relates the struggle among the Four Great Winds, the chiefs of the cardinal directions. The fight was resolved when the Winds agreed that each of them would have the Earth for three months. North Wind would have the winter months; South Wind, the autumn; West Wind, the summer; and East Wind, the spring.

Other traditions characterize the origin of seasons as the result of theft or trickery. In a Zuni legend, COYOTE and EAGLE stole LIGHT. When Coyote accidentally released the light, Earth's source of heat left with it, creating winter. In a Crow legend, a woman who lived in the south kept winter and summer in separate bags. She would release only winter to Crow country, while to the south it was always summer. OLD MAN COYOTE—with the aid of Jackrabbit, DEER, and WOLF—stole the bag containing summer and brought it back to Crow country. The two eventually agreed that each land would have both summer and winter. In another version of this tale, Old Man Coyote stole summer from a man far to the east who kept this season in a bag. In an Algonquian legend, the culture hero GLUSKAP was responsible for the origin of the seasons. Winter put Gluskap to sleep for six months by telling him stories. When he awoke, Gluskap traveled south to the land where Summer was queen. He captured Summer and brought her to Winter's house. When Winter tried to cast his spell on Gluskap again, the warmth of Summer overcame him.

In a Lakota story about the length of the seasons, Iktomi declared that winter would last for as many months as there were hairs in his wolfskin robe. FROG objected to that length of time and said that seven (in some versions, six) months of winter would be long enough. Iktomi flew into a rage and killed him. (In another version, Frog was merely stunned when Iktomi hit him with a club.) Although he was dead, Frog held out seven of his toes, and Iktomi gave in.

SEDNA *Inuit* A powerful sea goddess who ruled over sea mammals, lesser spirits, and MONSTERS; sometimes called Sea Woman. Among different groups in Alaska, Canada, and Greenland, Sedna was also known as Nuliajuk (Nuliayuk), Kannakapfaluk, Avilayoq, Immap Ukuua (Mother of the Sea), Takanakapsaluk or Takanaluk arnaluk (The Terrible One Down Under), and Unigumisuitok (The One Who Does Not Want a Husband). She was considered to be the mother of both land and sea creatures and was therefore the provider of all life. The Inuit credited Sedna with the power to create storms, control the migration of animals, and hold back the supply of fish and game as punishment when people failed to honor the animals properly. Sedna also had responsibility for ADLIVUN, the UNDERWORLD.

Tales about Sedna's beginnings differ. In one legend, as a young girl Sedna developed an uncontrollable appetite for flesh and tried to eat her own parents. They put her in an *umiak* (an open, hide-covered boat), took her out to sea, and pushed her overboard. When Sedna clung to the side of the boat, her parents cut off her fingers, joint by joint. The pieces of her fingers fell into the ocean and were transformed into fish, seals, whales, and all other sea animals. Sedna sank into the water with them and became their keeper.

In the Netsilik Inuit version of the tale, Nuliajuk (Sedna) was an orphan bullied by the other children. One day, while the people were moving to new hunting grounds on kayaks lashed together to form rafts, the children pushed Nuliajuk overboard. When she tried to climb back into the raft, her tormentors cut off her fingers and watched as she sank into the water.

In other versions of the story, Sedna was a beautiful young woman with many suitors, all of whom she refused. In one tale, she was tricked into marriage with a stormy petrel (a seabird) in the shape of a man. He took her far from her home, mistreated her, and made her miserable. In another story, she married a DOG who had transformed himself into a man (see DOG HUSBAND). In both of these tales, Sedna's father killed her husband; father and daughter then set sail for home. In the first tale, their boat was attacked by a flock of birds attempting to avenge the death of Sedna's husband. In the second tale, a great storm arose. To appease the birds or calm the storm, Sedna's father threw her into the sea. To keep her from climbing back into the boat, he cut off her fingers. All these tales end the same way, with Sedna's fingers severed and transformed into sea creatures.

SELU (Corn) *Cherokee*

The woman associated with the origin of CORN. Selu's two sons, the THUNDER BOYS, were always hungry, so each day she set out and returned with a basket of corn. Curious about where the corn came from, the boys followed her. They saw her place the basket on the ground and shake herself until corn came from her body and filled the basket. When her sons told Selu that they knew her secret, she told them that now she would have to die. She instructed them to drag her body around a field, which would cause corn to grow there. Then she died. The boys carried out her instructions, and wherever her blood fell, corn grew.

In a different version of the myth, Selu told her sons to kill and dismember her, then scatter the pieces of her body in the field. In another version, Selu discovered that her sons planned to kill her because they thought she was a witch. Selu instructed the boys to clear a large plot and, after they killed her, to drag her body around it seven times. They killed her and cut off her head, but instead of clearing one large plot, they cleared seven small ones and dragged her body around each plot twice. This explains why corn grows only in certain areas.

See also FIRST MOTHER; KANATI.

SHAMAN

A healer or MEDICINE person; someone with special abilities to communicate with the spirit world. Shamans directly experience spirits from different sources—ANIMALS, PLANTS, living persons, and ghosts of the dead; their experience enables them to gain sacred knowledge. They function as go-betweens for humans and supernatural forces. Through knowledge gained in visions, trances, and dreams, shamans are able to cure illness, see across time and space, predict the future, and control the weather.

The term *shaman*, which originated with the Tungus of Siberia, came to refer to healers of Native American cultures. (© *American Historical Society*)

In some cultures, shamans exercised considerable powers. Inuit shamans were believed to have the power to shake the ground, walk on clouds, make themselves invisible, fly, and assume the guise of animals. Shamans often have spirit helpers, such as *INUA* and *TUPILAK*, and use ritual objects, such as rattles, drums, wands, and MASKS. In most cultures, shamans had to learn a variety of ceremonies in order to carry out their functions. Powerful animal figures, such as BEAR, were sometimes seen as shamans. In a Northwest Coast tale, SALMON Boy became a shaman. Notable historical Native American shamans include HIAWATHA (Iroquois) and WOVOKA (Paiute).

SHIPAP *Keres* The FOUR underground chambers where the people lived before their emergence into the present world; also the name of the place of emergence. The traditional account of the origins of the Keres-speaking people is detailed in the ACOMA EMERGENCE AND MIGRATION account. MOUNTAIN LION guarded Shipap (called SHIPAPOLINA by the people of Cóchiti Pueblo, another Keresan pueblo).

See also SIPAPU; SIPOFENE.

SHIPAPOLINA *Zuni* A sacred place that was the home of the CULTURE HERO POSHAYANKI, the leader of the BEAST GODS. The Beast Gods—animal spirits or deities associated with the six directions—lived in Shipapolina with Poshayanki, his followers, and some KACHINAS.

SHIP ROCK A monolith in northwestern New Mexico that is the landmark of the traditional Navajo (Dineh) homeland. The Navajo (Dineh) call it *tse bit'a'i*, "rock with wings." In legend, a group of Navajo (Dineh) gathered on top of this rock to escape from an enemy's pursuit. The rock rose into the air and sailed across the sky, carrying its passengers to safety. Ship Rock was the home of Rock Monster Eagle, one of the MONSTERS killed by the WARRIOR TWIN heroes, MONSTER SLAYER AND BORN FOR WATER (see also MONSTERWAY).

SHIWANNA See CLOUD PEOPLE; KACHINA.

SHOOTINGWAY *Navajo (Dineh)* A ceremonial curing complex, or group of ceremonies (called chants, sings, or ways) conducted to heal illness and restore harmony (*hózhó*) in the universe (see NAVAJO [DINEH] CEREMONIALS). Shootingway is included in the HOLYWAY classification of ceremonials, which are used to restore health by attracting good.

The related traditional account centers on twin brothers called Holy Man and Holy Boy, whose travels and adventures parallel those of the WARRIOR TWIN sons of CHANGING WOMAN, MONSTER SLAYER AND BORN FOR WATER. Through their experiences, the twins gained powers and increased their knowledge of the world. They had many adventures, during which they got into difficulties and had to be rescued by the *DIYIN DINEH* (Holy People). Each time, they gained more knowledge of the rituals of Shootingway.

SILA (Air Spirit) *Inuit* The unseen, powerful spirit found throughout the universe; called Narssuk in some areas. Opinions of his powers vary. In some regions, Sila was a major deity with the power to give life and heal the sick. The Koniag viewed Sila as the highest power, who created the Earth and the SKY,

Ship Rock, New Mexico, marks the traditional homeland of the Navajo (Dineh). *(© Phil Degginger/ Animals Animals/Earth Scenes)*

caused earthquakes, and ruled over air and light. To the Chugach, Sila was an omnipresent power that controlled the weather and air. For the Copper Inuit, the lower regions of the sky were Sila's realm. Sila communicated with humans through the weather and the forces of nature feared by people—storm, snow, RAIN, and stormy seas. At any moment, he could raise a storm and make hunting impossible. When pleased with people, Sila sent no message; the Sun shone and the sea was calm.

SIPAPU (Shipapu) *Hopi* The place where the Hopi people emerged into the present world. Traditionally, Sipapu is located at the bottom of the Grand Canyon where the Colorado and Little Colorado Rivers meet. Sipapu is represented in KIVAS (ceremonial chambers) by a covered hole in the floor.

See also HOPI EMERGENCE AND MIGRATION; SHIPAP; SIPOFENE.

SIPOFENE *Tewa* The dark UNDERWORLD where the Tewa lived before their emergence into the present world. Humans, supernatural beings, and animals all lived together in Sipofene, where death did not exist. The Winter Mother and Summer Mother sent a man to explore the world above. He returned to tell the people that they could go there to live, but first he sent out six pairs of brothers to explore the world in all directions. When the people left Sipofene, they traveled southward, stopping 12 times to establish villages. When an epidemic struck the last village and forced the people to leave, they divided into six groups that went off and established the six Tewa villages that exist today.

See also SHIPAP; SIPAPU.

SKAN *Lakota* The SKY, an all-powerful spirit. In one legend, his daughter, WOHPE, gave the SACRED PIPE to the Lakota people. Skan created TATE, the WIND, as his companion. He also meted out punishment, as when he transformed the beautiful Ite into Anog Ite, DOUBLE-FACED WOMAN.

SKINWALKER *Navajo (Dineh)* A person who has turned away from the harmony (*hózhó*) of the Navajo (Dineh) Way and assumed the powers of witchcraft. Skinwalkers (*yenaldlooshi*) wear COYOTE

skins and travel at night. They are believed to be CANNIBALS and shape-shifters, people who can transform themselves.

SKY In most CREATION ACCOUNTS, Earth and sky are the first things created. The sky is often personified in Native American mythology, sometimes as a CREATOR (see MOTHER EARTH AND FATHER SKY) or a powerful spirit (see SKAN). Sky-dwelling creator figures appear in the accounts of many cultures. Among these figures are ABOVE-OLD-MAN (Wiyot), AKBAATATDIA (Crow), EARTHMAKER (Ho-Chunk, Tohono O'odham), ES-TE FAS-TA (Seminole), KODOYANPE (Maidu), KUMUSH (Modoc), and UTSITI (Keres).

In many traditions, the sky is the home of powerful sky spirits. BIRDS were seen as intermediaries between humans and the sky spirits. They were believed to be messengers that could carry prayers to the gods and return with the gods' blessings and guidance. For this reason, FEATHERS were viewed as a bridge between people and the sky spirit world and were used as offerings and on PRAYERSTICKS. According to Cherokee tradition, the sky spirits—represented by Great Hawk (TLANUWA)—were often in conflict with evil underground spirits—represented by Great Serpent (UKTENA).

In the Iroquois tradition, SKY WOMAN, the mother of humanity, fell from the sky world. To make a place for her to stand, the water animals created land.

SKY COYOTE *Chumash* The name the Chumash gave to POLARIS, the North Star. Sky Coyote was a powerful sky spirit who gambled with other sky spirits to determine the fate of life on Earth. His chief opponent was the SUN, who controlled the seasons and brought life to the world, but who could also bring death. When Sky Coyote won, he took all the food in the Sun's pantry—deer, geese, acorns, and other wild foods—and let the goods fall onto the Earth for the benefit of humans. The coming year would then be a good one, with plentiful rain and abundant food. When the Sun won, he collected human lives as his payment.

SKY WOMAN (Woman Who Fell from The Sky, Aataentsic, Ataensie, Eagentci) *Iroquois* The mother of humanity. Sky Woman was the pregnant wife of the Sky Chief. The many different versions of the Iroquois CREATION ACCOUNT provide various explanations of how she fell from the sky world. In one story, she fell while she was chasing a BEAR to obtain MEDICINE for her husband. In another account, her husband pushed her out of the sky world. Most versions involve a sacred tree with enormous roots that spread out from the floor of sky world. In one account, Sky Woman dreamed that the great sky tree must be uprooted, and her husband uprooted it for her. In a different version, she herself felled the tree. When Sky Woman looked through the hole left by the tree's roots, she slipped and fell. To stop herself, she clutched a tree branch but only managed to pull off a handful of seeds. In another version of the account, Sky Woman wanted bark from the tree's roots for medicine. Her husband, knowing that the tree should not be injured, dug a hole among the roots. He accidentally broke all the way through the floor of sky world, and Sky Woman fell through the opening, clutching at the tree's roots.

At that time there was no land, only the PRIMORDIAL WATERS covering the Earth. When the animals and birds of the waters saw Sky Woman falling, they knew they must help her. A flock of geese flew up to catch Sky Woman and bring her safely down. TURTLE told the other animals to bring up soil from the bottom of the water and put it on his back in order to create a place for Sky Woman to stand. Animal after animal dived and failed, until at last MUSKRAT emerged with soil in his paws. He placed the soil on Turtle's back, and it spread until it created an island. As a result, some tribes' name for Earth is Turtle Island. Carried by the geese, Sky Woman landed softly on the new island. She dropped the seeds from the sky tree onto the ground (or planted the roots she had clutched), where they grew into the first plants. Sky Woman later gave birth to a daughter, who became the mother of the TWIN sons of the West Wind, IOSKEHA AND TAWISCARA.

See also HUMANS, ORIGIN OF.

SLEEPING UTE MOUNTAIN *Ute* According to legend, Sleeping Ute Mountain in southwestern Colorado was once a great warrior god who came to help people fight against evil beings. As they fought, their feet pushed against the land, creating the mountains and valleys that characterize this region. Badly hurt in the battle, the warrior god lay down and fell into a deep sleep; he would awaken when he was needed again. The changing colors on the mountain—light green in spring, darker green in summer, red and yellow in autumn, and white in winter—were the colors of the blankets the sleeping warrior wore in each season. The RAIN from clouds on the mountain peak was a sign that the warrior god was pleased with his people.

SNAKE The snake is a potent symbol in Native American cultures across the continent. It is linked with healing, fertility, RAIN, and the knowledge of secret things. Snakes are often associated with flashes of lightning and feared for their speed and power. Through the shedding of their skins, snakes also symbolize renewal and rebirth.

For the Hopi, snakes have traditionally served as messengers to the UNDERWORLD and as guardians of spirits. In a Hopi ceremony to bring rain, members of the Snake and Antelope Societies dance with snakes, then place them in one large pile. Runners snatch as many snakes as they can from the pile, carry them off in the FOUR cardinal DIRECTIONS, and release them

Among the symbols painted on a rock in New Mexico is the figure of a snake. (© *Kim Newton/Woodfin Camp*)

in the desert so that the snakes can crawl down to the underworld and intercede with the rain gods. TIYO, the founder of the Snake Clan, taught the Snake DANCE to the Hopi. The Hopi recognize two additional directions, zenith (above) and nadir (below), and there is a guardian snake for each of the six directions.

During the Hopi migrations (see HOPI EMERGENCE AND MIGRATION), the people were protected on their journey through the South by Pálulukang, the Snake of the South. A ritual honoring the snake is still performed on First Mesa during the Pámuya ceremony. A giant effigy MOUND in the shape of a snake was constructed near Chillicothe, Ohio, during the time of the Adena MOUND BUILDERS (1000 B.C.–A.D. 200). Called Great Serpent Mound, it is the figure of an enormous snake with a coiled tail wriggling toward the north with its mouth open, trying to swallow a huge egg. The effigy extends for an amazing 1,348 feet. Some Hopi believe that their ancestors created this mound during their migration. The Snake Society interprets the "egg" as a hill that represents a village the snake is protecting.

In the Navajo (Dineh) CREATION ACCOUNT, there were four guardian snakes of the four cardinal directions, each of which was the COLOR of its direction. Snake People figure in the traditional accounts associated with some NAVAJO (DINEH) CEREMONIALS. BEAUTYWAY follows the adventures of a young woman who was tricked into marrying an elderly man named Snake. BIG STARWAY involves a family whose daughter married the son of Big Snake.

Snakes appear in many tales in which they eat people, make people ill, or turn into people. Among tribes of the Southeast, UKTENA, Great Serpent, figures in many tales in which he preys on humans and battles with TLANUWA, Great Hawk.

SÓTUKNANG *Hopi* The assistant of the Hopi CREATOR, TAIOWA. In the HOPI EMERGENCE AND MIGRATION account, Taiowa created Sótuknang to be the first power, the representation of things that are finite, or limited. Sótuknang was called the Nephew of the Creator. Under Taiowa's direction, Sótuknang first created nine universes, laying them out in their proper order—one for the Creator, one for himself, and seven for the life to come. He then created the water, land, and forces of air. When Sótuknang was done, Taiowa instructed him to create life and its movement to complete the four parts of his universal plan. Sótuknang then created SPIDER WOMAN to continue the process of creation. She made all the living things.

Because of human nature, Sótuknang was forced to become a destroyer as well as a creator. When the people who lived in the First World that Sótuknang created became warlike, he destroyed the world, saving just the people who still lived by the laws of the Creator. When the people of the Second World and then of the Third World also became corrupt, Sótuknang destroyed each world, again saving a few chosen people.

SPIDER Any of the many species of eight-legged arachnids, known for the intricate webs most members of the species weave. Because of this skill, spiders are traditionally linked to the skill of weaving. The spider's web-weaving ability gave it a prominent place in Native American mythology. In the form of SPIDER MAN or SPIDER WOMAN, a spider is a common and important character in Native American mythology, both as a helper and as a TRICKSTER, such as the Assiniboine and Lakota figure IKTOMI.

In a Cherokee tale, a water spider was the bringer of FIRE to the people. The Thunder Spirits sent lightning and created a fire in a hollow sycamore tree that grew on an island. The animals knew that the fire was there because they could see the smoke, but the water prevented them from reaching it. All the animals that could swim or fly tried to reach the fire, but they could not bring it back without being burned. Finally the water spider was given a chance. She wove a basket that she fastened onto her back. Then she spun a thread so that she could reach the fire. When she got to the island, she placed a burning coal in her basket and brought it safely back to the people. In another version of the tale, Grandmother Spider (Spider Woman) stole the fire.

SPIDER MAN A TRICKSTER who figures in many tales. The Lakota Spider Man, IKTOMI, could make himself invisible and often disguised himself as an old man. In an Assiniboine tale about the origin of SEASONS, Iktomi used animal helpers to steal summer from a man who kept this season in a bag. In a Lakota story about the seasons, Iktomi declared that winter would last for as many months as there were hairs in his wolfskin robe. FROG protested that no animal could live through that long a winter; seven (in another version, six) months was long enough. Iktomi flew into a rage and killed him (or, in one version, stunned him with a club). The dead Frog held out seven of his toes, and Iktomi gave in.

To the Assiniboine, who like the Lakota were members of the Siouan language family, Iktomi was a CREATOR figure as well as a trickster. In several versions of the Assiniboine CREATION ACCOUNT, Iktomi used mud retrieved from under the water by MUSKRAT to create the land.

In Navajo (Dineh) tradition, Spider Man showed First Man how to build a loom, and SPIDER WOMAN taught First Woman how to weave. (See also FIRST MAN AND FIRST WOMAN.)

SPIDER ROCK

An 800-foot-high sandstone spire in Arizona's CANYON DE CHELLY. According to Navajo (Dineh) tradition, the taller of the two needles that make up Spider Rock is the home of SPIDER WOMAN. The shorter needle is the home of TALKING GOD.

SPIDER WOMAN

(Spider Old Woman, Grandmother Spider) A powerful figure in many Native American tales. While generally appearing as a helper, she could also be dangerous. In Navajo (Dineh) tradition, Spider Woman taught FIRST WOMAN how to weave. Grandmother Spider helped AHAYUTA AND MATSILEMA, the Zuni WARRIOR TWINS, destroy the MONSTER CLOUD SWALLOWER. In the ACOMA EMERGENCE AND MIGRATION account, Spider Woman gave IATIKU and her sisters seeds to sow, which grew into the first PLANTS in the new world.

Grandmother Spider acts as a CULTURE HERO in Cherokee and Choctaw legends, bringing them FIRE and teaching them the art of making pottery. When the people emerged from the ground, the world was dark. There was no SUN, MOON, STARS, or fire. The people held a meeting at which someone said that the people to the east had fire. It was decided that the animal and bird people would try to steal it. After many different animals and birds were burned in their attempts, Grandmother Spider was allowed to try. She made a small clay bowl with a lid and spun a web to carry it in. Because she was so small, no one noticed her. She was able to take a small piece of fire and hide it in her bowl. When she reached home, the animals and birds—recalling the injuries fire could cause—decided that fire was not for them. The humans, however, said that they would take it. Grandmother Spider taught them how to use fire and keep it safe. (In some versions of this tale, it was the Sun that Grandmother Spider stole.)

Spider Woman sometimes assumed the role of a CREATOR figure. In the HOPI EMERGENCE AND MIGRATION account, Spider Woman created all living things, including humans.

SPRUCE

The spruce—members of the PINE family—are cone-producing evergreen trees with sharp, pointed needles. Various kinds of wildlife, including deer and rabbits, browse on spruce foliage in winter. The Hopi consider the spruce tree holy. According to Hopi tradition, Salavi, the ancient chief of the Badger Clan and a great holy man, transformed himself into a spruce tree when he died. The Badger Clan, which is the custodian of the sacred spruce, is one of the four most important Hopi clans. All Hopi KACHINAS wear branches and twigs of spruce and make a yearly pilgrimage to collect spruce.

The gum of the spruce tree figures in the Akimel O'odham CREATION ACCOUNT. When the Creator, EARTHMAKER, decided to destroy the people he had made with a FLOOD, a SHAMAN named Suha and his wife survived by sealing themselves inside a hollow ball made of spruce gum. This ark floated on the floodwaters until they receded.

STARS

The origin of the stars, as well as of other celestial bodies, is the subject of myths throughout North America. In the Navajo (Dineh) tradition, BLACK GOD was the CREATOR of the stars and CONSTELLATIONS. BLUE FEATHER, a Cóchiti Pueblo girl, became responsible for the appearance of the starry sky when she accidentally released the stars from a bag she had been entrusted with. The Pawnee Creator, TIRAWAHAT, created the SUN, MOON, stars, heavens, and Earth. A great deal of Pawnee mythology relates to star power. The Pawnee created a buckskin star chart that showed various constellations, such as Corona Borealis and Ursa Major, as well as

Morning Star—the morning phase of the planet Venus—is represented as a cross in this Southern Arapaho painted sheet worn as a robe during the Ghost Dance. *(Neg. No. 335998. Photo: Logon, courtesy Department of Library Services, American Museum of Natural History)*

the MILKY WAY. According to tradition, the star chart brought star power to the people when it was displayed and used during ceremonials.

Stars and planets—which were not distinguished from stars—are frequently personified in Native American mythology. For the Pawnee, the planet Venus was the powerful EVENING STAR, who with her husband MORNING STAR (the planet Mars) became the ancestors of the human race.

SUKU See BEAR.

SUN Because the Sun is crucial to life on Earth, it plays an important role in Native American mythology. The Sun is commonly depicted as the CREATOR of the world and of living things. For the Hopi, the orderly movement of the Sun each day from his eastern KIVA to his western kiva preserves the order of the world.

Many CREATION ACCOUNTS involve the creation of the Sun and other celestial bodies by a creator figure. AWONAWILONA, the Zuni Creator, first created mist and then transformed himself into the Sun, causing the mist to condense and fall as RAIN. The Maidu Creator, KODOYANPE, called the Sun and MOON into being. TIRAWAHAT, the Skidi Pawnee Creator, made

the Sun, Moon, STARS, heavens, and Earth. The APACHE EMERGENCE AND MIGRATION account offers several versions of the creation of the Sun and Moon.

The theft of the Sun in order to bring LIGHT to a dark world is described frequently. In a Northwest Coast tale, the world was in darkness except for one village until RAVEN stole caskets containing the Sun, Moon, and stars from that village's chief and gave them to his own people. In a Cherokee tale, various animals tried to steal the Sun but were burned when they tried to do so. Grandmother Spider (SPIDER WOMAN) made a clay bowl to hold the Sun and spun a web to enable her to carry it without being burned. (In a different version of this tale, Grandmother Spider stole fire.)

The Sun as the father of WARRIOR TWINS is a recurring theme. These tales feature the twins' journey to their father, the Sun, who tests them to determine whether they are indeed his sons. He then presents them with gifts, usually of weapons and armor. Warrior twins who were considered sons of the Sun include MAHAYUTA AND MATSILEMA (Zuni), HADENTHENI AND HANIGONGENDATHA (Seneca), KILLER-OF-ENEMIES and CHILD-OF-THE-WATER (Apache), MASEWA AND UYUYEWA (Keres), MONSTER SLAYER AND BORN FOR WATER (Navajo

[Dineh]), and PYUYKONHOYA AND PALUNHOYA (Hopi). Other sons of the Sun include AMCHITA-PUKA (Southeastern Yavapai), BEGOCHÍDÍ (Navajo [Dineh]), and ICTINIKE (Iowa, Omaha).

SUNAWAVI (Wolf) *Ute*   A CULTURE HERO responsible for bringing FIRE to humans and creating the SEASONS. COYOTE often appears as Sunawavi's brother and companion. In one tale, Sunawavi argued with Coyote over whether death should be permanent. Sunawavi believed that people should come back to life after death. Coyote, who argued for the permanence of death, won the argument. See also WOLF.

SUN DANCE *Plains*   The major ritual of the BUFFALO-hunting groups of the Plains region. Tribes that practiced the Sun Dance include the Arapaho, Arikara, Assiniboine, Blackfeet, Cheyenne, Comanche, Cree, Crow, Dakota, Gros Ventre, Hidatsa, Kiowa, Lakota, Mandan, Ojibway, Pawnee, Shoshone, and Ute. The name for the DANCE comes from the Lakota name, *Wiwanyag wachipi*, "Dance Looking at the Sun" or "Sun Gazing Dance." Other groups call the dance by different names. According to the Lakota, the Sun Dance was one of the FOUR sacred rites that WHITE BUFFALO CALF WOMAN foretold. A holy man received the rites in a vision. According to the Pawnee, the Sun Dance was given to them by a young man who learned the dance in a vision. In it, various animals presented him with special skills and sacred gifts. Among the purposes of the ceremony are to give thanks, pray for protection, pray for renewal and fertility, and fulfill vows.

Among the ritual elements of the Sun Dance were fasting, purification, and dancing before a sacred TREE or pole. For some groups, such as the Lakota, the ritual involved piercing the flesh of male dancers with skewers attached to rawhide ropes. The dancers were tethered to the central pole and danced until the skewers pulled free. The buffalo played an important role in the ceremony. A buffalo skull and other objects were a part of the ritual.

In this Teton Lakota painting, tribal members perform the Sun Dance, an important ceremony among Plains tribes. While dancing, the participants gazed steadily at the Sun and blew whistles made of eagle bone. *(Neg. No. 326847. Photo: Rota, courtesy Department of Library Services, American Museum of Natural History)*

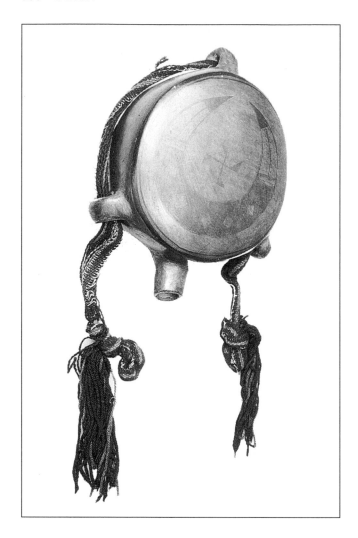

Hopi ceramic canteen with a representation of a swastika. (© E. R. Degginger/Animals Animals/Earth Sciences)

SWAN   The largest waterbird, the swan is characterized by a long, slender neck and brilliant white plumage. Swans figure in some earth-diver CREATION ACCOUNTS. In an Arapaho story, they were the third set of birds sent to bring up soil from under the water to create land, but they were unsuccessful.

SWASTIKA   An ancient symbol identified with motion, direction, and cyclical change. The form of the swastika is a Greek cross with the ends of the arms extended at right angles in the same rotary direction. One natural phenomenon that makes this shape is the rotation pattern of the BIG DIPPER, which is part of the CONSTELLATION Ursa Major, the Great Bear. Over the change of seasons, the Big Dipper rotates around POLARIS, the North Star, and maps out a swastika. This may explain why the symbol is a common traditional motif on pottery, baskets, and blankets in many cultures. The Navajo (Dineh) viewed the combination of Polaris and the Big Dipper as a constellation they called Whirling Male. The Akimel O'odham saw the swastika shape of this constellation as a record of their own history. Long ago, a powerful chief sent four of his subchiefs to journey to the cardinal DIRECTIONS and instructed them not to return until they had found people whose government was better than their own.

The migrations of the Hopi clans after their emergence into the present world formed a huge swastika (see HOPI EMERGENCE AND MIGRATION). Some clans headed south; others headed north. They then retraced their steps to the center, in order to go east and west and back again, forming a great cross with its arms pointing to the cardinal directions. As the clans turned at the ends of each of the four arms, the cross became a swastika. The leading Hopi clans turned right each time, creating a swastika with its arms rotating counterclockwise. This pattern corresponded with the movement of the Earth. The rest of the clans turned left, forming a swastika rotating clockwise. This pattern corresponded with the movement of the SUN and symbolized the clans' faithfulness to the Sun Father.

SWEET MEDICINE   *Cheyenne*   A famous legendary prophet and CULTURE HERO. According to tradition, Sweet Medicine spent FOUR years on Noaha-vose (BEAR BUTTE), where he received spiritual teachings and objects of power from MAHEO, the Above Spirit. Chief among the objects of power were the four sacred arrows of the Cheyenne that contained Maheo's teachings. When Sweet Medicine returned to his people, he instructed them in the sacred laws, social codes, and ceremonies he had received. He thus brought political unity to the Cheyenne.

In a story about Sweet Medicine's origins, he was abandoned by his mother at birth and raised by an elderly woman who found him. He grew and learned faster than ordinary children. He displayed supernatural powers early in life. He could travel long distances in an instant. When the people were starving because of the disappearance of game, Sweet Medicine taught them the sacred hoop-and-stick game and used the game to create a BUFFALO calf to feed the people. However, the people turned against Sweet Medicine when he fought with an elderly chief who whipped him and took the buffalo hide from Sweet Medicine's first kill. (Some say that Sweet Medicine killed the chief.) To avoid being killed, Sweet Medicine ran off. His ability to transform himself into an animal or a bird enabled him to escape his pursuers. Eventually he reached Noaha-vose, where he met powerful spirits who took him within the mountain. They gave him the four sacred arrows and taught him about their use. Sweet Medicine also learned the wise laws of the 44 chiefs, rules for the warrior societies, and many useful things. He returned home to teach his people and establish the way of the true Cheyenne nation. The governing body of the Cheyenne people—the Council of Forty-four Chiefs—can be traced to Sweet Medicine's teachings.

TABALDAK *Western Abenaki* The CREATOR of all living beings, including humans. Tabaldak first created people from stone. Disliking these creations, he destroyed them and made new people from wood.

TABOO Prohibition against touching, saying, eating, or doing something. (The word *taboo* comes from the Polynesian *tabu*.) Sometimes the prohibition comes from fear of harm from supernatural forces; sometimes it is meant as a protective measure. Often it is required by social or religious custom. Taboos restrict people's behavior in many areas of life: childbirth, puberty, ceremonies, hunting, religion, eating, and death. Hunters were forbidden to kill the TOTEM ANIMALS of their own clans. For some tribes, playing games and telling stories were forbidden in certain seasons. Observing taboos protected people from spirits that could harm them, cause illness, or bring bad luck. Among the Inuit, strict taboos were followed after a person's death, so that the dead person's soul would not turn into an evil being harmful to the community.

TAIOWA *Hopi* The CREATOR. According to the HOPI EMERGENCE AND MIGRATION account, once upon a time there was nothing, just an endless void in which Taiowa lived—no beginning or end, no time, and no life. Taiowa decided to create life in this emptiness. To help him carry out his plan, he created a being named SÓTUKNANG. Under Taiowa's direction, Sótuknang first created nine universes—one for the Creator, one for himself, and seven for the life to come. He then created the water, land, and forces of air. When Sótuknang was done, Taiowa instructed him to create life and its movement to complete the four parts of his universal plan. To carry out this instruction, Sótuknang created SPIDER WOMAN, who made all living things.

TAKUSKANSKAN (Changes Things) *Dakota* A being that personifies motion and lives in the Four WINDS. His spirit is in everything that moves. Takuskanskan makes things come alive. He is feared, because the spirits that help him—BUZZARD, FOX, RAVEN, and WOLF—are believed to bring disease and death.

TALKING GOD (Haashch'ééltiʼí) *Navajo (Dineh)* The YEI associated with the east, Talking God is one of the DIYIN DINEH (Holy People) who came up into this world with FIRST MAN AND FIRST WOMAN and is the leader of the *yei*. He was responsible for CORN and rare game animals. Because he was responsible for the eastern sky, he controlled the dawn. Talking God acted as a mentor to humans and other beings, guiding and directing them. He appears in the traditional accounts related to many Navajo (Dineh) ritual curing ceremonials, among them BIG STARWAY, EAGLEWAY, ENEMYWAY, FLINTWAY, NAVAJO WINDWAY, and NIGHTWAY.

TA TANKA See BUFFALO.

TATE *Lakota* The WIND, created by SKAN, the SKY, to be his companion. Tate married a beautiful woman named Ite, the daughter of FIRST MAN AND FIRST WOMAN. However, after bearing quadruplets, Ite plotted to take the place of the MOON, Hanwi, as the companion of the SUN, Wi. When Skan discovered her plot, he punished Ite by turning her into Anog Ite, the DOUBLE-FACED WOMAN, who had two faces, one beautiful and one ugly.

Skan directed Tate's four sons to establish the FOUR cardinal DIRECTIONS, at the center of which was Tate's home. After the brothers had many adventures traveling around the world, Skan assigned each of them a season associated with his direction and control over the weather for that season. Together, the four sons are known as WANI, "vigor." (See also SEASONS, ORIGIN OF.)

TATQEQ *Inuit* The MOON Spirit, who influenced the ocean's tides and currents and was thought to bring good luck to hunters. In the western part of the Arctic culture area, Tatqeq, not SEDNA, was believed to rule over game animals and control their supply. According to the Central Inuit, Tatqeq controlled fertility in women and enforced TABOOS related to childbirth. He was an object of fear to the Greenland Inuit, who believed that he observed human behavior carefully and punished people for improper behavior.

TAVWOTS *Paiute, Ute* A RABBIT that had many adventures while on a journey to fight the SUN. Angry because his back became sunburned while he was taking a nap, Tavwots set off for the Sun's home. On the way, he discovered and stole CORN and tricked both the BEAR and the tarantula. He shattered the Sun into many pieces, which started a FIRE that covered the entire world. Unable to escape, Tavwots was burned so badly that only his head was left. His eyes burst open and tears poured out, causing a great FLOOD that put out the fire.

In a Paiute legend, Tavwots was the father of the CINAUAU, two CREATOR brothers.

TAWISCARA (Taweskara, Tawiskaron) See IOSKEHA AND TAWISCARA.

THREE SISTERS *Iroquois* The three staple crops of tribes across the continent: CORN, beans, and squash. For the Iroquois, these three PLANTS were considered special gifts from SKY WOMAN, who came down to live on TURTLE Island, or Earth. They called the plants *johékoh*, "what we live on" or "those who support us." The link among the three plants is the way in which they are mutually sustaining. As the bean plant grows, it twines upward around the tall stalks of corn, which support it, and the squash plant spreads along the ground, choking out weeds and shading the soil to keep it moist.

THUNDERBIRD In many Native American cultures, the personification of thunder in the form of a giant bird with supernatural powers. Lightning flashed when Thunderbird opened and closed his eyes, and thunder rolled when he beat his wings. When the chief of a Thunderbird clan died, thunder rolled. The EAGLE and the HAWK were regarded as representatives of Thunderbird in the earthly realm. Thunderbirds often fought with other creatures, especially water serpents (see HORNED WATER SERPENT; UKTENA; UNCEGILA).

In the Yukon, Thunderbird (Tinmiukpuk) was powerful enough to carry off whales and reindeer and sometimes even humans.

For the Lakota, there were four different kinds of Thunderbird (Wakinyan): scarlet, black with a long beak, yellow with no beak, and blue with no ears or eyes. The Wakinyan traveled with the West Wind

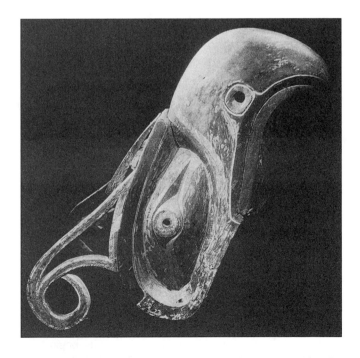

Thunderbird headdress, identified by downturned beak and feathered horns *(Werner Forman Archive/Art Resource, NY)*

and protected people from the North Wind blown by WAZIYA. People who dreamed of Wakinyan became *heyoka*, the Lakota contraries, who acted and spoke in backward ways (see also CLOWNS, SACRED).

In an Arapaho story, Thunderbird, as the symbol of summer, challenged WHITE OWL WOMAN, the winter bird, to determine whose powers were greater. The thick white clouds that White Owl Woman created overcame Thunderbird's towering black clouds, demonstrating that White Owl Woman was more powerful than Thunderbird.

THUNDER BOYS *Cherokee*

The TWIN sons of SELU and KANATI, the Hunter. Selu and Kanati had just one child until the day their son found a young boy by the riverbank. Selu and Kanati recognized the boy as their son's twin, created from the blood of animals killed by Kanati and cleaned by Selu. They named the boy Inage Utasuhi, which means "He-Who-Grew-Up-Wild" or "Wild Boy." The adventures of the Thunder Boys are related in various tales in which Inage Utasuhi is responsible for leading his brother into mischief.

In a story about the origin of CORN, the boys believed that their mother, Selu, was a witch and decided to kill her. She knew their plans and instructed them to drag her body around a cleared field. Corn grew wherever her blood fell. When Kanati discovered what the boys had done, he told them he would no longer live with them. Kanati went to the WOLF People, whom he sent to kill the boys. However, the boys killed all but two of the wolves, from which all wolves today are descended. Then the boys set out to follow their father and had many adventures. According to legend, the Thunder Boys went to live in the west. When thunder was heard in that direction, people said that the boys were talking to each other or playing ball.

The Thunder Boys are also associated with the loss and recovery of DEER. The boys let the deer and other game out of the cave where their father kept them. The deer ran off into the deep woods where no hunter could find them, and the people began to starve. They learned that only the Thunder Boys could bring back the deer. The people sent messengers to ask the boys to return, and they did. The boys then sang songs that called the deer back. Before they returned to the west, the boys taught the songs to the people so that they could always call the deer.

THUNDER SPIRITS *Navajo (Dineh)*

Powerful and dangerous spirits that were responsible for life-giving RAIN, which is created by thunder and lightning. Each Thunder Spirit was assigned to one of the FOUR cardinal DIRECTIONS.

TIH-KUYI-WUHTI (Mother of Game Animals) *Hopi*

The sister of MUYINWA, the deity that controlled the growth of PLANTS. Before every hunt, PRAYERSTICKS—ceremonially prepared sticks used as offerings—were offered to Tih-kuyi-wuhti to ensure the hunters' success.

TIRAWAHAT (Atius Tiráwa, Our Father Here Above, This Expanse) *Skidi Pawnee*

The highest and most powerful deity; the CREATOR of the SUN, MOON, STARS, heavens, and Earth. Tirawahat's agents, through which he acted, were WIND, clouds, thunder, and lightning. Tirawahat made the world in a thunderstorm. Lightning and thunder gave life to the Earth and its creatures. Tirawahat created human beings, taught them how to build a lodge and make FIRE, and gave them bows and arrows. He gave the people red, white, black, and yellow CORN and taught them how to cultivate and cook it.

TIYO (The Youth) *Hopi*

Founder of the Snake Clan and discoverer of the Hopi Snake DANCE. Tiyo set out on a journey to find the source of the Colorado River. Along the way, he was helped by SPIDER WOMAN and Great SNAKE, who revealed the river's source to him. After passing tests that were set for him, Tiyo learned many things, became part of the Snake Clan, and received Snake Maiden as his wife. Their descendants became the Hopi Snake Clan. When he returned to his people, he brought with him a MEDICINE BUNDLE and taught the Hopi the Snake Dance, an important RAIN-making ceremony. The Snake Dance is performed by initiates of the Snake and Antelope societies.

In another version of this tale, the young man set out to visit the Lower Place, or UNDERWORLD—the home of the deities—to determine whether the gods actually existed. Along the way, various beings appeared to him and warned him that the Lower Place was too far for him to reach. He was told that he could go only as far as Snake Village, where he ended up marrying a daughter of the snake chief.

TLANUWA *Cherokee*   Great mythic HAWKS. The conflicts between the SKY spirits and the evil underground spirits were symbolized by the battles between Great Hawk and Great Serpent, called UKTENA. The Tlanuwa often preyed on children, whom they fed to their young. In one tale, a woman rescued her grandchild from a Tlanuwa nest while the parent birds were absent. She threw the young hawks into the river, where Uktena began to eat them. When the Tlanuwa returned and saw what was happening, they attacked Uktena, dragged it from the water, and slashed it to pieces. Where the pieces landed, they turned into the unusual rock formations seen along the Tennessee River.

TOBACCO   With CORN, beans, and squash, one of the FOUR sacred plants. For Native Americans, both the pipe (see SACRED PIPE) and tobacco were sacred, and smoking was a holy ritual. Tobacco was used for a variety of ceremonial and religious purposes, such as to bless the harvest and to bind agreements between tribes. Tobacco also served medicinal functions and was used to treat a wide range of ailments, including toothache, earache, snakebite, wounds, and asthma. Tobacco smoke was seen as a way of communicating with the spirit world. Its rising fumes carried messages up to the Ones Above. Offerings of tobacco were made by smoking it or by placing unsmoked leaves on the ground, in water, in the fire, or in other places. Such offerings were made to request help and to give thanks. A man who killed a member of his own tribe was not permitted to join in ritual smoking with others.

The origin of tobacco, as well as knowledge about its cultivation and use, is the subject of many tales. In the Algonquian tradition, it was provided by the self-sacrificing FIRST MOTHER. The Anishinabe credited OKABEWIS with its origin. The Lakota received tobacco from WOHPE. A White Mountain Apache legend explains how COYOTE stole tobacco from the SUN and was tricked by the Apache into giving it to them.

A Cherokee myth deals with the loss and recovery of tobacco. Geese stole the tribe's only tobacco plant and caused great suffering. Many creatures tried to recover the plant from the geese, but all failed. Finally, HUMMINGBIRD used his tiny size and swiftness to get past the geese and strip off the top and seeds of the tobacco plant. (See also GOOSE.)

TORTOISE   See TURTLE.

TOTEM   An object, such as an animal or a plant, that serves as the symbol of a family or clan.

See also TOTEM ANIMAL.

TOTEM ANIMAL   An animal that is the guardian spirit of an individual or the symbol of a family. Totem animals, often acquired in the course of a VISION QUEST, accompany a person through life, endow him or her with the animal's wisdom, and

Thunderbird totem in Stanley Park, Vancouver, British Columbia, Canada (© *Terry Whittaker/Photo Researchers*)

nurture his or her talents and abilities. Because a totem animal is considered kin to a clan, there are TABOOS against killing the totem animals of one's own clan.

TOTEM POLE *Northwest Coast*

A pole or pillar carved and painted with symbols representing a family's ancestors. Totem poles frequently also contain symbols of mythical or historical incidents.

TREE OF LIFE

A symbol representing the first TREE and the powers associated with it: the bringing of RAIN, the spring renewal of life, and the fertility of women and the Earth.

TREES

Trees frequently play important roles in traditional tales. In one version of the Iroquois CREATION ACCOUNT, when the great sky tree was uprooted, SKY WOMAN—the mother of humanity—fell through the hole that was created in the clouds. In the Yavapai emergence account, a tree grew in the UNDERWORLD until it pierced the sky and created an opening to the upper world. In several tales, children trying to escape from a ferocious BEAR climbed into a tree that carried them up to safety as it grew toward the sky (see BIG DIPPER; DEVIL'S TOWER). DEGANAWIDAH, the Iroquois prophet whose efforts led to the creation of the Iroquois Confederacy, dreamed of a Tree of Peace under whose branches the warring tribes would meet to resolve their differences.

Some trees, such as the CEDAR, were considered to have special properties and were used in rituals. The Mesquakie believed that the spirits of their ancestors lived in trees and that the trees' murmuring in the wind was the ancestors' voices. For these people, wood was sacred, and so was everything wooden. Wooden bowls used in ceremonies were believed to contain a tree's spirit. These bowls were carved from burls, knotty growths on tree trunks; their rounded shape suggested pregnancy and thus made them symbols of fertility.

See also ASH; PINE; SPRUCE.

TRIBES, ORIGIN OF See HUMANS, ORIGIN OF.

TRICKSTER

A type of character known for trickery, deceit, and mischief-making. Almost every North American tribe has tales of tricksters. Tricksters can be male or female, human or animal. They are often shape-shifters with the power to transform themselves into other creatures. Sometimes they have other supernatural powers, such as the ability to regrow body parts. Trickster tales frequently involve layers of tricks, with the trickster himself often becoming the victim of a trick (sometimes his own).

The most common trickster figure is COYOTE, who appears in tales from the Southwest, Great Plains, Great Basin (almost all of Utah and Nevada; parts of Colorado, Wyoming, Idaho, Oregon, and California; small parts of Arizona, New Mexico, and Montana), Plateau (parts of Washington, Oregon, Idaho, Montana, northern California, and British Columbia), and California. In addition to his role as a trickster, Coyote also appears as a CULTURE HERO and CREATOR figure, as do some other tricksters, notably IKTOMI, the Lakota SPIDER MAN, and RAVEN in Northwest Coast and Alaskan tales.

In addition to Raven, bird tricksters include CROW (called CHULYEN by the Tanaina) and BLUE JAY (Chinook). RABBIT and HARE are common animal tricksters; examples are MAHTIGWESS (Algonquian), MISSAPOS (Ojibway), TAVWOTS (Ute), and Tsistu (Cherokee). Among other animal tricksters are MINK (Northwest Coast), RACCOON (Western Abenaki), and WOLVERINE (Micmac, Passamaquoddy).

Other tricksters include BEGOCHÍDÍ (Navajo [Dineh]), GLUSKAP (Algonquian), ICTINIKE (Iowa, Omaha), and OLD MAN (Blackfeet). LITTLE PEOPLE, tiny people who appear in the tales of many cultures, are usually depicted as tricksters.

TSUKU *Hopi*

Clowns who behave in backward or contrary ways (see CLOWNS, SACRED).

TUNGAK *(tunghak; plural tungat, tunghat) Yup'ik*

Powerful spirits that controlled the spirits of animals and therefore the supply of game animals. MASKS worn by SHAMANS often depicted *tungat* with symbols of the MOON, where they were said to live.

TUPILAK *(plural tupilek) Inuit*

Demons created by SHAMANS to eliminate their enemies. *Tupilek* were created by combining parts of dead humans and animals. Special charm songs brought them to life. *Tupilek* preyed on their victims by lying in wait

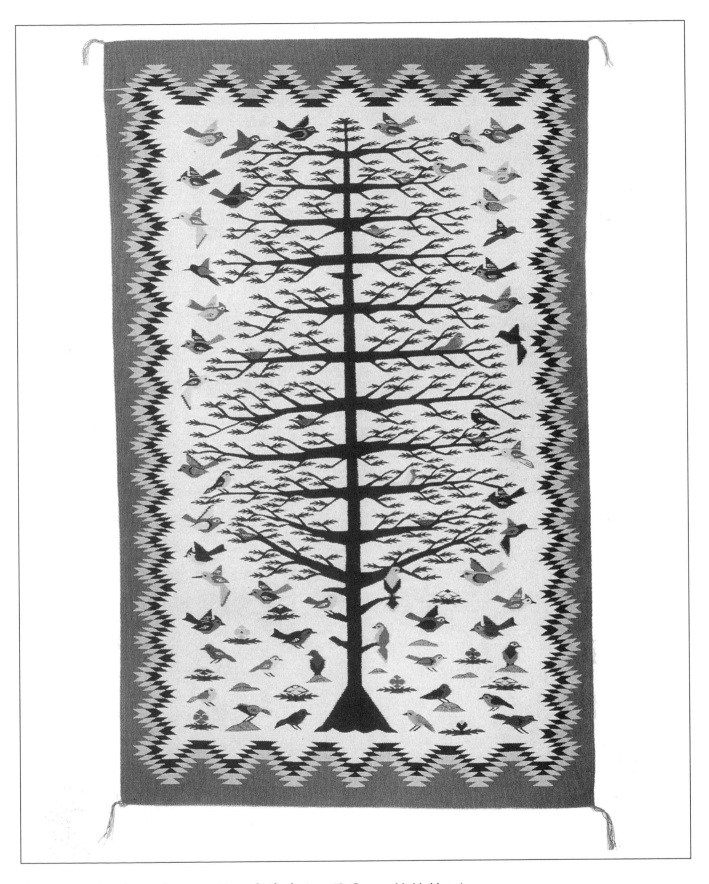

This Navajo (Dineh) rug features a Tree of Life design. *(© George H. H. Huey)*

under the ice. They could also sneak up on people by creeping along the ground, flying, or swimming.

TURKEY The wild turkey, unlike its domesticated counterpart, is able to fly and nests in trees. These large fowl run to avoid danger and feed on the ground on nuts, acorns, seeds, fruit, and insects. Among different tribes, the turkey took on roles associated with agriculture and warfare. In the Jicarilla Apache CREATION ACCOUNT, when BLACK HACTCIN created the birds, he gave Turkey responsibility for CORN and agriculture. A White Mountain Apache tale about the origin of corn describes how Turkey gave corn to human beings by shaking seeds of the four different colors of corn—black, blue, yellow, and white—from his FEATHERS. In a Cherokee myth, when Turkey gave FIRE to the world he singed off his head feathers, which explains why turkeys are bald.

Southeastern tribes related the turkey to warfare and ascribed magical properties to the bird. The war whoop of the Creek, Shawnee, and Yuchi imitated a turkey's gobble. SHAMANS used turkey feathers for both fans and capes. For the Hopi, turkey feathers symbolized the wildness and mystery of creation.

Turkeys figure in a Zuni tale that is similar to the familiar story of Cinderella. Long ago there was a poor young girl who herded other people's turkeys in exchange for scraps of food and pieces of worn-out clothing. Her clothes were dirty and ragged, and her appearance showed the results of years of neglect and poor nutrition. Yet the girl's kindness and devotion to her flock earned her the turkeys' love. Turkey Girl longed to attend an important ceremonial dance, but she knew that she could not go looking as she did. Much to her surprise, the turkeys told her that they would help her attend the dance. They turned her rags into beautiful garments and decorated her with gorgeous ornaments. Before Turkey Girl left for the dance, the turkeys made her promise to remember them and return soon. Once she began dancing, however, she forgot all about her flock. Only when the sun was setting did she recall her promise. She ran to the turkey pen as fast as she could, but it was too late. All the turkeys were gone. As she ran after them, her clothes became rags, and she turned back into the same poor Turkey Girl she had been before.

TURQUOISE WOMAN *Navajo (Dineh)* In the EAGLEWAY story cycle, CHANGING WOMAN created Turquoise Woman and WHITE SHELL WOMAN from skin she rubbed from under her breasts. *Turquoise Woman* is also an alternate name by which CHANGING WOMAN was known when her dress was blue.

TURTLE Turtle is a recurring figure in Native American mythology. Turtle is often associated with the earth-diver CREATION ACCOUNT, in which animals dived repeatedly into the PRIMORDIAL WATERS for soil to make the world. Frequently, Turtle was the successful diver. In the Iroquois creation account, mud was placed on Turtle's shell to create an island for SKY WOMAN to stand on. (The Iroquois name for Earth is Turtle Island.)

In a Maliseet-Passamaquoddy tale, Turtle was the uncle of the Algonquian CULTURE HERO GLUSKAP, who hardened Turtle's shell and gave him the gift of long life. Lakota mothers beaded turtle-shaped AMULETS to contain their daughters' umbilical cords and grant them the turtle's longevity. According to the Lakota, it is the turtle's task to lead the newborn safely into the world.

In a Cherokee tale reminiscent of a familiar Aesop fable, Terrapin (Turtle) beat RABBIT, the

A Lakota mother would make a turtle-shaped amulet in which she placed her newborn's dried umbilical cord. The amulet was intended to assure the child a long life like that of a turtle. (© E. R. Degginger/Animals Animals/Earth Sciences)

clever TRICKSTER, at his own game. The two were always boasting about their speed, so they decided to hold a race to see which of them really was faster. Terrapin had his family members and friends—all of whom looked exactly like Terrapin—hide along the path of the race and run out just before Rabbit reached them. As the exhausted Rabbit topped the last ridge, he saw Terrapin cross the finish line. Rabbit never guessed how he had been tricked.

TWINS The birth of twins is a frequent theme in Native American mythology. Many twins are WARRIOR TWINS, sons of the SUN with supernatural powers; they are destined to save the world from MONSTERS and perform many wonderful tasks. Other twins play opposing roles: One twin symbolizes goodness and is even a CREATOR figure, while the other twin is evil and tries to overcome the good that his brother does. In Iroquois tradition, IOSKEHA AND TAWISCARA were the twin sons of SKY WOMAN.

Ioskeha was the good twin, a creator and CULTURE HERO; Tawiscara was the evil twin and was associated with winter. Of the Yuma twins KOKOMAHT AND BAKOTAHL, Kokomaht was the good twin and creator; Bakotahl was evil. The Algonquian culture hero GLUSKAP had an evil twin, MALSUMSIS, who killed his mother during birth and tried to kill Gluskap on several occasions.

In other stories, twins are complementary rather than opposite and act in tandem. In Cherokee tales, the THUNDER BOYS, the twin sons of KANATI and SELU, were jointly responsible for the death of their mother. They were also associated with the loss and recovery of DEER. Twins named Holy Man and Holy Boy are central to the traditional account of the Navajo (Dineh) SHOOTINGWAY ceremonial, and "stricken twins" (one blind, the other lame) figure in the NIGHTWAY ceremonial. In a Lakota tale, twin brothers, one of whom was blind, killed UNCEGILA, a female water serpent.

U

UKTENA (Great Serpent) *Cherokee, Creek* A monstrous water serpent that preyed on children and fishers. Uktena is described variously as having horns, a magic crystal in his head, and seven bands of color around his neck or head or along his whole length; having antlers like a stag; and being able to move by land, water, and air. Anyone who approached Uktena would be dazed by the light of the crystal in his head and would run toward the serpent rather than away from it.

In one myth, Uktena was slain in a battle with the TLANUWA, the Great HAWKS. According to another legend, a Shawano SHAMAN named Aganunitsi killed the serpent by shooting an arrow through the seventh band of color on the monster. Aganunitsi told the birds to feed on the serpent's flesh for seven days; then he picked the magic crystal from Uktena's bones and returned it to the Cherokee. The power of the crystal filled the rivers with fish, made CORN grow, and healed the sick.

UNCEGILA (Uncegilah, Unkcheghila) *Lakota* A huge female water serpent with a curved horn on her head, glittering scales of mica, a sparkling crest along her back, and a row of many-colored spots on her sides. A person who looked upon Uncegila would become blind, go mad, and then die on the fourth day. The only way to kill Uncegila was to shoot a MEDICINE arrow through the seventh spot from her head. Her heart—a flashing red crystal—was behind that spot. Many warriors wanted to kill her in order to obtain that crystal, which would give great power to the person who won it. TWIN brothers, one of whom was blind, slew Uncegila with the help of a medicine woman who gave them sacred arrows.

One story about Uncegila describes how she fought with and killed a giant BEAR. His body, cov-ered with earth, created BEAR BUTTE in the Black Hills of South Dakota. Another legend says that Uncegila emerged from the PRIMORDIAL WATERS and flooded the land, causing great devastation and loss of life. This angered THUNDERBIRD, who created a great storm by flapping his wings. His lightning bolts dried up the water and killed Uncegila. Her crystal heart was shattered, but her bones can still be seen scattered throughout the BADLANDS of South Dakota.

UNDERWORLD In various Native American cultures, the place from which people emerged onto the Earth, the home of gods and spirits, or the place of the dead.

For many cultures, the underworld is where people lived before they came out into the present world. In the Choctaw and Creek CREATION ACCOUNTS, people emerged from a watery underworld through a hole in the ground. Their flesh was pale and damp, and they had to bask in the sun until their skin darkened. In the Southwest, creation accounts universally involve people rising through a sequence of worlds or underground chambers into the present world. Among emergence accounts are those of the ACOMA EMERGENCE AND MIGRATION, APACHE EMERGENCE AND MIGRATION, HOPI EMERGENCE AND MIGRATION, NAVAJO (DINEH) EMERGENCE, and ZUNI EMERGENCE AND MIGRATION.

The underworld was also a place where spirits resided. The DIYIN DINEH, the Navajo (Dineh) Holy People, lived in the underworld. For the Lakota, spirits that lived in the underworld kept the BUFFALO and other game animals there, releasing them as needed through the WIND CAVE. For the Hopi, the underworld was the home of the RAIN gods and other deities, to whom members of the Snake Society appealed for rain by releasing SNAKES in the desert. The Modoc Creator, KUMUSH, visited the underground world of the spirits and retrieved bones from which he created the Klamath, Modoc, Shasta, and other California tribes.

The underworld is, in many traditions, the place where people go after death. For the Apache, the Hopi, and the Navajo (Dineh), the place of emergence was also where people returned after they died. In the Navajo (Dineh) creation account, after giving the MEDICINE BUNDLE to CHANGING WOMAN, FIRST MAN AND FIRST WOMAN returned to the underworld to become the chiefs of death and witchcraft. When they die, the Zuni go to KOLHU/WALA-WA, the village of the KACHINAS under a lake. For the Inuit, anyone who disobeyed the sea goddess SEDNA would be sent to ADLIVUN, the underworld, after death. The underworld was not always easy to reach. For the Yup'ik, a dead soul had to undergo many tests and pass obstacles in order to reach it.

UNKTEHI *Lakota* Huge, cattlelike creatures that figured in the conflict between the above world, represented by THUNDERBIRD, and the below world. Their battles, which were said to take place in the BADLANDS, were fought in thunderstorms and lightning. The *unktehi* were created by WAKAN TANKA, who tore a rib from his right side, threw it into the ocean, and created male *unktehi*. He created female *unktehi* from a rib taken from his left side. The ribs symbolize the semicircles of the Earth's surface, and the *unktehi* represent the Earth's hemispheres. According to legend, male *unktehi* lived in the water—primarily deep water and under waterfalls—and were addressed as "grandfather." Female *unktehi* lived primarily on the Earth and were addressed as "grandmother." The *unktehi* were essentially malevolent water spirits responsible for FLOODS and drowning. They fed on the spirits of human beings and on animals that were sacrificed to them.

URETSETE (Uretsiti)   See IATIKU.

URSA MAJOR (Great Bear)   The CONSTELLATION containing the star pattern called the BIG DIPPER.

UTSITI (Uchtsiti) *Keres*   The CREATOR of the universe, also known as the Great Father and Lord of the SUN. Utsiti made the Earth by throwing a clot of his own blood into the heavens. He then planted IATIKU, the Mother of the Pueblo people, and her sisters in the soil of this newly created world. Utsiti germinated the souls of the CORN MOTHERS in the Earth, where a spirit named Thought Woman raised them.

UWANNAMI (*uwanam aasiwani*) *Zuni*   Cloud spirits associated with the six DIRECTIONS and represented by clouds, fog, dew, and rainstorms. After death, members of the RAIN priesthoods are said to join the *uwannami*.

According to a legend about the origin of the rain priesthoods, six men went to the village of the KACHINAS to gamble with them. The kachinas won and trapped the losing men. The people realized that this fate would happen to anyone who lost to the kachinas. The people sent a young man they wanted to get rid of to gamble with the kachinas. They were unaware that he had obtained the support of SPIDER WOMAN by making an offering to her. With Spider Woman's help, the young man beat the kachinas. However, the six losing men had to remain in the kachina village. These men became rain priests.

See also CLOUD PEOPLE.

UYUYEWA (Oyoyewi)   See MASEWA AND UYUYEWA.

VISION QUEST   A person's search for knowledge and spiritual power in the form of a vision from the spirit world. Although rites vary among cultures, preparation for a vision quest usually involves praying with the SACRED PIPE, fasting, and making offerings to the spirits. The quest usually takes place in a natural setting, frequently a sacred place. For example, the Crow figure BURNT FACE retreated to a mountaintop to undertake his vision quest. The traditional goal is to acquire a guardian spirit that will share its power with the seeker. The vision may be of an animal, a bird, or another being that then becomes the seeker's spirit guide. One such spirit guide in legend was the Pawnee figure MOON WOMAN, who responded to a young man's vision quest with gifts of CORN and BUFFALO.

Crow Sun effigy doll used in a ceremony to assist the pledger in obtaining a vision (*Plains Indian Museum, Buffalo Bill Historical Center, Cody, Wyoming, Werner Forman Archive/Art Resource, NY*)

Crow eagle medicine bundle. It is made of the skin of a bird that appeared in a vision. (*Museum für Völkerkunde, Werner Forman Archive/Art Resource, NY*)

WABOSE (Wabasso, Waboos) *Algonquian* The third brother of the CULTURE HERO MANABOZHO. In different tales, Wabose ran away to the north and was changed into a RABBIT or simply disappeared.

WAKAN TANKA (The Great Mystery) *Lakota* The highest power, representing all the spiritual beings and powers; the CREATOR. *Wakan* means "something mysterious" and is often translated as "holy." Wakan Tanka is represented in the creation of the world, the SUN, SKY, STARS, Earth, WIND, THUNDERBIRDS, and the journey people take after death.

WAKINYAN   See THUNDERBIRD.

WAMPUM   *Algonquian, Iroquois* Beads of polished shells in several colors that were made into strands, belts, or sashes. They were used for trade, money, decoration, and religious purposes.

A Seneca legend links HIAWATHA to the origin of wampum. Sent to make peace with the warring tribes of the Five Nations, Hiawatha had trouble remembering the points he wanted to make in his speech. He guided his canoe onto shore and plunged his paddle into the sand to stop it. As he raised the paddle, he

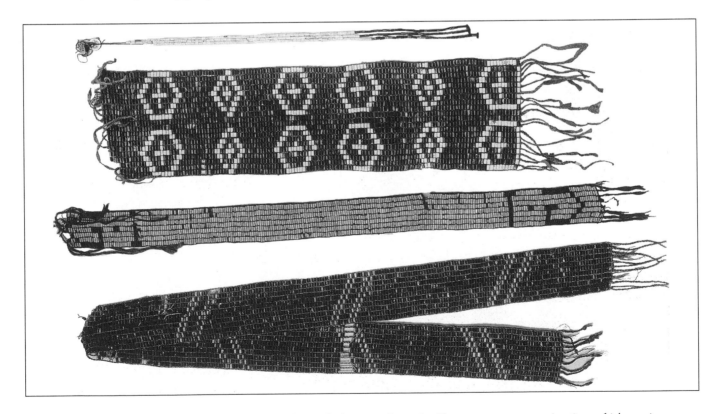

Wampum belts such as those shown were used in tribal councils to signify acceptance or rejection of ideas. A speaker ended his remarks by passing a belt across the council fire. If a listener tossed a belt aside, it meant that he rejected or doubted what the speaker said. The wampum became part of the official tribal record. *(Neg. No. 17292. Photo: J. Kirschner, courtesy Department of Library Services, American Museum of Natural History)*

saw some small shells on the blade. He noticed a white shell with a hole in it, and he absentmindedly strung it on a thong of his belt. Immediately inspiration came to him, and the thought was represented by the white shell. He added other shells to the strand, and as he ran his fingers over them, his speech fell into place. Thus wampum came to be used to convey messages and thoughts.

At the council that established peace among the Five Nations, ATOTARHO, the Chief Firekeeper, raised strings of white wampum high in prayer and thanksgiving. This act closed the first Council Fire of the newly formed Iroquois League of Five Nations, the Iroquois Confederacy.

WANI *Lakota* The Four WINDS, which have power over the weather. They are the sons of TATE, the Wind. Because of the association between wind and breath, the Wani are also associated with power over life. *Wani* means "vigor."

SKAN, the SKY, directed the Wani to establish the FOUR cardinal DIRECTIONS, at the center of which was Tate's home. After the brothers had many adventures traveling around the world, Skan assigned each of them a season associated with his direction and control over the weather for that season. (See also SEASONS, ORIGIN OF.)

WARRIOR TWINS Twin warrior brothers are a common theme in Native American mythology. Typically, they are sons of the SUN (even though one may have had a different father), to whom they make a journey. After passing tests that the Sun set for them in order to prove that they were his sons, the TWINS were given gifts of weapons and armor. They then had many adventures, often ridding the world of MONSTERS. The power to make RAIN was usually associated with warrior twins. Warrior twins of various cultures include AHAYUTA AND MATSILEMA (Zuni), HADENTHENI AND HANIGONGENDATHA (Seneca), KILLER-OF-ENEMIES and CHILD-OF-THE-WATER (Apache), MASEWA AND UYUYEWA (Keres), MONSTER SLAYER AND BORN FOR WATER (Navajo [Dineh]), and PYUYKONHOYA AND PALUNHOYA (Hopi).

WATER SPRINKLER (Tó neinilí) *Navajo (Dineh)* The YEI who controlled RAIN and water.

Water Sprinkler helped MONSTER SLAYER AND BORN FOR WATER when they made their journey to the SUN, their father. In the NIGHTWAY ceremonial, Water Sprinkler appears as a CLOWN who is dressed poorly, dances out of step, and gets in the way of other dancers.

WAZIYA *Lakota* A giant who guarded the entrance to the place where the northern lights (AURORA BOREALIS) danced. Waziya blew the cold North WIND from his mouth, was responsible for snow and ice, and constantly battled with the south winds.

WEE-SA-KAY-JAC *Cree* The CREATOR, who created the world twice and made the first human. After Wee-sa-kay-jac created the Earth, evil spirits dug into the ground and released all the water it contained. The FLOOD that resulted swept over the world until only a small island remained. Wee-sa-kay-jac hastily organized the surviving animals to build a giant canoe that could hold them all. There they lived until the waters stopped rising.

Then Wee-sa-kay-jac decided to create the Earth anew. He sent BEAVER, OTTER and MUSKRAT down to retrieve clay from the bottom of the waters. All three drowned in the attempt, but when Muskrat's body rose to the surface, Wee-sa-kay-jac found a bit of clay lodged between its claws. He brought the three diving animals back to life, then cooked the clay in a pot until it overflowed the sides and spread out to create the world. When the world was large enough, Wee-sa-kay-jac took a lump of clay from the pot and used it to create the first man.

See also CREATION ACCOUNTS; HUMANS, ORIGIN OF.

WHALE The largest of the marine mammals and, in the blue whale, the world's largest mammal. There are two families of whales—the baleen whales, which strain tiny animals called plankton or krill from seawater, and the toothed whales, which feed on fish, squid, sharks, seals, and other sea life.

Whales—especially killer whales—appear frequently in tales from the Northwest Coast, subarctic, and Arctic. In a Yup'ik tale, AKHLUT was a killer whale that went on land in the form of a wolf to

Orca—killer whale—on a totem pole in Cowichan Native Village, Duncan, British Columbia, Canada (© 1997 Inger Hogstrom/Danita Delimont, agent)

hunt. In a Bella Bella tale, the killer whale QANEKE-LAK changed into a human. In an Inuit creation story, land was formed from the body of a whale harpooned by RAVEN.

WHITE BUFFALO CALF WOMAN   *Lakota*

The woman credited with bringing the SACRED PIPE and the BUFFALO to the Lakota; also known as White Buffalo Calf Maiden, White Buffalo Cow Woman, and White Buffalo Woman. White Buffalo Calf Woman appeared to two hunters as a beautiful young woman dressed in white buckskin. At that time, there was no game and the people were starving. One hunter behaved properly toward her. The other one, however, desired her and reached out to touch her. He was immediately struck by a bolt of lightning and burned to ash. (In a different account, White Buffalo Calf Woman enveloped him in a cloud. When the cloud dissolved, all that was left of the man were his

bones and snakes that had eaten him.) The woman told the remaining hunter that she had a message from the buffalo nation. She instructed him to tell the chief to prepare a MEDICINE lodge with 24 poles for her arrival.

When White Buffalo Calf Woman arrived in the village, she presented the chief with the sacred pipe and instructed the people in its proper use in prayer. She taught the women how to make a hearth fire and how to cook CORN and meat. After teaching the people the first of seven sacred rites, the Ghost Keeping Ceremony, she left. As she walked away, she stopped and rolled over (or sat down) FOUR times. Each time she stopped, she turned into a buffalo of a different color: black, brown, red, and white. As a white buffalo calf, she galloped away. After White Buffalo Calf Woman vanished, great herds of buffalo appeared and gave themselves to the people.

WHITE CORN MAIDEN   See CORN MOTHERS.

WHITE HACTCIN   *Jicarilla Apache*   One of the HACTCIN, supernatural beings that created the Earth and the SKY. In one version of the APACHE EMERGENCE AND MIGRATION account, White Hactcin gave Holy Boy the SUN. In a tale about the adventures of the hero CHILD-OF-THE-WATER, White Hactcin helped Child-of-the-Water use two blue-eyed fish he caught to make white people. First, Child-of-the-Water traced an outline of his own body on the ground and placed the fish inside it. White Hactcin then gradually changed the fish into a man and a woman.

WHITE OWL WOMAN   (Nankubaccin) *Arapaho*   The winter bird, the symbol of winter and bringer of snow. THUNDERBIRD, who was the symbol of summer for the Arapaho, challenged White Owl Woman to a contest to determine whose powers were greater. Thunderbird created towering black clouds accompanied by loud thunder and high wind. White Owl Woman countered Thunderbird's clouds with thick, white clouds that built up snow in high drifts. The black clouds were completely overcome, and White Owl Woman was shown to be the more powerful figure.

WHITE PAINTED WOMAN *Apache*   The mother of the CREATOR and CULTURE HERO KILLER-OF-ENEMIES. White Painted Woman is the Apache counterpart of the Navajo (Dineh) figure CHANGING WOMAN and is sometimes called by that name as well.

In the Jicarilla Apache CREATION ACCOUNT, after the emergence into the present world, the people began to wander around the world (see APACHE EMERGENCE AND MIGRATION). Two girls, White Painted Woman and WHITE SHELL WOMAN, went to a mountaintop where they lived for some time. One night, SUN came to the mountaintop and slept with White Painted Woman, and Water came and slept with White Shell Woman. Each woman gave birth to a son—Killer-of-Enemies and CHILD-OF-THE-WATER. Tales about the two heroes contain themes common to stories of WARRIOR TWINS, such as making a journey to their father, the Sun, and killing MONSTERS.

In another version of the account, the Creator warned White Painted Woman that a great FLOOD would destroy the world. She took refuge in an abalone shell that floated on the floodwaters until they receded. The shell came to rest at WHITE SANDS in New Mexico, where White Painted Woman gave birth to two sons, Killer-of-Enemies and Child-of-the-Water.

White Painted Woman also figures in a Jicarilla Apache legend that says the Earth will someday become unfit for life, and the people will ascend to two other worlds above the present one. The first time the world is destroyed it will be by water; the second time it will be by FIRE. White Painted Woman is the protector of the materials from which the new worlds will be made.

WHITE SANDS   White Sands National Monument in New Mexico is an expanse of dazzling, white gypsum sands that drift into dunes 10 to 60 feet high. According to an Apache legend, it was here that WHITE PAINTED WOMAN gave birth to the WARRIOR TWINS KILLER-OF-ENEMIES and CHILD-OF-THE-WATER.

WHITE SHELL WOMAN   The name of women in several different traditions. In the Apache CREATION ACCOUNT, White Shell Woman gave birth to the CULTURE HERO CHILD-OF-THE-WATER at the same time as WHITE PAINTED WOMAN gave birth to KILLER-OF-ENEMIES. In some versions of the Navajo (Dineh) stories about CHANGING WOMAN, White Shell Woman is the name by which Changing Woman is known when she is dressed in white. In other versions, White Shell Woman is Changing Woman's sister and another of the SUN's wives. In the EAGLEWAY story cycle, Changing Woman created White Shell Woman and Turquoise Woman from skin she rubbed from under her breasts. In Zuni tales, White Shell Woman is identified as either the mother or the maternal grandmother of the Sun Father.

WHITE STAR WOMAN   See EVENING STAR.

WIDAPOKWI *Southeastern Yavapai*   A female CREATOR figure and grandmother of the CULTURE HERO AMCHITAPUKA; called Kamalapukwia (First Woman) by the Yavapai-Apache. When the Yavapai people emerged from the UNDERWORLD, they failed to seal the opening behind them. Water poured up from the underworld and flooded the world above. (In the Yavapai-Apache version, Gwi, the Cloud, poured RAIN into the opening before the people emerged and flooded the underworld.) Everyone was drowned but Widapokwi, who was sealed in a hollow log (or placed in a log canoe) with enough food to keep her alive until the FLOOD receded.

With the SUN, Widapokwi had a daughter, the first person born on the present world. When her daughter was grown, Widapokwi wanted her also to have a child with the Sun. Knowing that the girl was his daughter, the Sun refused. However, Widapokwi tricked him so that his rays would enter the girl. The child she conceived was Amchitapuka, whose name means "first man on Earth." In the Yavapai-Apache account, the Sun sent his daughter to Gwi, the Cloud, who became the boy's father.

WIND   A powerful force of nature, wind is personified in myths across the continent. Because of its association with breath, speech, thought, and even movement, wind is commonly believed to have power over life. Consequently, wind figures in the CREATION ACCOUNTS of various cultures.

NILCH'I (Wind) is a CREATOR and major figure in the NAVAJO (DINEH) EMERGENCE account. Nilch'i was one of the *DIYIN DINEH* (Holy People) who emerged into the present world. He provides all living things with the means of life. Nilch'i ligai (White Wind) blew over two ears of CORN to create FIRST MAN AND FIRST WOMAN. Nilch'i also gave life to CHANGING WOMAN.

In the Apache account of the origin of HUMANS, BLACK HACTCIN sent Wind to give breath to First Man and bring him to life. ESAUGETUH EMISSEE, (Master of Breath), the Creek Creator and god of the wind, was also believed to have power over the breath of life. For the Dakota, TAKUSKANSKAN, a being that lived in the Four Winds, personified motion and made things come alive. WANI, the Four Winds of the Lakota, had power over life as well as the weather. Their father, TATE, was the companion of the all-powerful sky spirit SKAN.

In some traditions, the winds served as intermediaries between the sky spirits and humans. In the Akimel O'odham CREATION ACCOUNT, when the Creator, EARTHMAKER, decided to destroy the quarrelsome people with a FLOOD, he first sent warnings through the voices of the winds. One at a time, the winds went to the people and told them to change their ways and live in peace. Only one man, Suha, paid attention to the winds' warnings and followed their instructions. Only he and his wife survived the flood.

Some traditions attribute the origin of SEASONS to the wind. According to the Lakota, Skan, the Sky, assigned a season to each of the Wani (the Four Winds) and gave them control over the weather for that season. A giant named WAZIYA blew the cold North Wind from his mouth and was responsible for snow and ice. The Four Great Winds of the Tsimshian created the seasons by dividing up the year among themselves.

In many cultures, the wind was ruled over by powerful beings. In the Algonquian tradition, the CULTURE HERO MICHABO (Great Hare) ruled the wind. Wind was one of the agents through which TIRAWAHAT, the most powerful deity of the Skidi Pawnee, acted.

WIND CAVE   A cavern in a ravine at the southern edge of the BLACK HILLS of South Dakota, now Wind Cave National Park. The Lakota called it Washun Niya, "The Breathing Hole," for the sighing sounds that come from it. Wind Cave was said to be a link between the surface world and the UNDERWORLD, where the spirits that kept the BUFFALO and other game animals lived. For countless generations, these spirits had sent an abundance of game out of the cave to the people, ensuring their survival. After white people arrived, however, the spirits released fewer and fewer buffalo until almost none were left.

WINDIGO (*witiko*)   *Cree, Northern Ojibway*   A feared cannibalistic being who was the personification of winter famine. The *windigo* is described in many different ways, but usually it is portrayed as a giant with bulging eyes, a mouth filled with long, jagged teeth, and a heart of ice. Sometimes moving as a whirlwind, the creature stalked the northern woods during winter, hunting humans just as humans hunted animals. People who became CANNIBALS out of hunger were said to have "turned *windigo*" and were driven from the band or killed.

WINDIGOKAN   *Plains Ojibway*   Sacred CLOWNS, or contraries, whose name comes from WINDIGO, a feared CANNIBAL.

WINEBOZHO (Waynaboozho, Winabojo)   See MANABOZHO.

WISKE   *Potawatomi*   A CULTURE HERO who created the Potawatomi clans and gave each clan its MEDICINE BUNDLE. Wiske's TWIN brother, CIPYAPOS, guarded the afterworld and received the souls of the dead.

WITCH   A being that used its magical powers for evil, such as killing or causing illness. Most Native American cultures have tales of witches and witchcraft. Witches are often depicted as shape-shifters who can transform themselves into animals or other creatures. In Navajo (Dineh) tradition, SKINWALKERS are considered to be people who have turned away from the Navajo (Dineh) way and taken on the powers of witchcraft. They are believed to be CANNIBALS and shape-shifters. In the Northeast, witches were said to acquire their powers through a process of initiation. Candidates had to promise to sacrifice a family member before being accepted into the craft.

WOHPE *Lakota*   The daughter of SKAN, the SKY. Wohpe lived with TATE, the WIND, in the center of the world and cared for Whirlwind (Yum), the son of Anog Ite (DOUBLE-FACED WOMAN). According to one legend, Wohpe gave the SACRED PIPE to the Lakota, showed them how to prepare TOBACCO for it, and taught them how to use it in ceremonies.

WOLF   This largest member of the dog family ranges from four to seven feet in length and 30 to 100 pounds in weight. A powerful predator, the wolf has been both honored and feared for its strength and hunting ability. The Cherokee revered the wolf as the companion of KANATI, the Hunter, so Cherokee hunters never killed wolves.

In Native American tales Wolf is often portrayed as a CREATOR or CULTURE HERO. Wolf appears in some tales as the older brother of COYOTE. In the Paiute CREATION ACCOUNT, Wolf, feeling lonely, created Coyote and called him his brother. At that time the world was covered with water, and Wolf and Coyote could only paddle around in a canoe. The two of them piled dirt on the water until they created the Earth.

As a culture hero, Wolf is frequently associated with the origin of SEASONS. In a Ute legend, Wolf (SUNAWAVI) brought FIRE to humans and created the seasons. In a Crow tale, Wolf was one of the animals that helped OLD MAN COYOTE steal summer from its keeper so that the Crow people could have both summer and winter.

Among Algonquian-speaking tribes, Wolf (MAL-SUMSIS) was the evil twin brother of the culture hero GLUSKAP. For the Zuni, Wolf was the BEAST GOD symbolizing the east. In Dakota myth, Wolf was one of the spirit helpers of TAKUSKANSKAN, the being that personified motion and gave life to things.

WOLVERINE   The solitary, fierce wolverine is the largest member of the weasel family. Wolverine—called MASTER LOX (or Master Leux) by the Micmac and Passamaquoddy—usually appears in tales from

Wovoka, the Northern Paiute prophet who founded the Ghost Dance of 1890 *(National Anthropological Archives)*

the Northeast as a TRICKSTER and thief and is often depicted as the companion of WOLF. Master Lox was killed many times but always came back to life.

WOMAN-WHO-FELL-FROM-THE-SKY See SKY WOMAN.

WOODPECKER   A bird that clings to trees with its strong toes, the woodpecker uses its powerful bill to hammer the bark and capture insects. Because of its brilliant red head, the woodpecker symbolized the SUN for some West Coast tribes. The crimson FEATHERS of woodpecker scalps were treasured for use in making headdresses, ceremonial feather belts, and ornaments. Among some tribes woodpecker scalps were so valuable that they became a medium of exchange.

WOVOKA (Wuvoka, Jack Wilson) (ca. 1856–1932)   The Paiute prophet who instituted the GHOST DANCE OF 1890. Born in Nevada, Wovoka was the son of a visionary named Tavibo. On January 1, 1889, Wovoka had a vision during a solar ECLIPSE in which he saw the Creator and was given a message for his people. If the people underwent ceremonial purification and lived without warfare or other negative ways, then the world would be as it had been before the arrival of Europeans. The landscape would look as it did before, the BUFFALO would return, whites would disappear, and people would be reunited with their dead loved ones.

Wovoka's message of hope spread from tribe to tribe. Ghost Dance followers met periodically for five days of ritual—praying, chanting, and dancing in open circles. Nervous settlers, worried that the Native Americans might turn violent, sent for military help. Government efforts to suppress the movement came to a head on December 29, 1890, when Seventh Cavalry troops rounded up a band of Hunkpapa (Teton Lakota) at Wounded Knee in South Dakota and slaughtered more than 200 men, women, and children. Open practice of the religion declined sharply after the massacre, but Wovoka continued to correspond with Ghost Dance followers and traveled to different reservations, serving as a SHAMAN and healer.

X Y Z

XOWALACI (The Giver) *Northwest Coast* A CREATOR figure. In the beginning, the world was covered with the PRIMORDIAL WATERS. Xowalaci and his helper, First Man, lived in a lodge on the water. Growing bored, Xowalaci created land and then tried to make people. His attempts were unsuccessful, producing only sea mammals, dogs, and snakes. First Man then tried to create people by using TOBACCO smoke. After three days, a beautiful woman appeared from the smoke. The children of First Man and the woman he created were the first humans.

YEI (*ye'ii*) *Navajo (Dineh)* The DIYIN DINEH, or Holy People, deities that emerged from the lower worlds before humans were created. They are considered kindly beings that guided people. The *yei* include TALKING GOD, CALLING GOD, Male God and Female God (six of each), BLACK GOD, MONSTER SLAYER AND BORN FOR WATER, Gray God (also called WATER SPRINKLER), Humpback, Fringe Mouth, Red God, Whipping God (also known as Destroyer), Whistling God, and Shooting God. People in masks and costumes play the part of the *yei* in public ceremonials such as NIGHTWAY. The *yei* are represented in human form in SANDPAINTINGS made during curing rituals. (See also NAVAJO [DINEH] CEREMONIALS.)

ZUNI EMERGENCE AND MIGRATION
Zuni The people lived in the dark, crowded UNDERWORLD FOUR levels below the surface of the present world. The WARRIOR TWINS AHAYUTA AND MATSILEMA led the people into the daylight. The people were not entirely human until the twins completed their transformation.

Following the emergence, the people migrated to find a place to live. During the journey, the son and

Yei impersonator costumed as Zahadolzha (Fringe Mouth) for a performance of the Nightway ceremonial (© Bettmann/CORBIS)

daughter of a chief became the parents of the Koyemshi, Mudhead sacred CLOWNS. Eventually the people settled at Zuni, which is south of present-day Gallup, New Mexico.

ZUNI SALT LAKE   A sacred lake of the Navajo (Dineh), located in the crater of an extinct volcano in New Mexico. The lake is said to be the home of SALT WOMAN, an important figure in the traditions of the Navajo (Dineh), Pueblo, and Zuni people. In the Southwest, procuring salt has always been associated with solemn ceremonies. The Hopi, Navajo (Dineh), Zuni, and other tribes make annual pilgrimages to Zuni Salt Lake to gather salt for ceremonial purposes.

SELECTED
BIBLIOGRAPHY

Abbott, Kathryn A. "Hiawatha," *Encyclopedia of North American Indians*. Houghton
  Mifflin Co. Available on-line. URL: http://college.hmco.com/ history readerscomp/
  naind/html/na_015000_hiawatha.htm. Downloaded on April 18, 2003.

Brown, Jason Keith. "Klouskap and the Origin of the Penobscot," Acacia Artisans.
  Available on-line. URL: http://acaciart.com/stories. Downloaded on March 15, 2002.

Duncan, Dayton. *People of the West*. Boston: Little, Brown and Company, 1996.

Encylopedia Mythica. Available on-line. URL: http://www.pantheon.org. Updated on April
  7, 2002.

Giese, Paula. "Wampum—Treaties, Sacred Records," Native American Indian Resources.
  Available on-line. URL: http://www.kstrom.net/isk/art/beads/wampum.html. Updated on
  December 17, 1996.

Gill, Sam D. *Native American Religions: An Introduction*. Belmont, Calif.: Wadsworth, 1982.

Gill, Sam D., and Irene F. Sullivan. *Dictionary of Native American Mythology*. New York:
  Oxford University Press, 1992.

Harrod, Howard L. *The Animals Came Dancing*. Tucson: University of Arizona Press, 2000.

Hazen-Hammond, Susan. *Spider Woman's Web: Traditional Native American Tales About
  Woman's Power*. New York: Berkeley Publishing Group, a division of Penguin Putnam,
  1999.

Hirschfelder, Arlene, and Paulette Molin. *Encyclopedia of Native American Religions*. New
  York: Facts On File, Checkmark Books, 2000.

Kokopelli Stables. "Kokopelli: The Legend," Kokopelli Stables. Available on-line. URL:
  http://www.totalaccess.net/~kokopele/legend. Downloaded on April 10, 2002.

Lapahie, Harrison, Jr. "The Navajo Creation Story," Lapahie.com. Available on-line. URL:
  http://www.lapahie.com/Mythology.cfm. Downloaded on May 8, 2002.

Leeming, David Adams, and Jake Page. *The Mythology of Native North America*. Norman:
  University of Oklahoma Press, 1998.

Mails, Thomas E. *Sundancing: The Great Sioux Piercing Ritual*. Tulsa: Council Oak Books,
  1998.

Manitou Cliff Dwellings. "Major Anasazi Regions and Sites," Manitou Cliff Dwellings.
  Available on-line. URL: http://www.cliffdwellingsmuseum.com/sites.htm. Downloaded
  on April 16, 2003.

Miller, Dorcas S. *Stars of the First People: Native American Star Myths and Constellations*.
  Boulder, Colo.: Pruett Publishing, 1997.

Milne, Courtney. *Sacred Places in North America: A Journey into the Medicine Wheel*. New
  York: Stewart, Tabori & Chang, 1995.

Momaday, N. Scott. *The Way to Rainy Mountain*. Albuquerque: University of New Mexico Press, 1969.

Mooney, James. *Myths of the Cherokee*. 1900. Reprint, New York: Dover Publications, 1996.

Neihardt, John G. *Black Elk Speaks: Being the Life Story of a Holy Man of the Oglala Sioux*. 1932. Reprint, with an introduction by Vine Deloria, Jr., Lincoln: University of Nebraska Press, 1988.

Owusu, Heike. *Symbols of Native America*. New York: Sterling Publishing Co., 1997.

Penn, W. S., ed. *The Telling of the World: Native American Stories and Art*. New York: Stewart, Tabori & Chang, 1996.

Rahr, Tammy, with Sparo Arika Otis-Vigil. "The Hiawatha Belt: Unity Among Nations," Peace X Peace. Available on-line. URL: http://www.peacexpeace.org/peacepapers/rahr.html. Downloaded on April 18, 2003.

San Juan School District. "Navajo Starlore," San Juan School District. Available on-line. URL: http://dine.sanjuan.k12.ut.us/string_games/significance/nav_starlore. Downloaded on February 7, 2003.

Seppa, Nathan. "Ancient Cahokia: Metropolitan Life on the Mississippi," *Washington Post*, March 12, 1997, p. H01. Available on-line. URL: http://www.washingtonpost.com/wp-srv/national/daily/march/12/cahokia.htm. Downloaded on November 27, 1999.

Sharp, Jay W. "The Early Formative Period: A Season of Change," "The Great Puebloan Abandonments and Migrations," "The Hohokam: Farmers of the Desert," "The Mogollon: Their Magic," "The Paleo-Indians: Shadows in the Night," DesertUSA. Available on-line. URL: http://www.desertusa.com/ind1. Downloaded on February 25, 2003.

Snowder, Brad. "Starlore of Native America," Western Washington University Planetarium. Available on-line. URL: http://www.ac.wwu.edu/~skywise/ legends.html. Downloaded on May 11, 2002.

Spirits of the Snow: Arctic Myth. New York: Time-Life Books, 1999.

Stonees WebLodge. "Native American Lore," Stonees WebLodge. Available on-line. URL: http://www.ilhawaii.net/~stony/loreindx.html. Downloaded on July 8, 2002.

Strom, Karen M. "Blessingway," Hanksville. Available on-line. URL: http://www.hanksville.org/voyage/navajo/BlessingWay.php. Downloaded on April 6, 2002.

———. "Navajo Ceremonials," Hanksville. Available on-line. URL: http://www.hanksville.org/voyage/navajo/ceremonials.php. Downloaded on April 6, 2002.

Taylor, Colin F., ed. *Native American Myths and Legends*. New York: Smithmark Publishers, 1994.

Thomas, David Hurst, et al. *The Native Americans: An Illustrated History*. Ed. Betty Ballantine and Ian Ballantine. Atlanta, Ga.: Turner Publishing, 1993.

Through Indian Eyes: The Untold Story of Native American Peoples. Pleasantville, N.Y. Reader's Digest Association, 1995.

Twin Rocks Trading Post. "Discussion of 'Ways'," Twin Rocks Trading Post. Available on-line. URL: http://www.twinrocks.com/stateartist/legends/introways.html. Downloaded on February 6, 2003.

Uhler, John William. "Mesa Verde National Park Information," Mesa Verde National Park. Available on-line. URL: http://www.mesa.verde.national-park.com/info.htm. Downloaded on May 12, 2002.

Ute Mountain Ute Tribe. "Legends and Children's Stories of the Ute Tribe," Ute Mountain Ute Tribe. Available on-line. URL: http://www.utemountainute.com/ legends.htm. Downloaded on March 23, 2002.

Waldman, Carl. *Atlas of the North American Indian*. New York: Facts On File, 2000.

————. *Encyclopedia of Native American Tribes*. New York: Facts On File, 1999.

Welker, Glenn. "Apache Creation Story," "How the Buffalo Were Released on Earth," "Origin of Fire," Indigenous People's Literature. Available on-line. URL: http://www. indigenouspeople.org/natlit. Updated on September 9, 1998.

Western U.S. for Visitors. "Diyin Dine'é," "Changing Woman (Asdzáá nádleehé)," "The Holy Wind," "The Hooghan of First Man," "Monster Slayer and Yé'iitsoh," "Rock Monster Eagle (Tsé nináhálééh) and Monster Slayer (Naayéé neizghání)," Western U.S. for Visitors. Available on-line. URL: http://www.gocalifornia.about.com/cs/navajostories. Downloaded on April 6, 2002.

World of the American Indian, The. Washington, D.C.: National Geographic Society, 1974, 1979, 1989.

Yavapai-Apache Nation. "Creation Story," Yavapai-Apache Nation. Available on-line. URL: http://yavapai-apache-nation.com/Pages/creation.html. Downloaded on March 23, 2002.

INDEX

Boldface page numbers indicate main headings; *italic* page numbers indicate illustrations.